Why Rich Women Shoplift
- When They Have It All!

JOHN C. BRADY II, PHD., D. CRIM.

Uniform Resource Locators (URL's)

All URLs were verified at the time of printing as being representative, accurate and retrievable. However, the author and publisher cannot guarantee that these referenced URL's will not change or be altered nor be retrievable as cited in this book in the future.

Acceptable Citation

No portion of this book may be reproduced by any means including electronically without the express written approval of the author and publisher. However, for limited academic research purposes, this material may be used and quoted when proper attribution is given to both the author and publisher.

If further information concerning this book or other books written by Dr. Brady access: johncbrady.com

ISBN: 0615686176

ISBN 13:   9780615686172

Library of Congress Control Number: 2012954505
Western Psych Press
San Jose, CA

We are all responsible, defiled, unhappy. We have stolen with the burglar whose face we do not know, we have murdered with the parricide about whom we read in the newspapers, raped with the lewd, cursed with the blasphemous.

—Henry Troyat, *Firebrand:*
The Life of Dostoevsky

DISCLAIMER

The names of people and other identifying background information about the cases presented in this book have been changed to establish anonymity and ensure confidentiality. The same is true concerning the presentation of police reports and the various loss-prevention reports; even though they are available to the public, they have been redacted. Each case here also has an altered California Superior Court docket number. Other possible identifiable information such as the geographic location of the cases has been changed, and the patients as described are composites.

DEDICATION

This book is dedicated to my patient wife, Vanessa, who put up with the many months that I was "missing in action" while working on this project. The same is true of my two children, Johnny III and Spencer, who encouraged me to write a book by asking, "What kinds of cases are you working on now?" Finally, this book is dedicated to William Chestnut, J.D., a very good friend and professional colleague for thirty-five years.

TABLE OF CONTENTS

CHAPTER 1

CHAPTER 2

CHAPTER 3

CHAPTER 4

CHAPTER 5

CHAPTER 6

CHAPTER 7

Figures and Tables

Figures

Tables

ACKNOWLEDGEMENTS

Many individuals have contributed to this study, and my professional colleagues have proffered many helpful suggestions to make this a better book.

I particularly want to express appreciation not just to the four highlighted shoplifters presented here but to the more than 100 shoplifter-patients whom I have treated over the years and from whom I have learned so much. In the end, I discovered there is much more to glean from their stories.

Jane Tyler read and then reread the early drafts of this book from the beginning to the end. Her suggestions made the book a truly "readable feast." Thanks also go to Cindy Gustafson, whose fingers did the necessary dancing to polish fairly rough drafts into a finished format. In fact, she also typed up the original cases, so she deserves double credit. The finishing touches done by Molly Dougherty made this a better book. For this effort, I extend my thanks.

Mr. Terrence Shulman, who kindly wrote the Foreword to this book when the manuscript was in process, also made a positive contribution as a peer reviewer, and for that I extend my gratitude.

FOREWORD

TERRENCE D. SHULMAN,
J.D., L.M.S.W., A.C.S.W., C.A.A.D.C., C.P.C.
Founder and Director,
Shulman Center for Compulsive Theft, Spending and Hoarding

Dr. John Brady asked me to write a foreword to his new book, *Why Rich Women Shoplift—When They Have It All!* After reading his manuscript, I am honored and eager to do so.

I first became acquainted with John Brady when he called me in the metropolitan Detroit area from his office in Milpitas, California, where he practices forensic psychology. He introduced himself and told me he specialized in impulse control disorders such as kleptomania and shoplifting and that he'd read several online articles about my work with shoplifters as well as my 2003 book, *Something for Nothing: Shoplifting Addiction and Recovery*. He expressed his appreciation for the breadth of information in my book and for the two decades of work I'd spent treating various shoplifters. Brady also knew that I was a recovering shoplifter myself and that I'd founded Cleptomaniacs and Shoplifters Anonymous, or CASA, in 1992. (I changed the *k* in *kleptomania* to a *c* to form the word *casa*, or "home" in Spanish.)

Dr. Brady and I quickly discovered that we were among a rare subset of mental health professionals who'd had the privilege of diagnosing and providing treatment for hundreds of shoplifters—most of whom came to our attention through contact with the court system after an arrest. As is noted in both our books, there's often much more to shoplifting than meets the eye. Stereotypes persist that most shoplifters are reckless youth, poor, drug addicts, plain thieves, or professional boosters; however, Winona Ryder and the countless other high-profile shoplifters prove that something deeper often is at play.

Brady brings his unique academic and professional background to this book—he has doctorate degrees in criminology and psychology—and to the study and treatment of shoplifters. After spending two decades studying the etiology of shoplifters' actions, he has written one of the most important and in-depth professional tomes on the social-psychological factors that influence people to shoplift. This book presents new clinical information that should be of great interest to a wide readership: judges, attorneys, law enforcement and loss prevention professionals, academies, colleges and universities offering criminal administration and justice classes, and, last but not least, shoplifters themselves.

In Chapter 6 of Brady's book *Case Studies: Not Deprived and Definitely Not Happy Campers*, he keenly notes what I have also found: that most shoplifters have no clear idea why they steal; thus, our job is to mine the unconscious for clues. For example, Brady describes the strange case of "Shari Nelson," a middle-aged Southern California woman who loss prevention and law enforcement personnel initially determined was "an ordinary shoplifter." She turned out to be anything but ordinary when her psychiatric hospital records revealed that on many occasions she'd engaged in exsanguination (the intentional extraction of her blood) to basically commit suicide on the installment plan. She'd devised such a macabre method, Brady later discovered, so that her physically and emotionally abusive mother wouldn't know her daughter was a career shoplifter and a failure/

loser in her mother's eyes. Because of early intervention and psycho-therapy, there was a positive outcome for Nelson as well as for the judicial system.

Brady asserts something else I've also theorized: the vast major-ity of shoplifters do not meet the specific psychological criteria nec-essary for a diagnosis of kleptomania as described in the American Psychiatric Association's current *Diagnostic and Statistical Manual of Mental Disorders* (4th ed., text rev.; *DSM–IV–TR*; 2000). In Chapter 2 of his book *The Shoplifting Dilemma: It's a Big Deal*, Brady presents research, including some of my book's material. He concludes,

Shoplifting researchers continue to reveal inadequacies in the current DSM–IV–TR diagnostic criteria (for kleptomania) when diag-nosing patients who steal. At best, the DSM–IV–TR nosology of klep-tomania as an impulse disorder accounts for no more than 4–5% of those patients identified as taking things that do not belong to them.

Brady holds out hope that the drafters of the next (2013) edi-tion of the diagnostic manual, *DSM–5*, might better account for the descriptive dynamics of people who shoplift or steal from others. If nothing changes, we may need to rely on Brady's book for deeper and clearer analyses, diagnoses, and much-needed hope and help for roughly 10% (or 30 million Americans) who continue to shoplift in shame, ignorance, and secrecy. In the "Goals of the Study" portion of his book, Brady states that one goal is to "establish whether shoplift-ers reflect serious criminogenic, psychopathic, or antisocial tenden-cies." To test this assumption, all four women shoplifters in his sample were presented with the Carlson Psychological Survey (CPS). One measure on this instrument, the Antisocial Tendency Scale, taps act-ing-out, aggressive, and psychopathic behaviors. Most of the shop-lifters Brady and I have treated were well educated, financially com-fortable, hardworking, and family oriented; in addition, most were generous and giving to a fault and quite ethical in nearly all aspects of their lives. In addition, most shoplifters have not stolen and would not steal from individuals or places other than stores. The results of the CPS confirm that none of the tested shoplifters demonstrated any antisocial behaviors in addition to their penchant for theft.

Brady adds to the field of shoplifting research with the "shoplifting zone" outlined in detail in Chapter 5. He contends that this zone is comprised of four distinct and progressive stages: (1) anticipation/readiness; (2) neutralization: moral decision versus moral erosion; (3) action (the theft act); and (4) postexcitation/depression. Brady articulates a theory with which I concur: "Progression through these often confusing and painful stages results in a psychosocial reidentity stamping procedure whereby the shoplifter surrenders his or her positive preshoplifting self-identity and mentally replaces it with a very negative postshoplifting identity."

This new shaping of our professional thinking on how shoplifters move through these four psychosocial stages may help explain the true identity crises in most nonprofessional shoplifters. In a personal interview with Brady on August 10, 2011, I shared with him that after I'd started shoplifting around age fifteen, my identity morphed from feeling like the hero and good son to a Jekyll and Hyde–like hypocrite, living a life of secrets, lies, and escalating conflict. During my initial nine months of psychotherapy, my therapist helped me peel back the onion layers of my life and theorized that my stealing was closely related to my deep and repressed anger toward my father, my lost childhood, and my learned pattern of taking care of everyone else except me. Further, my therapist also suggested—it was a lightbulb moment—that I'd become addicted to shoplifting itself.

So, if shoplifting could be understood as a potentially addictive behavior, then it makes sense for Brady to address the central question in his book's title, *Why Rich Women Shoplift—When They Have It All!* He states that almost all the shoplifters he has treated during the past 20 years were not fully in control of themselves at the time they committed their theft acts. Brady's book documents his use of the Rotter Locus of Control Scale to assess the personal control of shoplifters and where his results reflected high scores on externality—the degree to which they felt that their lives were driven by such exogenous factors as luck, chance, fate, and fortuitousness. This external orientation was highly prevalent in the people I treated and, again, was something I experienced during my own decade of stealing. I felt there were a number of outside factors that were exerting control over my life, such as the pain connected to my father's alcoholism, my parents' divorce, my father's death, and feelings of rejection by others—for no apparent reason.

Those with an interest in human nature and behavior will enjoy and feel challenged by *Why Rich Women Shoplift—When They Have It All!* Brady aptly supports his theories from both anecdotal patterns as well as from the results of the psychological instruments he used. Although he does not direct specific attention in his book to the treatment process, our longing may soon be rewarded: he notes in Chapter 7 that he intends to produce a sequel tentatively titled: *Treatment for Rich Women Who Shoplift.* I hope I am able to play some part in the production of that book. I predict that it will equal, or even surpass, his present effort.

Terrence Daryl Shulman, J.D., L.M.S.W., A.C.S.W., C.A.A.D.C., C.P.C.

Southfield, Michigan

March 2013

WHAT THE PROFESSIONALS ARE SAYING—PEER REVIEWS

- ## Doug R. Lipton, J.D., Defense Attorney, San Jose, California

John Brady has been an integral part of my legal team when defending all categories of criminal defendants, including those who have stolen. I rely on his comprehensive psychological reports, which have proven to be effective in the fight for justice for my clients. Brady's insight, expertise, and forensic opinions are well respected in the criminal justice system, and his reputation as an authority in forensic psychology is legendary throughout California. In a recent case, Brady provided test results, and his opinion as to the defendant's culpability and character led to the criminal charges being drastically reduced, resulting in a probation sentence in lieu of prison. Brady was certainly a hero to this client, and there are countless other cases like this one, where his brilliant analysis has positively altered the direction of the case.

- ## Pat Potter-McAndrews, M.A., B.F.P.C., San Jose, California

During the past 20 years of clinical practice, I have diagnosed hundreds of patients experiencing a wide variety of self-control issues, many involving petty theft and shoplifting. John Brady's book, *Why Rich Women Shoplift—When They Have It All!* serves as a clinical guide for answering an important question: Why do affluent women steal and, in the process, risk ruining their reputations, perhaps the destiny of their families, and even the loss of their personal freedom via incarceration? Women's shoplifting has remained a taboo subject for too many years, and now Brady has helped us unravel why people who do not need to steal, in fact, do.

• Stewart B. Nixon, Ph.D., Clinical Psychologist, San Jose, California

John Brady's long-awaited book *Why Rich Women Shoplift—When They Have It All!* discusses theft issues from multiple perspectives, including psychosocial, psychodynamic, and learning theory. I've always wondered why so many affluent women steal. Now, thanks to Brady's insightful analysis, I have my answer. His book is a great resource for patients afflicted with the problem of shoplifting, for criminal justice personnel, judges, mental health professionals who treat this disorder, and, of course, for college classes in sociology, criminology, and psychology. I read with great interest the seminal cases outlined in this valuable text, which at times are both humorous and devastatingly tragic.

• Ingo Brauer, J.D., Criminal Defense Attorney, San Jose, California

In *Why Rich Women Shoplift—When They Have It All!* John Brady examines the myriad psychological symptoms that turn ordinarily law-abiding people—in this case, affluent women—into career thieves. What I found of most interest from a professional standpoint (I have represented many clients charged with theft and embezzlement) is that shoplifters, during the stealing or just after, experience a chemical rush of adrenaline that can alleviate depressive symptoms. Brady has provided psychological consultation with me on a number of criminal cases in which my clients were charged with theft. His psychological evaluations with these cases have proved very beneficial for sentencing purposes. This book is a must read for law enforcement professionals, attorneys, and judges who deal with women who steal but in large measure don't know why.

• Michael A. Nichols, J.D., Criminal Defense Attorney, Sunnyvale, California

We all think we know what shoplifting is, but with John Brady's capable guidance, we learn *why* it is. His book, *Why Rich Women Shoplift— When They Have It All!* gives us insight into a social-legal epidemic of huge proportions. The shoplifting addict is not the person who is often portrayed, especially in the media: He or she is your neighbor, son, wife, husband, or even pastor. Learn the psychological triggers pushing people toward a life of stealing, including cases in which the person wants to be caught and punished.

• Martin W. King, J.D., Criminal Defense Attorney, San Jose, CA and Adjunct Professor of Law, Lincoln Law School of San Jose

John Brady's clinical exposition as noted in the case of Mrs. Nelson (case 4 in Chapter 6) chronicles a difficult case legally and psychologically that, with his expertise and insightful diagnosis, was satisfactorily resolved within the criminal justice system. All too often the system cares not for the cause of the defendant's behavior—in this case shoplifting. Here, however, a caring judge and understanding prosecutor and defense attorney worked together with Brady to fashion a workable remedy to address the myriad and complex issues facing Mrs. Nelson. My thanks and appreciation for a job well done!

PREFACE

What's New Here?

When talking to professional colleagues, friends, and family members about my work as a forensic psychologist, the same question invariably comes up: "What kinds of court cases have you been working on recently?" I have, on occasion, described some shoplifting cases, how puzzling and tragic some of them were, and the fact that none of those arrested who came to my attention stole for economic reasons. Almost all my shoplifting cases involved women who had stable financial backgrounds (some with a financial net worth of about $2 million), came from functional family backgrounds, and were well educated, yet all faced jail sentences for theft of private property, and all of them, to some degree, had lost control of their lives. They then often prompt me, "Why don't you write a book about some of the most interesting cases?" Indeed, why not? So here it is: *Why Rich Women Shoplift—When They Have It All!*

After I decided to undertake this project, I conducted appreciable research to find out more about what has been written concerning the intriguing psychological world of the shoplifter. When surfing the web and accessing the University of California library system using the general search topic "shoplifting," I found more than 600 references to the subject. Looking for a little guidance, I consulted with a number of shoplifting experts, especially Terrence Shulman, himself a recovering shoplifter and the author of four excellent books on the subject; he also conducts shoplifter treatment groups in Michigan. Unfortunately, this background research did not yield much in terms of empirical, evidence-based results concerning the psychology of the shoplifter. How do they get started down this very slippery path? And of most interest to me was whether there was a definitive and measurable chain of psychological events that propels normally law-abiding people into the world of shoplifting. Hopefully this book will provide some pragmatic answers to these and other pertinent questions about shoplifting that have not been addressed in the works of previous researchers.

Over the years, there have been innumerable popular portrayals of the shoplifter. Most of those accounts have been highly descriptive and narrative, one even chronicling the history of shoplifting; yet they were not explanatory, nor were they psychologically oriented often times written by well-intentioned journalists. The seminal investigation on the subject was conducted by Mary O. Cameron in 1964. Although she dealt with many important sociological and psychological shoplifting variables, including the co-occurring psychiatric conditions described in Chapter 1 of the present volume, she and other researchers had not, it seemed to me, addressed in any unified theory exactly how a person becomes a shoplifter. Are there patterns or social-psychological commonalities shared by all shoplifters? And, on their way to becoming career shoplifters, do they enter into and pass through a sequence of shoplifting stages?

It seemed to me, based on the diagnosis and treatment of at least a hundred shoplifters, that a person had to progress psychologically from nonshoplifter status (law-abiding) to shoplifter status (law-violating). But how does this happen? Is there a process? Are there common pathways or a sequence of identifiable steps? It became evident that the shoplifters referred to me did evidence an ill-defined shoplifting track—that is, a beginning, a midpoint, and a late stage in their thought process that contributed to their shoplifting pattern. This shoplifting sequence is discussed in detail in Chapter 5.

The enigma seemed to be how sincere, morally directed, previous nonoffenders can become thieves and can simply stroll out of multiple stores with merchandise they have not paid for. This problem was always on my mind when I was called to diagnose and treat innumerable nice people who were criminally charged with serious crimes against property and who faced jail time. I wanted to further explore this and other areas to find an answer.

Some type of a self-identity shift or transformation had to occur for the nonshoplifter to be willing to assume the negative status of a shoplifter. What would make them surrender their law-abiding identification as nonoffenders and then have it replaced with new psychological and criminal labels that cast them as societal outsiders or deviants? I could comprehend why material need or even greed might, in certain cases, be a factor, but the people charged with theft crimes referred to me by attorneys were well educated and came from affluent, high-status, backgrounds. All the shoplifters in this research were upper-middle-class women of a wide range of ages.

How did these usually well-intentioned women get from there to here? This aspect of the shoplifting dynamic had not been the focal point of previous researchers' attention. In addition to identifying the shoplifter's psychological stages, this study used three psychological testing instruments to evaluate the mental status of shoplifters. This important assessment aspect, as undertaken in this study, has also received very little attention from prior shoplifting investigations, most of which have been highly anecdotal or related to the use of controversial drugs to treat shoplifters.

From the detailed information presented to me by shoplifters, it appeared the single common factor they all shared was their impression of being "out of control" at the time they offended. Certainly I was not the first psychologist to notice the absence-of-control aspect of shoplifting, but this study may be the first one in which the out-of-control issue has been directly addressed in a research study employing psychological tests.

Additionally, almost all the shoplifters I treated had little or no idea why they stole, how or when they began, and sometimes were so confused that they did not recollect where they were at the time of their stealing and arrest. The degree to which one is or is not in control of one's life is a psychological concept termed *locus of control* and is explained in Chapter 4. It seemed to follow that a compendium or casebook approach to explain the shoplifter's road map was the logical organizational format for the book.

GOALS OF THE STUDY

The goals of this study are threefold:

1. To meet the need for further investigation into the relationships between the locus-of-control dimension and the psychology of the shoplifter. Chapter 4 explores this relationship and defines *locus of control* and its measurement.

2. To establish whether shoplifters reflect serious psychopathic, criminogenic symptoms or antisocial tendencies, and to determine whether they reflect clinical depression in addition to their identified theft behavior. Chapter 6 explores these issues using four case studies.

3. Despite many previous attempts to describe and diagnose shoplifters, no studies address an important missing aspect: Is it possible to identify or somehow classify the psychological steps or stages that a shoplifter necessarily passes through on the way to becoming a career shoplifter? The third goal is thus to identify and describe the sequence of the shoplifting stages. These four stages are explained in Chapter 5.

Each case study in Chapter 6 presents a psychiatric diagnosis as well as a case analysis based on the results of the psychological testing and presented to the court at the time of the defendant's hearing, either at trial or later at a sentencing hearing. These referenced diagnoses are derived from the psychiatric nomenclature as presented in the *DSM–IV–TR*.

RESEARCH SAMPLE

The inferences, psychological opinions, and shoplifter diagnoses advanced in this study are based on a total sample of more than 100 shoplifters I have seen during the past 25 years of forensic practice. The specific research data, including the results of psychological testing presented in this book, have been derived from four specific cases that were referred to me by defense attorneys for psychological shoplifter assessments. These four cases, which are referenced throughout the book, are described in detail in Chapter 6. In order of presentation, they are:

1. Mrs. Daio

2. Mrs. Konvitz

3. Mrs. Chow

4. Mrs. Nelson

To maintain continuity when I refer to these cases in the text, the reader may choose to directly access the complete cases as presented in Chapter 6.

PREFACE AND GOALS REFERENCES

American Psychiatric Association. (2000) *Diagnostic and statistical manual of mental disorders* (4th ed., text rev.). Washington, DC: Author.

Beck, A. T., Steer, R. A., & Brown, G. K. (1996). *Manual for the beck depression Inventory-II*. San Antonio, TX: Psychological Corporation.

Cameron, M. O. (1964) *The booster and the snitch: Department store shoplifting*. New York-London: The Free Press of Glencoe, A Division of The Macmillan Company.

Carlson, K. A. (1982). *Carlson psychological survey manual*. Port Huron, MI: Sigma Assessment Systems.

Rotter, J. B. (1966). Generalized expectancies for internal versus external control of reinforcement. *Psychological Monograph, 80,* 1–28.

CHAPTER 1

SHOPLIFTERS: OUT OF CONTROL? CRIMINALS? OR JUST DEPRESSED?

In the theory of psychoanalysis we have no hesitation in assuming that the course taken by mental events is automatically regulated by the pleasure principle.

—SIGMUND FREUD, *BEYOND THE PLEASURE PRINCIPLE*, 1920

What Attorneys and Judges Want to Know About Shoplifting

As a forensic psychologist, I have been called hundreds of times to help "figure this person out" in terms of why someone committed a crime as well as how to get him or her to stop doing so. Usually my work has involved representation of criminal defendants, charged or sometimes "overcharged" by the prosecution with criminal offenses. These cases, about a hundred of them to date, involved shoplifters. Usually I was asked by a defense attorney to help with the preparation of a comprehensive defense position for the person charged with theft. Generally, this meant using psychological assessment tools to determine whether psychological variables could help explain why a financially well-situated and nice person decided to steal. The goal of this work was designed not exculpate those charged with shoplifting, because that responsibility rests with the trial court, but to determine how psychological processes are often key to understanding the dynamics of non–economically oriented shoplifting.

Several California attorneys I have worked with have emphasized how important it is to have a shoplifter evaluation done on behalf of their clients. As William Chestnut, a prominent San Jose based attorney with 30 years of experience, concluded:

It's been my experience with almost all of my shoplifting, petty theft cases that a psychological assessment can make all the difference in two critical areas:

1. Help determine what psychological factors may have affected my shoplifting clients, and

2. Case disposition, including the ability to negotiate a plea bargain with the district attorney to reduce the criminal charges, or at sentencing, to argue for probation in lieu of jail time. Without this type of an evaluation, the defendant and attorney are at a big disadvantage (Chestnut, 2013).

Another attorney and former Santa Clara County prosecutor, Mike Nichols, J.D., currently in private practice, framed the shoplifting dilemma a different way in August 2012:

> Why is there currently such an epidemic of shoplifting cases? After all, the shoplifter may be your neighbor, son, daughter, or even your pastor. Let's face it, we have all been tempted, but why some of us do it and others use restraint are questions every defense attorney representing a shoplifter must come to terms with. I suspect most come and argue to Dr. Brady that shoplifting is not what we usually think it is. And I believe that every shoplifter needs to have a complete shoplifting psychological workup done to help with the preparation of his or her defense. Dr. Brady has provided this important service for my clients, achieving favorable results.

As stated, all the shoplifting cases analyzed in this book either were referred by defense attorneys, self-referred, or sent by superior court judges to establish whether, in lieu of jail sentencing, probation placement might be a more appropriate option. The chief questions in every case, and my professional charge as a forensic psychologist, was to answer, "Why did they do it, and how should they be treated within the criminal justice system?" Quite literally, I had superior court judges say to me in open court, "Dr. Brady, if you don't think Mrs. Jones is a klepto or a criminal, then explain to the court exactly what she is and why she shouldn't be sentenced to jail for stealing?" Sometimes I was hard-pressed to deliver an answer.

Superior courts and judges over the years have become woefully frustrated with what they label repeat "petty offenders" who clog up court dockets. After being involved with the criminal justice system for 25 years, I could understand their consternation, especially because the same shoplifters appeared in court time after time.

After these accused shoplifters were referred for psychological evaluation, they were presented with a standard battery of three psychological tests (in some situations, additional tests were necessary). The results of these tests are discussed in Chapter 6. These tests were designed and used to measure three areas of the defendants' personalities:

1. Are they in control or out of control of their lives?

2. Do they demonstrate antisocial, or criminogenic behavior in addition to shoplifting?

3. Are they depressed? If they are, to what extent?

To best understand the four shoplifters presented in this investigation, the three distinct questions listed here have been posed. However, the main psychological variable investigated here is psychological control and how being out of control negatively impacts the shoplifters' lives, driving them to steal.

Are Shoplifters Out of Control? The Locus-of-Control Concept

The first question raised here is, "Are shoplifters measurably out of control?" The four shoplifter cases described in Chapter 6 were evaluated in order to determine if, in fact, they were out of control when they offended. This control factor was assessed using the Rotter Locus of Control IE scale (Rotter, 1966). Full descriptions of the locus-of-control concept and locus-of-control descriptors are presented in Chapter 4.

The specific work of the forensic psychologist is to help not only the shoplifter but also to assist the courts, attorneys, and, in some cases the prosecution, when interested, to determine why shoplifters engage in self-defeating, high-risk, low-reward behavior that is against their self-interest and often leads to public humiliation and possible incarceration. This book is devoted to this work.

The limited research on shoplifting has proven quite clearly that there is no single psychological profile or category of all people who shoplift. And there is no one-size-fits-all theory to account for a behavior as diverse and complex as shoplifting. Although varied, the

4

shoplifting cases described in this book do share one common measurable psychological factor: the shoplifters being out of personal control. One psychological construct seen as a recurring thread uniting these cases was the shoplifters being out of control at the time they offended, a state otherwise known as being "external." Being externally driven by outside forces is one causal theory as to why people shoplift, and in some psychological ways, this external control theory is commensurate with the compulsive shoplifting typology explained in Chapter 3. Few other studies have measured locus of control within the shoplifter population.

A variety of causal or explanatory theories of shoplifting have been explored, such as generalized anxiety (Beck & McIntyre, 1977), impulsiveness (Bradford & Balmaceda, 1983), psychological stressors (Arboleda-Florez, Durie, & Costello, 1977), overcompensation for personal (or perceived) losses (Cupchik, 1997), or simple kleptomania as described in the American Psychiatric Association (2000) *DSM- IV-TR*.

Why Can't I Stop?

One pervasive psychological state of mind consistently reported by shoplifters is their perception of not being in control of their actions, motivations, behaviors, thoughts, or even their lives while stealing. Thus, being out of control (external) at the time of the shoplifting act is the one psychological factor reported by all the shoplifters I have diagnosed and treated. This out-of-control dimension is often accompanied by subjective feelings such as a rush, a thrill, a high, euphoria (perhaps even sexual euphoria), intoxication, or manic feelings. All of these feelings are underscored by a sense of an underlying control abdication and feelings of being controlled by outside, external, anxiety-eliciting forces.

A recovering shoplifter, attorney, and treatment specialist, Terrence Shulman (2004) characterized his feelings of being out of control and personally powerlessness:"I was so out of control, I scared myself. I couldn't believe what I was doing," he says. "And I actually contemplated suicide."

Additionally, being out of control can be representative and symptomatic of an *impulse control disorder* as defined in the *DSM–IV– TR*. Shoplifting occupies a lonely diagnostic space, but it is certainly a common failure of personal control for those who engage in it. This has been confirmed from anecdotal accounts of people who state they have kept their theft impulse a secret until they were arrested. According to shoplifting researchers Grant and Kim, psychological control is a key factor in the shoplifting process:

> These conditions tend to go unreported because of sufferers' ignorance of the behavior as a psychological problem. Distressed by their lack of control over their actions, yet too ashamed to tell others, they suffer in silence. Not surprisingly, they are likely to have low self esteem, to the extent that they might turn to alcohol or substance abuse, become depressed or "suicidal" (2003, p.1).

Stated another way, being out of personal control is symptomatic of a person's inability to cope with a multitude of stressful life events, including some that have deep psychosocial historical roots. Because shoplifters are out of control, their drive to steal becomes so intense they cannot stop.

According to Berlin:
> Shoplifting for millions of citizens is simply another maladaptive way of coping with stressful life circumstances…ways similar to overeating, drinking, drugs or becoming withdrawn. It is not an issue of good vs. bad people, rich vs. poor people, young vs. old people, or education vs. illiteracy (1996, pp. 3–4).

Many admit that it will be hard for them to stop shoplifting, even after getting caught. All shoplifters possess incredibly strong defense systems, making them resistant to change.

Berlin also states:
> A person's predilection to shoplifting can develop quickly when the excitement generated from "getting away with it" produces a chemical reaction (i.e. adrenaline, etc.) resulting in what shoplift- ers describe as an incredible "rush" or "feeling high", which many

shoplifters will tell you is the "true reward," rather than the merchandise itself. In addition to feeling good, shoplifters quickly observe that this "high" temporarily eliminates their feelings of anger, frustration, depression, or other unhappiness in their life (1996, pp. 3–4).

More recently, Shulman (2011) has again commented that being out of control or being "powerless" over one's life is characteristic of the many shoplifters treated in his group therapy sessions. Moreover, his research has shown that only a small percentage of shoplifters can be diagnosed with kleptomania. He contends that most shoplifters see the world as "unfair, cruel, and many are angry."

The shoplifter's perception of seeing the world as unfair directly corresponds to feelings of being out of control—that is, having an external locus of control. What does it mean to feel as if outside forces are pushing you around like a billiard ball, compelling you to bad, illogical, and illegal moral decisions? Shoplifting is specifically driven by a person's reaction to not being in control of his or her life, culminating in the theft act.

Are Shoplifters Just Like Other Criminals?

A second question arises concerning the shoplifter's criminal proclivity: *Are shoplifters psychologically similar to other persons charged with nonshoplifting criminal offenses?* After all, they have been arrested and criminally charged, so psychologically it would seem to follow that shoplifters should reflect criminal traits. The present study examined whether four shoplifters had psychological test scores that were consistent or inconsistent with a property offender (burglary) criminal sample comprised of nonshoplifters. It was concluded that these four shoplifters, although all had been arrested, had quite different profiles from other property offenders. They did not generally show psychological profiles similar to identified, acting-out, aggressive, psychopathic, dangerous, or property-offense criminals.

Accordingly, the second goal of this study was to establish whether shoplifters reflect psychopathic or criminogenic symptoms or serious antisocial tendencies and whether shoplifters indeed commit crossover offenses in addition to acts of theft. It was hypothesized that shoplifters would commit very few crossover crimes in addition to stealing. The application of Palmer and Hollin's (2003) criminal thought patterns confirms that external-oriented shoplifters do have thought patterns similar in some ways to other nonshoplifter offender populations. However, this finding about thought patterns does not imply that shoplifters proceed to actually commit other offenses. There is no reason to assume that shoplifters have not contemplated engaging in other criminal offenses, but despite this, they do not necessarily mirror dangerous or psychopathic personality traits.

This is especially germane to objective measures of antisocial behavior or psychopathy. For many years, this trait has been directly connected to criminal behavior, and even—in limited cases—to shoplifting. Research has also demonstrated that being out of control is connected to deviant or procriminal thought patterns, thereby lowering a person's threshold to steal (Brady, 1990).

What effect, if any, does an out-of-control, external orientation have on the cognitive mind-set of the shoplifter? And does this orientation contribute to criminal thinking patterns developed by shoplifters? The results of this study present evidence that shoplifters do bear out definitive patterns associated with the surrender of personal control, and consequently they may adopt thinking patterns both associated with externality and cognition conducive to criminal thought ideations, including a tendency to steal.

This cognitive shift from an internal to an external orientation leading to criminal thought formation has been pointed out by Palmer and Hollin (2003) with a wide variety of offenders, including those convicted of crimes against property. Notwithstanding the difference in samples, their research results are germane to this study.

Palmer and Hollin (2003,pp.175-187) identify at least 10 thinking styles supporting criminal lifestyles. These factors mirror the factors attributable to external descriptors presented in Chapter 4. They are:

1. Confusion—psychological distress and mental confusion.

2. Defensiveness—defensive style attempting to conceal difficulties or deficiencies.

3. Mollification—externalizing blame rationalizing criminal behavior.

4. Cut-off —low frustration tolerance, tendency to remove barriers to criminal behavior with drugs, or use of short phrases such as "I couldn't stop myself."

5. Entitlement—an attitude of privilege or ownership, tendency to misidentify wants as needs.

6. Power orientation—need for control over others.

7. Sentimentality—belief that one is really a "good person" despite involvement in criminal behavior.

8. Super-optimism—belief that the negative consequences of crime can be avoided indefinitely.

9. Cognitive indolence—poor critical reasoning.

10. Discontinuity—inconsistencies between thinking and behavior.

Recidivist shoplifters (60–80%) are observed to acquire a set of weakened moral values that differentially support their criminal behaviors.

The application of Palmer and Hollin's criminal thought pattern theory confirms that shoplifters do exhibit thought patterns similar in some ways to other nonshoplifter offender populations. Yet this finding, as well as the results of the present study, do not corroborate the notion that shoplifters commit other offenses. However, it does support the notion that shoplifters idiosyncratically select only one form of deviant violation.

Three Psychological Tests Used in This Investigation

In this investigation, three well-established individual psychological tests were administered to the four shoplifters. (Subsequent references to these tests as used with the shoplifter sample will present the tests' abbreviations. For example, the Carlson Psychological Survey is referred to as the CPS). These psychological tests were used to answer the following three questions:

1. Are shoplifters out of control? Personal control was measured using the Rotter Locus of Control Scale.

2. Are shoplifters just criminals? The Carlson Psychological Survey was measured for criminogenic factors.

3. Are shoplifters depressed? Depression was assessed using the Beck Depression Inventory II and the CPS self-depreciation scale. Studies have established that the Rotter Locus of Control Scale also can detect depressive symptomatology; thus, it was also considered as a measure of shoplifter depression.

The Rotter Locus of Control Scale

Because so many of the shoplifters whom I have diagnosed and treated have stated that they "felt almost totally out of control of their lives" when they stole, the inclusion of the Rotter Locus of Control IE Scale seemed clinically appropriate to this study. The IE test determines whether the patient is driven by *internal* or *external* psychological factors. External locus of control as compared with internal locus of control has been connected to many malappropriate and criminal behaviors, including sexual acting out, crimes against property, shoplifting, gambling, rape, domestic aggression, white-collar crime, substance/alcohol abuse, anxiety, anorexia and bulimia, posttraumatic stress disorder, and many other psychological conditions associated with interpersonal conflict. I have used the Rotter Locus of Control Scale for 30 years to evaluate criminals, drug addicts, sex offenders, car thieves, alcoholics, and now shoplifters (Brady, 1999). A full definition of locus of control and a description of the IE scale are presented in Chapter 4. Also included in Chapter 4 is a list of the 20 important locus-of-control psychological descriptors (see Table 4.1).

The Carlson Psychological Survey

To determine whether shoplifters have criminal-oriented personalities, the four patients whose cases are described here were also given the Carlson Psychological Survey (Carlson, 1997). The CPS was selected for use with this shoplifting population because it was developed and standardized using criminal-deviant groups. The test was also selected as the measure of acting-out and antisocial behaviors because the four shoplifters evaluated in this study had long histories of both shoplifting and exposure to the criminal justice system. Collectively, they reported more than 400 theft acts and 30 arrests. At the time of assessment, they had been criminally charged with either petty theft (shoplifting) or grand theft.

According to Carlson, the developer of the CPS:
> The Carlson Psychological Survey (CPS) is an instrument for the assessment and classification of criminal offenders, persons charged with crimes, and others who have come to the attention of the criminal justice system or social welfare systems. The CPS was designed to reflect the unique situations of these individuals as well as the atypical reasons for referral (Carlson,1997,p.1).

More generally, the CPS is comprised of 50 items, organized into four psychological content areas:

1. Chemical Abuse (CA)—This dimension reflects the degree to which the person abuses drugs or alcohol and the relevance of these chemicals to antisocial behavior.

2. Thought Disturbance (TD)—This dimension reflects disorganization of thinking, confusion, perceptual distortions, hallucinations, and feelings of unreality. These traits may manifest themselves in unusual affect, including anxiety. High scorers on this scale indicate unusual problems in dealing with reality because they cannot organize themselves.

3. Self-Depreciation (SD)—This dimension reflects the degree to which a person degrades himself or herself and is a measure of depression. The high scorer on the SD scale generally does not value him- or herself and refuses all outside credit for life accomplishments.

4. Antisocial Tendencies (AT)—This scale reflects hostile animosity and socially defiant attitude in a person, as well as the overt willingness to be assaultive or threatening to others. Assaultiveness may or may not culminate in actual physical aggression; it may be clearly demonstrated by malicious conversation, mocking, or by an unfriendly manner toward others. High scorers on the AT scale are also likely to be cynical about other individuals, interpreting their behavior as unjust or self-serving. Inherent in this scale is an acceptance of criminal thinking or actual behavior. That is, the person acts in an unethical and untrustworthy manner, but feels little or no guilt (1997, pp.1–2).

The last two content areas—self-depreciation and antisocial tendencies—are particularly germane to the goals of the present study. Carlson later added a CPS validity scale measuring honesty that has also been used in this study.

The CPS presents patient profiles of criminal offenders that can be used for comparison to the present shoplifting population. The Carlson Type 3 property offender profile, appropriate for use with shoplifters, for example, has been used here to compare shoplifter scores with other identified property offenders. Carlson notes:

These individuals are usually described as immature and rebellious but not decidedly antisocial. They commonly look for support from their peers and get into trouble while looking for this approval if they think some antisocial act will be looked upon with favor. That is, their offenses are generally unplanned, impulsive reactions to situations with little financial gain (Carlson, 1982, p. 11).

This emphasis on the CPS Type 3 profile helps differentiate those persons who engage in shoplifting for economic gain (common property, or theft offenders) from those who are driven by pervasive underlying psychological variables such as an external locus of control or depression. The primary use of the CPS in this study is as a means of measuring acting out, potentially criminal behavior using the results from the CPS antisocial (AT) tendency scale. Carlson Type 3 individuals reflect elevated scores on the AT scale. Graph 1 depicts the Type 3 profile for the property offender. The antisocial range falls between 75 and 99.

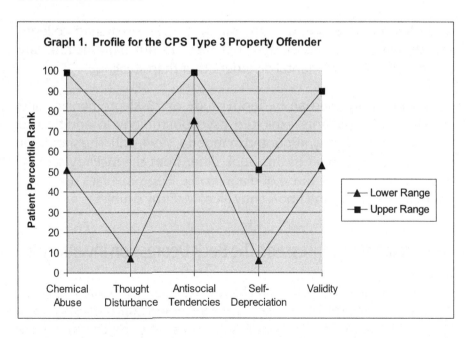

Graph 1. Profile for the CPS Type 3 Property Offender

Of the four shoplifter cases presented in this study, only one was diagnosed with a serious psychopathological disorder, a delusional diagnosis, and major depression that contributed to both her shoplifting and her suicidal attempts via the slow extraction of her own blood (Mrs. Nelson, Chapter 6, Case 4).

Other researchers contend that shoplifters, in addition to their theft behavior, have other criminogenic traits that lend themselves to assessment. For example, over the last 15 years Cupchik (1997) has maintained that shoplifters manifest identifiable psychopathological symptoms. Using the Minnesota Multiphasic Personality Inventory (MMPI), Cupchik established that both men and women shoplifters had significantly high MMPI depression scales, after-noting that,

> 67% of the women and 43% of the men had significantly high psychopathic (PD) scales on the MMPI. This finding suggested that these individuals may have been inclined to act out without much remorse as might the average person when subjected to excessive stress (Cupchik, 1997, p. 36).

In another shoplifting study, Moore (1983) researched college-age shoplifters and concluded that they do not demonstrate any diagnosable signs of mental disorder other than stealing.

McElroy published an in-depth study of 20 kleptomaniacs and found that "all patients exhibited psychopathology in addition to kleptomania" (McElroy, as quoted in Yagoda, 1994, p. 2). The shoplifter case studies presented in this book differ from the McElroy sample because they are not those of diagnosable kleptomaniacs using the *DSM–IV–TR* criteria, and apparently all of McElroy's subjects were.

Are Shoplifters Depressed? The Beck Depression Inventory II

The third important question that has been posed here is: *Are shoplifters depressed?* Several previous researchers, including Cupchik (1997), have found that diagnosed depression as well as other psychopathology was evident in at least one-third of the shoplifters studied. In fact, depression was the most frequently found diagnostic problem. This may help explain why some shoplifters "get a rush or lift" from stealing on their birthdays and around holidays (Berlin, 2006). The theft experience provides the shoplifter with a quick feeling of exhilaration that momentarily lifts feelings of depression. This diagnosis of shoplifter depression is in keeping with the results of the present study.

Although investigators have focused on depression as a central shoplifting driver, the diagnosis of ongoing depression was usually done without the benefit of psychological testing, yet was thought to be consistent with the classification of depression contained in the *DSM–IV–TR*. The three psychological tests used with the four cases presented here did assess depression; thus, I have presented a measurable way to more accurately examine whether shoplifters are depressed. These results are presented in Chapters 6 and 7.

There is no doubt that many of the shoplifters I have seen and treated were chronically depressed; my purpose with this study is to determine how this condition influenced their shoplifting behavior and, if it did, to what extent. An accepted, reliable method or test was needed. The Beck Depression Inventory II (BDI-II) was selected for this purpose. Both the BDI-II and the self-depreciation scale of the CPS collectively provided the results of the depression levels of the four cases in this study.

The decision to include the BDI-II (Beck, Steer, & Brown, 1996) was based on innumerable shoplifters self-reports that prior to, during, and even after stealing, they felt depressed as well as out of control. The BDI-II was the third instrument used in this study and was administered to the four shoplifting patients. The test is described as:

> An assessment of the severity of depression in psychiatrically diagnosed adults and adolescent patients aged 13 years and older. The BDI-II was developed as an indicator of the presence and degree of depressive symptoms consistent with the DSM-IV, not as an instrument for specifying clinical diagnosis. The BDI-II should be used cautiously (Beck, Steer, & Brown, 1996, p.1).

The BDI-II has been used with compulsive buyers or persons with compulsive buying disorder to assess for psychiatric comorbidity—that is, to determine whether shoplifters also have other serious psychiatric disorders. In one study, Kuzma and Black (2006) concluded that compulsive buyers have comorbid psychiatric disorders—particularly mood/depression, anxiety, substance abuse, and eating disorders.

The BDI-II is a widely used self-report instrument for measuring the severity of a patient's depression. It is designed to correspond to the *DSM–IV–TR* criteria for depression. It is a 21-question, multiple-choice, self-report inventory that constitutes one of the most reliable and valid instruments for measuring the severity of depression. The current version of the questionnaire was designed for individuals, ages 13 and older and is composed of items relating to depression symptoms such as hopelessness and irritability and cognitions such as guilt or feelings of being punished; physical symptoms such as fatigue, weight loss, and lack of interest in sex are also tapped. There are three versions of the BDI: the original BDI, first published in 1961 and later revised in 1971 as the BDI-1A, and the BDI-II, published in 1996. Today, the BDI-II is used as an assessment tool by mental health professionals and researchers in a variety of settings. The BDI-II takes 10 minutes to self-assess depressive symptoms.

Studies have demonstrated that the external locus of control of shoplifters correlates positively with elevated depression measures (Brady, 1990). Thus, the BDI-II results can be positively correlated with the locus of control score on externality.

The Cases Tell the Tale

The four cases presented in Chapter 6 are not just those of shoplifters in isolation; rather, they are very real people with families and full lives, including careers and life goals that are negatively impacted by feelings of being out of control and depressed. These people did not wake up one morning and suddenly tell themselves, "this is the day I'll lose control and begin to ruin my life by shoplifting." Losing control, or having feelings of being out of control, is an insidious, progressive psychological process that, if not treated, can yield very negative consequences.

Chapter 1 References

American Psychiatric Association. (2000) *Diagnostic and statistical manual of mental disorders* (4th ed., text rev.). Washington, DC: Author.

Arboleda-Florez, J., Durie, H., & Costello, J. (1977). Shoplifting—an ordinary crime. *International Journal of Offender Therapy and Comparative Criminology, 21,* 201–207.

Beck, A. T., Steer, R. A., & Brown, G.K. (1996). *Manual for the Beck Depression Inventory-I.* San Antonio, TX: Psychological Corporation.

Beck, E. & McIntyre, S. (1977). MMPI patterns of shoplifters within a college population. *Psychological Reports, 41(3f),* 1035–1040.

Berlin, P. (1996). Why do shoplifters steal…and why do so many continue to steal even after getting caught? In *The National Report on Shoplifting* (pp. 3–4). Jericho, NY: Shoplifters Alternative.

Berlin, P. (2006). Why do shoplifters steal? National Association for Shoplifting Prevention. Retrieved June 20, 2009 ,from http://www.shopliftingprevention.org

Bradford, J. & Balmaceda, R. (1983). Shoplifting: Is there a specific psychiatric syndrome? Canadian Journal of Psychiatry, 28, 248–254.

Brady, J. C. (1990). Drug addicts: Are they out of control? San Mateo, CA: Western Book/Journal Press.

Brady, J. C. (1999). Shoplifting: It's not what you think. San Jose, CA: PSI Press.

Carlson, K. A. (1982). Carlson psychological survey manual. Port Huron, MI: Sigma Assessment Systems.

Carlson, K. A. (1997). Carlson psychological survey manual (2nd ed.). Port Huron, MI: Sigma Assessment Systems.

Chestnut, W. Personal communication. (June 10, 2013)

Cupchik, W. (1997). Why honest people shoplift or commit other acts of theft. Toronto: Tagami.

Grant, J. E., & Kim, S. W. (2003). Stop me because I can't stop myself: Taking control of impulsive behavior. New York: McGraw-Hill.

Kuzma, J. M., & Black, D. W. (2006). Compulsive shopping: when spending begins to consume the consumer. Journal of Family Practice, 5(7), 27–40.

Moore, R. (1983). College shoplifters: Rebuttal of Beck and McIntyre. Psychological Reports, 53, 1111–1116.

Nichols, M. Personal communication. (June 10, 2013)

Palmer, E. J., & Hollin, C. R. (2003). Using the psychological inventory of criminal thinking styles with English prisoners. Legal and Criminological Psychology, 8, 175–187.

Rotter, J. B.(1966). Generalized expectancies for internal versus external control of reinforcement. Psychological Monographs, 80, 1.

Shulman, Terrence D. (2004, October 22). Appearance on CBS News The Early Show [television broadcast].

Shulman, Terrence D. (2011, March 6). The truth about shoplifting [Television broadcast]. CNBC TV Productions.

Yagoda, B. (1994, February). Addicted to stealing. Retrieved July 3,2013, from http://.ahopliftingprevention.org/whatnapffers/nrc/articlestoread/addicted to stealing

CHAPTER 2

THE SHOPLIFTING DILEMMA: IT'S A BIG DEAL!

There is only one...principle that can preserve a free society: namely, the strict prevention of all coercion, except in the enforcement of general abstract rules equally applicable to all.

—Friedrich A. Hayek, *The Road to Serfdom,* 1944

The Shoplifting Dilemma: Exactly What Is It? Kleptomania or Not?

Nationwide, shoplifting and petty theft has reached epidemic proportions. Shoplifting is a legal and psychosocial dilemma for all involved in the criminal justice system—defense attorneys, prosecutors, probation departments, judges, and, of course, defendants.

It has been estimated that in North America these types of theft crimes claim 20 victims every minute. More than 10 million acts of shoplifting are committed each year, with an annual dollar loss estimated at $20 billion (Glasscock, Rapoff, & Christophersen, 1988). An already bad situation has been made worse by the fact that shoplifting as a subtype of larceny is increasing at a far greater rate than the general population figures would suggest (Coid, 1984).

Research studies have attributed this dramatic increase in shoplifting to marginal detection, low prosecution rates, underreporting, and a bad economy. The shoplifting phenomenon is experienced by both male and female offenders from all social classes. Yet there is compelling evidence that upper middle class or affluent are overrepresented in certain shoplifting categories. This fact seems paradoxical. Why would well-to-do people engage in behavior that could result in their going to jail and suffering personal humiliation?

What exactly is the generally accepted definition of *shoplifting*? *Shoplifting* is a nonpsychological term used to describe an act of theft that occurs when an individual steals merchandise from a retailer while the store is open to the public. California has its own laws that address these types of crimes, and more often than not shoplifting is statutorily defined as petty theft.

Common Shoplifting Acts

The most common types of shoplifting acts include, but are not limited to:

1. Secreting and/or hiding unpaid-for merchandise on one's person or in one's handbag, store bag, umbrella, newspaper, or other container carried by the offender.

2. Wearing unpaid-for merchandise out of the store.

3. Openly carrying unpaid-for merchandise out of the store.

4. Switching price tags and paying a lesser price for an item.

5. Exchanging the contents of a package for merchandise of a higher value (for example, putting Nikes in a box of cheaper athletic shoes).

6. Selecting an item of merchandise from its display and presenting it for an exchange or refund (Sennewald, 2000, p. 4).

Maybe They Are Just Kleptos

Some shoplifting investigators have connected this particular type of theft to an impulse control disorder. Shoplifting as a discrete diagnostic classification appears in the *Diagnostic and Statistical Manual of Mental Disorders* (4th ed., text rev.; *DSM–IV–TR*; American Psychiatric Association, 2000, section 312.32) as kleptomania, along with intermittent explosive disorder, pyromania, pathological gambling, and trichotillomania (pulling out one's hair for the pleasure of it). The diagnosis of kleptomania is discussed at length later in this chapter. There seems to be no doubt that the phenomenon of shoplifting almost by definition is an expression of an impulse control disorder— that is, it involves the unchecked urge to steal. Yet, in addition to this simple reasoning, almost all shoplifting researchers, including me, believe that most shoplifters are not kleptomaniacs—their emotional state is inconsistent with the psychological definition—and are instead are given to illogical thoughts of overcompensation. These erroneous thoughts contribute to counterproductive and negative ends such as being apprehended, and arrested, and experiencing embarrassment because of shoplifting. After counseling innumerable shoplifters, I have seen a common motivational pattern of overcompensation patterning emerging. But, why the overcompensation? And to what is this overcompensation tied?

Over the years, shoplifters have reported vivid dream sequences during which they were stealing, constituting a form of overcompensation. Lorand (1950), for instance, recaptured the dream of one of his shoplifting patients. The case involved the simple theft of a library book. The patient had unconscious fears of her public exposure as a thief but nevertheless desired to steal the book because she felt she somehow deserved it: "Things have been stolen from me in the past, so I did it." As he describes her dream, "I come home. A boy is stealing everything in the house that belongs to mother and sister—jewels, furniture, etc. Mother and sister are not home. Then they come in. Father comes home…" (Lorand,1950, pp. 30–31). Lorand's patient falls into the category which I have termed the *equalizer shoplifter*. These shoplifters demonstrate a motivation to steal based on retaliatory justification; they have long memories of past perceived or real losses that have been taken from them, and symbolically they seek to regain them. To do this, they steal. (For a complete description of this shoplifter typology, see Chapter 3).

Lorand comments on another one of the shoplifter's psychological overcompensatory conflicts. This time the case involved a man who stole business equipment from his workplace:

When the conflict became very acute, he tried gradually to bring some of the equipment back, but that which was already incorporated in finished work could not be replaced. The stolen objects were of such small value, and to him, who was quite well to do, they obviously meant so little, that their stealing could not have been anything but compensation for the lack of something else—primarily of recognition for his work and more deeply for the lack of love at home (Lorand, 1950, pp. 30–31).

The overcompensation or equalization of the shoplifter as demonstrated by the Lorand cases is tied directly to underlying feelings of inadequacy or inferiority. Under normal circumstances, overcompensation is usually connected to a socially accepted goal. For example, a boy of small physical stature may engage in an extreme regimen of bodybuilding in order to compete with larger, more muscular boys, sometimes for the attention of girls. For shoplifters, the compensatory pattern chosen is not reflective of normal circumstances and is very likely one that is motivated by both selfish drives and unconscious wishes to possess something they do not have.

Many of the shoplifters I have treated voice opinions concerning their impression that they had been treated unfairly, and powerless to improve their life situation. This is consistent with persons who are directed by an external locus of control force. Because of their exigent need to rebalance their out-of-control lives, they seek psychological reparation within the illegal context of shoplifting. Theft was chosen as an inappropriate channel to overcompensate for their personal mistreatment and unfairness. To a large extent, these shoplifters felt their needs were blocked; therefore, they obtained a measure of relief by stealing (symbolic reparation).

Mrs. Daio (Chapter 6, Case 1) that for reasons she did not comprehend shoplifting purses temporarily relieved feelings of anxiety and worthlessness:

Most of my life I felt inferior to others. Almost nothing I did made me happy. I was empty inside and always fearful that something bad was going to happen to me. Of what I wasn't exactly sure, but in a strange way when I stole those purses, damn it, I felt better. At least I was good at something. It was like I didn't feel I was a second-class person any longer until I was arrested.

This theme of overcompensation was voiced many times by the shoplifters referred to me. It seemed that, in one way or another, each shoplifter was striving to achieve for him- or herself an improved status to compensate for intense feelings of inferiority, low self-esteem, and rejection. This is tantamount an external on locus of control. These strivings seem to be equated with a type of willpower to counteract some real or imagined social disability. Yes, shoplifting reflects elements of an impulse control problem and perhaps some characteristics of kleptomania; however, the concepts of being out of control and overcompensation, it seems to me, serve as better explanation of why certain people chose to steal.

Kleptomania: An Impulse Control Disorder? Maybe

At various times, shoplifters have been labeled "kleptos," a popular but socially pejorative term derived from the descriptive but not explanatory psychological and diagnostic word *kleptomania*. But are all shoplifters kleptomaniacs? As one superior court judge asked, "Is Mrs. Jones a 'klepto' or a criminal?" Considerable descriptive research, including the results of the present study, concludes that the preponderance of shoplifting behavior falls outside the psychological definition of kleptomania presented in the *DSM–IV–TR(312.32)*, which defines the disorder as follows:

    A. Recurrent failure to resist impulses to steal objects that are not needed for personal use or for their monetary value.

    B. Increasing sense of tension immediately before committing the theft.

    C. Pleasure, gratification, or relief at the time of committing the theft.

    D. The stealing is not committed to express anger or vengeance and is not in response to a delusion or hallucination.

    E. The stealing is not better accounted for by Conduct Disorder, a Manic Episode, or Antisocial Personality Disorder. (American Psychiatric Association, 2000, p.669).

The *DSM–IV–TR* further describes the kleptomania diagnosis and prevalence: "Kleptomania is a rare condition that appears to occur in fewer than 5% of identified shoplifters. It appears to be much more common in females" (American Psychiatric Association, 2000, p.668). The question is then raised, what about the other 95% of shoplifters who do not meet the diagnostic criteria of kleptomania? Chapter 3 presents a description of 16 shoplifter typologies, including kleptomania, as well as important new shoplifter categories: (1) the trophy collector, (2) the externalizer, (3) the provisional delinquent, (4) the binge-spree shoplifter, (5) the equalizer, and (6) the Alzheimer's sufferer/amnesiac. The trophy collection category helps explain why some shoplifters steal and covet very expensive items that they may later use as sexual pleasure objects (Mrs. Daio, Chapter 6, Case 1).

The shoplifters presented in this book were, in fact, demonstrably angry, vengeful, frustrated, and at times hostile at the time of their shoplifting offenses (Kleptomania, Criterion D). Because of these intensely negative emotions, these patients do not meet the psychiatric definition of kleptomania as outlined by the American Psychiatric Association. As stated by Cupchik, a major researcher in the field of shoplifting, "In 1991, Dr. Atcheson and I estimated that less than four or five of the hundreds of shoplifters we had assessed over a period of 12 years between 1979 and 1991 would legitimately qualify as suffering from kleptomania" (Cupchik, 1997, p. 24).

Further commenting on the *DSM–IV–TR* definition of kleptomania, especially as it relates to the element of anger and in agreement with my clinical findings, Cupchik states, "Dr. Atcheson and I have been entirely convinced that the vast majority of theft offenders we have assessed have been very angry indeed at the time of their offenses, and that there existed a strong psychodynamic relationship between the person's underlying anger and his or her subsequent theft behavior" (Cupchik,1997, p. 24).

In 1964, sociologist Mary O. Cameron effectively dismissed the hypothesis that shoplifting is synonymous with kleptomania. She further suggested that the term *kleptomania* may be only a catch-all, nonexplanatory diagnosis: "At this point it seems worthwhile to discuss a term I have not found necessary or useful to employ in this study, 'kleptomania.'" She further points out that, at least in her opinion, "There neither are (nor in terms of modern psychology, ever were) 'kleptomaniacs', i.e., people whose only form of maladjustment is an obsessive-compulsive desire to steal" (Cameron, 1964, pp. 116–117). "On the basis of these findings," she noted, "it appears that psychiatric diagnosis did not reveal any characteristic trends of neurotic personality deviation among those shoplifters who were examined" (pp.116-117).

Terrence Shulman, a recovering shoplifter and currently a shoplifting therapist in Detroit, Michigan, provides an understandable comparison of kleptomania and addictive-compulsive stealing/shoplifting. His description of the compulsive shoplifter fits well with the out-of-control or external shoplifter construct as defined in the present volume. His analysis is shown in Table 2.1.

Table 2.1. Comparison between Kleptomania and Addictive-Compulsive Stealing/Shoplifting

Kleptomania (DSM–IV–TR)	Addictive-Compulsive Stealing
• Recurrent failure to resist *impulses* to steal objects *not needed* for personal use/monetary value—no premeditation.	• Recurrent failure to resist *addictive compulsive* urges to steal objects that are used—some premeditation.
• Increasing sense of tension *just before* committing the theft.	• Generally, *already ever-present tension*.
• Pleasure or relief *at the time of the theft or during* the theft.	• Generally, pleasure or relief *shortly after* committing the theft.

• The stealing is *not* committed to express anger or vengeance.	• Generally, the stealing *is* a means of acting out anger or to make life fair.
• The stealing is not due to Conduct Antisocial Personality Disorder.	• Same. Generally, most people are honest and law-abiding.

Source: Shulman 2004, p. 72.

Frosch and colleagues, in one study of shoplifters, state: "Kleptomania must be distinguished from ordinary shoplifting... most shoplifters are not kleptomaniacs" (as cited in Cooper et al, 1986, p. 317). In a detailed psychological study of 50 shoplifters, Bradford and Balmaceda(1983) also found that only two of their many shoplifting patients fit the diagnostic criteria for kleptomania as outlined in the *DSM–IV–TR*.

The DSM–IV–TR Totally Misses the Point

These results from Frosch et al. (1983), as well as almost every other shoplifting researcher, continue to reveal inadequacies in the current *DSM–IV–TR* diagnostic criteria for kleptomania when diagnosing patients who steal. Frankly stated, the American Psychiatric Association's definition is inadequate and misses the point, because most shoplifters are indeed angry at the time of their theft. At best, the *DSM–IV–TR* nosology of kleptomania as an impulse disorder (this appears obvious) accounts for no more than 4–5% of those patients identified as taking things that do not belong to them.

Other psychologists who have treated large numbers of theft offenders claim that only 3% of their patients fit these limited *DSM* criteria (Fugere, D'Elia, and Philippe cited in Cupchik,1997). They conclude that only a small percentage (3–5%) of theft patients they treated could be diagnosed with kleptomania. This represents an initial and major diagnostic problem that somehow must be overcome for theft offenders to be diagnosed with any degree of clinical accuracy. If this same diagnostic percentage rate was applied, for instance, to a dental decay diagnosis, then we would all be toothless! There is a case to be made for the inclusion of shoplifting as separate and distinct diagnosis differentiating it from the current definition and diagnosis of kleptomania as currently established in the *DSM–IV–TR*.

In particular, an examination of the *DSM–IV–TR* definition of kleptomania 312.32, Criterion D—"The stealing is *not* committed to express anger or vengeance"—eliminates almost all shoplifters, because research, including this study, as well as experience in the diagnosis and treatment of hundreds of shoplifters, has verified that shoplifters are frequently bubbling over with both anger (sometimes expressed as self-hatred), vengeance ("Who gives a damn about Nordstrom anyway? They've got millions"), and retaliation ("Now I got back at them for short-changing me last time"). The real problem with the poorly crafted defining criteria for kleptomania in the *DSM–IV–TR* is that, as proven by researchers, up to 97% of all patients who steal are currently misdiagnosed. How can this be true? Returning to the dental misdiagnosis analogy, this might mean that when you send your children for a dental checkup, the well-intentioned, good doctor will miss up to 97% of your child's cavities. This is not very comforting, to be sure—these are not favorable odds! Even when examining psychological diagnoses in general, which historically have been fraught with a multitude of definitional issues, the classification of shoplifters with a 97% error rate is not acceptable.

As Cupchik states:
It is the opinion of both Dr. Atcheson and myself that, of the hundreds of theft offenders we had seen between 1979 through 1986, there were only two or three who could possibly be said to be suffering from true kleptomania. In other words, less than 3% of the theft offender cases we assessed may have warranted the label of "kleptomania" (1997, p. 230).

Is it any wonder that the fields of psychology and psychiatry maintain such bad reputations and poor histories when called upon to diagnose shoplifter patients? Cupchik, almost 30 years ago, strongly argued that the *DSM-III* (which was current at that time) diagnostic category of kleptomania be expanded to include the category of atypical theft offenders, a typology which corresponds to Typology 3 presented in Chapter 3.

Commenting on the potential for modification of or the inclusion of new categories of theft behavior, Cupchik continues:

> Fortunately, the DSM represents an evolving clinical database and clinical decision-making process, and in a sense must therefore always be playing 'catch-up' since it takes its cues from the growing body of clinical findings. It is the hope of this writer that, with the additional findings of my own and those of other clinical investigators, that some alteration in the listings pertaining to theft behavior will be forthcoming in a near future edition of DSM (1997, p. 231).

At the time that Cupchik proffered these comments concerning the fleeting notion of the "evolving clinical database," he was being more than charitable. It must be disappointing for Cupchik that, after all these years, nothing has changed in the *DSM–IV–TR* diagnosis of shoplifting including the new DSM-5.

At this time, an American Psychiatric Association task force is no doubt hard at work on the development and revision of the *DSM-5*. The task force is charged with reviewing the entire *Diagnostic and Statistical Manual of Mental Disorders*. In its effort to redefine and hopefully improve this important diagnostic manual, it is hoped the task force will also address and clarify the confusing classification of impulse control disorders, including the category of kleptomania. Of central importance to this effort is the collective opinion of most clinicians who are called on to diagnose and treat persons accused of theft that, because of the current, confusing description of kleptomania, the preponderance of all shoplifters (up to 97%) do not meet the diagnostic criteria.

To this end, it is my intent to forward to the task force the results of this study along with additional shoplifting research results conducted by professional researchers such as Cupchik and Shulman. Their research

results generally support those expressed here—that the present kleptomania diagnosis fails to describe or accurately depict the subjective
emotional state of the shoplifter at the time of the theft; additionally,
that it fails to account for many other psychological factors connected
to the shoplifting experience. While I am sure   that this so called army
of experts must have had some sound theoretical reasons for the inclusion of certain diagnostic criteria, particularly that "The stealing is not
committed to express anger or vengeance, is not done in response to a
delusion or hallucination." But where did this information come from?
It is unclear where this information came from. It certainly could not
have been derived from direct therapeutic conversations with a shoplifter population, because research shows at the time they offend it is
well understood that shoplifters are frequently angry, hostile, vengeful,
retaliatory, and sometimes fairly nasty characters.

The description of this disorder under the *DSM–IV–TR* section
"Differential Diagnosis" cautions that : "Kleptomania should be distinguished from ordinary acts of theft or shoplifting. Ordinary theft
(whether planned or impulsive) is deliberate and is motivated by the
usefulness of the object or its monetary worth." The dilemma here, of
course, is that most professionals who diagnose and treat kleptomania patients have voiced their disagreement with this definition.

During the time I spent conducting the research on this book, I
consulted with a wide variety of professionals who made it crystal
clear that, as a group, few shoplifters were motivated by any material gain. In fact, it seems that just the opposite seems to be more
representative—that is, the thefts are perpetrated because of mostly
unconscious psychological drivers and not because Mrs. Smith needs
a new jewelry accessory to go with her new stolen designer dress.

I recommend the inclusion of a new diagnostic category—shoplifting—that would be substantively different from the present *DSM's*
coding for kleptomania, within the section "Impulse Control Disorders,
Not Elsewhere Classified." It is apparent that a new approach is
required to create both a descriptive and explanatory diagnosis that
can accurately capture this mental condition.

Let's Change Things

I suggest the following:

1. Retain both the *DSM–IV–TR* and *DSM-5* (2013) kleptomania diagnosis within the diagnostic section "Impulse Control Disorders, Not Elsewhere Classified" for use with the small number of cases it does accurately capture. After all, the term *kleptomania* has been in popular use since the 1880s. Maintain all five criteria for kleptomania, A–E, as stated earlier in this chapter.

2. Develop a new *DSM* category to better describe *shoplifting*— a term, amazingly enough, that was coined by the offenders themselves. Pursuant to this new category, delete Criterion D from the current *DSM–IV–TR*, "the stealing is not committed to express anger or vengeance."

3. For the present, use the available and more applicable *DSM–IV–TR* coding 312.30, "Impulse Control Disorder, Not Otherwise Specified." As stated in the *DSM–IV–TR*, "This category is for disorders of impulse control that do not meet the criteria for any specific Impulse-Control Disorder or for another mental disorder having features involving impulse control described elsewhere in the manual (e.g. Substance Dependence, a Paraphilia)" (p.677**).**

Impulse Control Disorder Identifiers

It is my opinion that the diagnostic category, "Impulse Control Disorder, Not Otherwise Specified, "can more closely capture the recurrent, maladaptive failure to resist stealing characterized but not limited to these 10 psychological identifiers:

1. Preoccupation with shoplifting

2. Shoplifting equals excitement

3. Unsuccessful efforts to stop

4. Irritability, anger, hostility, vengeance, retaliation

5. Uses shoplifting as escape device

6. Feels helpless to stop

7. Even when caught, shoplifter repeats

8. Lies about or covers shoplifting events

9. Jeopardizes everything, (security and reputation) to shoplift

10. Feels sudden gratification after shoplifting

It has been my clinical experience in 25 years of private practice that the kleptomania diagnosis has rarely been applicable. Alternatively, I have had many occasions on which it was more appropriate to use the coding "Impulse Control Disorder, Not Otherwise Specified" to better capture the representative behaviors of people who steal.

A second pervasive drawback of the existing classification system concerns the criminality aspect implicit with using the kleptomania diagnosis, which it fails to account for. This criminal issue is of paramount importance, because theft is an act that has already taken place where the person has already committed the criminal act of stealing. The clinician is then called upon to reach back in time to render a present diagnosis for a past criminal event. The *DSM–IV–TR* indirectly addresses the issue of diagnosing retrospective theft or criminal behaviors only a few times in the entire 943-page coding manual, and only the conduct disorder diagnosis specifically addresses theft or criminogenic issues connected directly with shoplifting. Five of these principal diagnoses from the *DSM–IV–TR* include:

1. Conduct disorders, 312.89, unspecified onset: aggression to people and animals, Criteria 6: "has stolen while confronting a victim."

2. Adjustment disorders, 309.3: "disturbance in conduct in which there is a violation of the rights of others."

3. Borderline personality disorder, 301.83, Criterion 4: "impulsivity in at least two areas that are potentially self-damaging (e.g. spending, sex, substance abuse, reckless driving, and binge eating)."

4. Antisocial personality disorder, 301.7, Criteria 1 and 7: "failure to conform to social norms with respect to lawful behaviors as indicated by repeatedly performing acts that are grounds for arrest… rationalizing having hurt, mistreated, or stolen from another."

5. Manic episodes, classified under mood disorders: "Adverse consequences of a Manic Episode (e.g. involuntary hospitalization, difficulties with the law, or serious financial difficulties) often result from poor judgment and hyperactivity," ethical lapses, and engaging in unrestrained buying sprees. There are only "baby steps" from unrestrained buying sprees to shoplifting.

It is safe to conjecture that the preponderance of crimes against property—shoplifting—are not committed based on altruistic Robin Hood–like motives. In my experience, these acts are in the main committed based upon the thief's underlying negative psychological drivers, which embrace anger, aggression, retaliation, open hostility, and vengeance. Therefore, using the definition of *kleptomania* in the current *DSM–IV–TR* (Now replaced by the DSM-5) places the diagnostician in a corner. It is clear that when called upon by an attorney or a court, the clinician has little choice when differentially diagnosing the shoplifter defendant. Instead of kleptomania, I prefer the coding "Impulse Control Disorder, Not Otherwise Specified," which can be tailored to match the individual elements of each shoplifter's history of stealing and presenting psychological symptomatology, thus better accounting for his or her criminal transgressions.

The *DSM-5* drafters have included hoarding behavior as a new diagnosis. This will be a new diagnosis to classify people who have significant difficulty discarding personal possessions. Hoarding can lead to anxiety and distress, and including it in the *DSM-5* is expected to increase public awareness and stimulate new research into this area. Currently there is evidence to validate a new psychological condition related to the retention of computer files, digital hoarding. This condition, which reportedly affects millions of people worldwide, centers on why people, both men and women alike, for no obvious reason, simply can't hit the delete key on their computers, thereby eliminating forever the accumulating mountain of unread and no doubt useless e-mails they receive. This new phenomenon is, of course, a close cousin to the condition historically familiar to many: "Why can't Joe clean out the garage and toss out all that piled-up junk?" Nationwide, and perhaps even internationally, the same answer is given: "You just never know when you'll need it," or, in the case of the digital hoarder, "I'll read them later!" But, in fact, "later" never really comes.

Hoarding, while it can be an important issue in society, is certainly less prevalent than shoplifting. However, the two behaviors are related. Therefore, inclusion of hoarding behavior and the exclusion of new and more descriptive definitions of shoplifting might be an oversight. An analysis of the many thousands of shoplifting cases compared with the relatively few cases of hoarding demonstrates that shoplifting as a separate diagnostic category warrants its own unique diagnosis, perhaps predicated on the reasons presented here.

Maybe It's a Capitalist Plot

In addition to theft patterning based on kleptomania, it is true that economic drivers may influence a small percentage (about 5%) of shoplifters. Left-leaning economist Gordon (1973) offers one version of theft, including shoplifting, as indigenous to the capitalist way of life. He argues, "the social relations of production in capitalistic societies help define an economic class structure and that one cannot therefore adequately understand the behavior of individuals unless one examines the structure of institutionally determined opportunities."He continues,"Driven by the fear of economic insecurity and by competitive desire to gain some of the goods unequally distributed throughout the society, many individuals eventually become criminals" (Gordon,1973, p.174). Gordon's perspective may be particularly relevant given the present state of the U.S. economy.

Shoplifting Is a Big Deal

Whether classified as kleptomania, external behavior, atypical, out of control, or an impulse control disorder, shoplifting is obviously a widespread phenomenon. Current statistics suggest that 1 of every 11 people have shoplifted at some time in his or her life, which amounts to millions of dollars in merchandise per day, according to the National Association for Shoplifting Prevention (2009). All forms of shoplifting are rampant in society today and are reaching epidemic proportions. Sixty-one percent of the nation's largest retailers report that the incidence of "opportunistic shoplifting" increased tenfold during the 2008–2009 economic downturn and recession, despite the fact that these retailers have collectively spent $15 billion per year in loss-prevention efforts (Harper, 2009).

Even with these enhanced loss-prevention techniques, more than half of all U.S. retail stores have been victimized by organized retail crime, an umbrella term for grand-scale shoplifting (Retail Industry Leaders Association, 2009). The present analysis does not address the issues associated with organized retail crime offenses or those cases where monetary gain is a central factor related to theft; it does, however, address those offenders who steal without any apparent economic incentives that could serve as drivers for their theft behavior.

Celebrities Really Do It!

The psychological drivers in the cases I present are, in all probability, similar to those compelling the celebrity shoplifters we read about in the popular media. The celebrity cases are not merely paparazzi fodder, but represent personal psychological histories and pain (loss of control) that are, in many cases, exactly the same as the cases of the four women presented in this study.

When we hear the news that another celebrity has been arrested for shoplifting, nonfinancial psychological factors such as overcompensation, depression, loss, sexual tension relief, revenge, and loneliness are often detailed. Consider, for example, the statements made by Winona Ryder on ABC News' *20/20* to Diane Sawyer. Despite being a Hollywood star, Ryder described her personal sadness, loneliness and alienation: "I'd drive around L.A. at night and listen to music when I couldn't sleep, and I wish I had someone to talk to, a friend or someone, and I didn't" (Ryder, 1999). Ryder was convicted in 2002 of felony grand theft and vandalism for the theft of several thousand dollars' worth of merchandise from a Saks Fifth Avenue store in Beverly Hills. A judge later reduced her convictions to misdemeanors and said she could finish her probation unsupervised ("Winona Ryder's Conviction Reduced," 2004). It is apparent that this successful and highly compensated movie star did not steal because she needed the clothing.

More recently, in 2008 Ms. Ryder in was accused of either misplacing(as she contends) or the outright theft of $124,000 worth of Bulgari diamond-encrusted jewels, a braclet and a ring. These items were loaned to the star to wear during a swank photo shoot in Madrid, Spain sponsored by Marie Claire magazine. Regardless of the fact that Ms. Ryder has given several plausible reasons as to why the jewelry went missing, and before the case could be adjudicated, the media jumped all over the story, in their usual, nasty manner: "Winona Did It Again," "Caught In The Middle Of Jewelry Theft-Winona Accused," "Here We Go Again-Winona And The Missing Jewels," and perhaps the most biting headline- "Once A Thief-Always A Thief-The Continuing Story Of A Troubled Actress."

Another well publicized case of "trial-by-media" concerns the former teen Mouseketeer, and pop-singer, Britney Spears. Not eliciting much media sympathy either, Ms. Spears, who has by most accounts, experienced ups-and-downs in her personal life, exhibiting at times some odd behaviors such as shaving her trademarked golden blond hair, and appearing a little drunk in public, was accused of stealing a cheap lighter from a gas station (do they sell any others?) and equally as strange, taking a wig off a store mannequin in an accessory store then leaving without paying.

A newsworthy case involving fashion model and socialite Peaches Geldof (daughter of rock musician Bob Geldof and granddaughter of famous British T.V. host, Hughie Green) who is well recognized strolling down a fashion designer's catwalk, or as a writer for "The London's Daily Telegraph", was accused of stealing an expensive couture dress from a trendy London boutique. Similar to the accusations made against Ms. Ryder, Peaches, was suspected of stealing expensive clothing after her photo shoot a year earlier.

Another controversial, gossip-fueled case is that of Lindsay Lohan, who was charged with felony grand theft for shoplifting a one-of-a-kind $2,500 necklace from Kamofie & Company, an exclusive Venice Beach, California, jewelry store. She pled not guilty and was released on $40,000 bail. Ms. Lohan did not steal because she could not afford the necklace. On April 22, 2011, Los Angeles Judge Stephanie Sautner sentenced Ms. Lohan to 120 days in jail and 480 hours of community service, including 360 hours at the downtown Los Angeles Women's Center on Skid Row and 120 hours at the Mission Road Coroner's office, as part of a probation violation for the alleged jewelry theft. The judge ruled that Lohan had violated the conditions of her 2007 probation for drunk driving.

An additional aspect of Ms. Lohan's case centers on the revocation of her probation, which could result in Ms. Lohan being sentenced to up to 245 days in jail. Although facing jail time, the *San Jose Mercury News* reported that the probation commissioner in charge of Ms. Lohan's case, Jane Godfrey, believes in rehabilitation in lieu of confinement. Since being placed on probationary status, Ms. Lohan has been accused of misdemeanor lying to police, reckless driving, obstructing a police officer after she crashed her Porsche on the Pacific Coast Highway, and misdemeanor assault charges stemming from a brawl in a New York City nightclub (Hicks, 2012). An update of her case in a *San Jose Mercury News* headline, (Hicks, 4, 2013) pejoratively reads: "Lindsay Lohan Lands in Familiar Spot-Betty Ford." The article continues to describe Ms. Lohan's substance abuse battle, emphasizing her many relapses, rather than any positive steps that she has made to combat her long-standing addiction.

Indeed, Peaches, Britney, Winona and Lindsay who apparently are accustomed to having a cohesive script ready to follow when acting, are "scriptless" and clueless as to why they continually seem to put themselves into bad situations (like shoplifting), that are not in their best self-interest. The sub-title of this book, "When They Have It All !" is an apt description of these tragic, popular women who appear externally to "have it all" yet have, for uncertain reasons, have fallen from grace. Although convicted many times over by the paparazzi, before they had their day in court, these women, as well as hundreds of others like them, on a psychological-level, simply have no idea of what drives their inappropriate actions. Instead of mindlessly condemning these easily targeted, vulnerable women to sell more tabloids, in my professional opinion, they deserve respect, personal regard, compassion and comprehensive understanding of why they act as they do. In fact, their real stories probably have never been told to professionals for de-construction and interpretation, even though at times they have given shallow interviews to TV personalities and print reporters. Instead of an interview with a morning TV anchor on Channel 4, I extend an open, professional invitation to help these often confused women (and who of us aren't at times?) to help them better arrange the pieces of their torn lives viewed within the framework of seeing them more as sinned against than as sinners.

Additional cases making the news include former Miss USA, Shannon Marketic and baseball pitcher Mike Leake. Shannon Marketic was charged with shoplifting in Denton, Texas, in 2010. As she explained it to the *Dallas Morning News*, "The items, including skin treatment products, had been rolled beneath her purse in her shopping basket without her knowledge. She denied shoplifting" ("Ex–Miss U.S.A. Charged with Shoplifting," 2010).

On April 18, 2011, Mike Leake, a starting pitcher for the Cincinnati Reds, was arrested at a Macy's department store in downtown Cincinnati. He was charged, with shoplifting six T-shirts valued at

$58.99. His teammates and fans were shocked at this news likely due to his $2.3 million signing bonus in 2009 and monthly salary of $425,000 at the time of his arrest ("Reds Pitcher Mike Leake Arrested alleged theft", 2011). Again, it is obvious that Mr. Leake could have paid for the six shirts that he allegedly stole. His case is one that makes us look for the noneconomic variables that serve as the mainspring of shoplifting behavior for people with money.

While these shoplifting cases are newsworthy, they are not sparked by dollar-driven motivation. Rather, certain psychological commonalities affect both the celebrity shoplifter as well as on the less newsworthy shoplifters included here. And not all shoplifters are the same. My research has established that there are up to 16 shoplifter typologies (see Chapter 3). It is important to be able to differentiate these sixteen types and determine the motivational factors underlying the shoplifting act, which can also facilitate later treatment choices.

Chapter 2 References

ABC. 20/20. Interview Part 1 with Winona Ryder by Dianne Sawyer. [YouTube video]. Retrieved December 1,2009, from www.youtube.com/watch?V=ZogBCYILm3A

American Psychiatric Association. (1980). Diagnostic and statistical manual of mental disorders, 3rd edition. Washington, DC: Author.

American Psychiatric Association. (2000). Diagnostic and statistical manual of mental disorders (4th edition, text rev). Washington, DC: Author.

Associated Press. (2010, August 4). Ex-Miss U.S.A. charged with shoplifting in Denton. Star Chronicle—Houston, Texas.

Berlin, P. (1996). Why do shoplifters steal…and why do so many continue to steal even after getting caught? Reprinted from The National Report on Shoplifting. Jericho, N.Y.: Shoplifters Alternative, pp. 3–4.

Bradford,J. & Balmaceda,R.(1983). Shoplifting: Is it a specific psychiatric syndrome? Canadian Journal of Psychiatry, 28,248-254.

Cameron, M. O. (1964) The booster and the snitch: Department store shoplifting. New York-London: The Free Press of Glencoe, A Division of The Macmillan Company.

Coid, J. (1984). Relief of Diazepam-withdrawal Syndrome by Shoplifting. British Journal of Psychiatry, 145, 552–554..

Cupchik, W. (1997) Why honest people shoplift or commit other acts of theft. Toronto: Tagami Communications.

Frosch, W.K., Frosch, J.P., & Frosch, J. (1986) Cited by Cooper, A.M., Francis, A.J. &

Sacks, M.M. (1986). Psychiatry: The personality disorders and neuroses. New York: Basic Books, (p.317).

Glasscock, S., Rapoff, M. & Christophersen, E. (1988). Behavioral methods to reduce shoplifting. Journal of Business and Psychology, 2 (3), 343–354.

Gordon, D. M. (1973, April). Capitalism, class, and crime in America. Crime and Delinquency, 19 (2), 173–174.

Harper, J. (2009, May 11). One industry still booming. Washington Times, p.2.

Retrieved November 20, 2012, from http://www..washingtontimes. com/news/may/11/shoplifting-growing-in-poor-economymdl

Hicks, T. (2012, December 13). Jail time in Lindsey Lohan's future? San Jose Mercury News . com/celebrities, p. A-2.

Hicks, T.(2013), Lindsay Lohan lands in familiar spot-Betty Ford. SanJose Mercury News. com/celebrities, Section 1, p. 2.

Lorand, S. (1950). Clinical studies in psychoanalysis. New York: International Universities Press, Inc.

Reds pitcher Mike Leake arrested. (2011, April 8). Los Angeles Times, p.4.

Sennewald, C. A. (2000). Shoplifting vs. retailers. Chula Vista,CA: New Century Press.

Shulman, T. D. (2004). Something for nothing: Shoplifting addiction and recovery. West Conshohocken, PA: Infinity Publishing.

Swertlow F. & Silverman, S.M. June,18, 2004. People Magazine. Judge reduces Winona Ryder's conviction, p.1. Times, Inc. 2013.

SIXTEEN SHOPLIFTING TYPOLOGIES AND SEVEN SHOPLIFTING PSYCHOLOGICAL CATEGORIES

Most people are unconscious of their thoughts or they may be prone to "stinking thinking." All behavior—whether freely chosen or stemming from an addictive-compulsive mind set—originates from our thoughts, beliefs, and values.

—TERRENCE D. SHULMAN, SOMETHING FOR NOTHING, 2004

Shoplifters Are Not All the Same

A number of shoplifting investigators, including Schulman (2004), have developed shoplifting typologies. The shoplifting typologies and subdivisional psychosocial category classifications are viewed as non–mutually exclusive—that is, they tend to share certain psychological characteristics with each other. This categorization or mapping of shoplifters is seen as emergent to the extent that continuous research likely will confirm additional shoplifter typologies not included here. Thus, this listing is not meant to be exhaustive, yet it has expanded the number of validated shoplifter categories identified previously by other researchers in the field to sixteen from six or seven. This is not to suggest that previous researchers have failed to establish or diagnose the additional shoplifter typologies outlined here. The fact remains that as more types of shoplifters are diagnosed and treated, invariably they will present with new psychological symptomatology that lends itself to the development of additional typologies. This is especially true of Typology 14, the Alzheimer's/amnesiac shoplifter. As the U.S. population ages, we can anticipate that the percentage of this type of shoplifter will correspondingly increase.

Table 3.1 delineates the 16 shoplifter typologies into seven psychological subcategories. Each typology is characterized by certain identifiable elements. The single commonality shared by all the typologies is the fact they include a definitive and measurable psychosocial or adjustment problem. Almost counterintuitively, these adjustment issues are turned around by shoplifters and become what they believe are solutions to their problems, while in reality these adjustments lead to their subtle acceptance of a deviant lifestyle. Shoplifting as a form of deviant behavior may appear methodical, compulsive, goal-oriented, specifically directed, or as a conscious attempt to cheat society by getting something for nothing. In reality, none of the four women whose cases are presented in depth in Chapter 6 knew why they had committed the thefts, even though their behaviors certainly represent what appears to be, at least on a surface level, a conscious contempt for the rights of others and nonconformity with society's laws. None of these four patients, when queried, had any initial insights as to why they offended, risking it all and perhaps facing a jail sentence.

Most shoplifters today can be categorized into one or more of these 16 overlapping typologies based on clinical observations and prior research conducted by treating professionals. This observational methodology is descriptive but not psychologically explanatory for the purpose here. Therefore, the question presents itself: Why do some shoplifters engage in one distinct form of stealing or fall into a discrete typology such as binge shoplifting, while others fall into the thrill seeker category and yet others become compulsive, out-of-control shoplifters?

This study supports the position that the level of personal risk attached to each typology is affected directly by the individual's measure on the locus-of-control variable. Correspondingly, the more out-of-control or external shoplifters, as measured on the Rotter Locus of Control Scale, would generally fall into a higher shoplifter risk typology, such as the thrill seeker. Those less externally oriented shoplifters, on the other hand, might fall into a lower-impulse risk category, such as the situational shoplifter. In some shoplifting cases some behavior is shared by one or more of these typologies; thus, the boundaries between the typologies may be porous. A complete analysis as to why shoplifters follow one track and not another, especially when considering the evaluation of psychological risk taking, is a fertile area for further research.

Table 3.1. Sixteen Shoplifter Typologies and Seven Correspondent Psychological Categories

Sixteen Shoplifter Typologies	Seven Psychological Categories
1. The Externalizer*+	
2. The Compulsive▪	1. Impulse Driven
3. The Atypical Shoplifter	
4. The Kleptomaniac▪	

5. The Thrill Seeker▪

6. The Trophy Shoplifter*

7. The Binge-Spree Shoplifter*

8. The Equalizer*

> 2. Psychosocially Motivated

9. The Situational Shoplifter

10. The Professional▪

11. The Impoverished
(Economically
Disadvantaged) Shoplifter▪

> 3. Economically Influenced

12. The Provisional/Delinquent
Shoplifter

> 4. Age Determined

13. The Drug or Alcohol Addict▪

> 5. Alcohol and Substance
Connected

14. The Alzheimer's Sufferer/
Amnesiac*

15. The Chemically/Alcohol
Driven Shoplifter

> 6. Mentally/Medically Impaired

16. The Inadvertent/Amateur
Shoplift*

> 7. No Identifiable
Psychosocial Drivers

▪These shoplifter categories have been previously researched by Shulman (2004, p. 80).

+ The externalizer shoplifter is the primary focus in the present research.

* This is a new category.

These sixteen shoplifter typologies are not exhaustive and were not designed to be mutually exclusive but are meant to serve as descriptive psychological categories. The often-asked question regarding shoplifters was posed by Berlin: "Is it need, or is it greed…or is it something entirely different that tempts millions of people to steal from retail stores each year? Except for the drug addicts and hardened professionals who steal for resale and profit as a business, most shoplifters are decent people who are otherwise law-abiding citizens" (1996, p. 2).

The preponderance of the shoplifters that I have treated can provide only vaguely defined surface reasons for their stealing. These reasons are not the same as those deeply buried in their unconsciousness as to why they even began to think about stealing in the first place. It is the position here that the behavior of shoplifters falls into a certain typology and that shoplifters traverse through four shoplifting stages (detailed in Chapter 5). This represents a life-changing experience for them.

Retailers, the police, prosecutors, attorneys, and judges see thousands of apprehended shoplifters who, for a variety of reasons, don't always fit the profile of a typical criminal. More often than not, they don't use shoplifting paraphernalia, they don't use drugs, they carry proper identification, they have no prior criminal record (except perhaps for shoplifting), they don't associate with known criminals, they don't steal for resale, they usually have the money to pay for the item(s) they stole, they frequently have a job and a family, they steal things they don't really need and often don't use, they know what they did was morally wrong and against the law, and frequently they feel ashamed and remorseful. Their overall lifestyle is not that of a typical thief or criminal. These people are processed through the criminal justice system, as they should be, but with little understanding of exactly why they committed the offense and what kind of treatment is appropriate to help reduce recidivism.

The focus of this book is a reinterpretation of the shoplifter as a person who is directed by external factors that reinforce, help determine and direct his or her stealing behaviors. This is compared with the internally controlled person who feels that the reinforcement for his or her behavior comes from personal effort and not from outside, random forces driving him or her in unpredictable directions.

These researched shoplifter typologies are representative of the current status of shoplifting investigation. Yet, there are no doubt additional typology descriptions still to be identified. The inclusion of the first typology, "the external shoplifter" or "the externalizer," is supported by the locus-of-control research done with the four cases presented in Chapter 6. In turn, each of the sixteen typologies is discussed. More attention is devoted to those definitive shoplifting categories for which there are ample research data to support their inclusion. For example, much attention has been focused on the external and compulsive shoplifter typologies. This review is especially focused on those areas because direct, empirical psychological research with these two typologies has been feasible. The category of "thrill seeker," although a representative class of shoplifting, is not so easily investigated using standardized psychological instruments.

Sixteen Shoplifting Typologies
Impulse-Driven

1. The Externalizer

Regardless of the motivation to shoplift, I have found, using psychological testing, that the majority of shoplifters engage in these self-defeating, illegal acts not based on criminal intent, financial incentive, material need, or greed but as a response to the perception that they are not in control of their lives. The four shoplifter cases presented in Chapter 6 all demonstrate an external locus-of-control orientation. This group of shoplifters has been termed *externalizers*. These shoplifters feel they are controlled by outside forces that serve as negative psychological drivers, lowering their moral threshold against not stealing and resulting in their chronic theft behaviors. Research pertinent to this study indicates that the preponderance of shoplifters fall into this category. Similar to the classification of external nonoffenders, these shoplifters share many identifiable crossover psychological characteristics.

Research on locus of control specifically with deviant or criminal groups strongly indicates that externalizers are more aggressive

48

and show a greater criminal tendency when compared to internal-izers (Brady, 1990). To some degree, the external shoplifters use their theft behavior as an illegitimate channel to express their anger or as a means to legitimize their personal aggression. Thus, shoplifting is not simply interpreted as a passive event. In many of the cases, there is direct confirmation of what in psychological theory has been labeled the frustration/aggression hypothesis. This well-established the-ory postulates that shoplifters, similar to other criminal subcultural groups, displace their aggression perhaps generally at society for not giving them equal access to material goals and redirects it at substi-tute targets, such as Macy's, Saks Fifth Avenue, or Nordstrom. In the end, most shoplifters display copious amounts of anger, resentment, and even open hostility towards themselves and society.

2. The Compulsive

The compulsive shoplifter shares many maladaptive traits with the external shoplifter. Hipp (2010) presents the behavioral characteristics of compulsive shoplifters:

- A recurrent failure to resist obsessive, addictive, or com-pulsive out-of-control thoughts.

- The act of shoplifting brings pleasure and relief during or just after the event.

- They usually feel guilt or shame afterward.

- The stealing is often acting-out behavior based on anger, or a way of trying to dissipate anger/frustration.

- The stealing is not due to conduct disorder or antisocial personality disorder.

- This group of people is at risk of cross-addiction.

- They are usually law-abiding persons aside from their shoplifting (p. 5).

49

This group of shoplifters demonstrate repressed anger and often exhibit signs of other addictions such as gambling and compulsive shopping or buying disorders. They are often extremely generous to others, yet paradoxically don't care about themselves. If caught and confronted, they will break down and become quite emotional. Compulsive shoplifters are also seen as externalizers or as people who cannot gain self-controlled power over their own actions, maintaining a belief system influenced by capriciousness, chance, and unpredictability. I have found that compulsive shoplifters often have repressed memories of a past traumatic life event that results in current theft episodes. This event has negatively predisposed them to performing quite irrational acts.

This compulsive aspect has also been tied to compulsive buying or what Black (2007) has termed *compulsive buying disorder*. The validity of this classification continues to be debated by psychologists. According to Black, the symptoms of compulsive buying disorder involve "an increasing level of urge or anxiety that can only lead to a sense of completion when a purchase is made" (2007, p. 3). I have found that compulsive shopping or buying may serve as a gateway for later, more troubling theft behavior. One of the shoplifters presented in Chapter 6 had a history of compulsive buying that antedated her shoplifting and that made her "feel important and less alienated." As stated by Shulman (2004, p.101), "If a person starts out with a shopping addiction, it becomes tempting to start shoplifting as a way of budgeting money, rationalizing that one isn't buying as much or spending as much if one is stealing."

Lending support to the hypothesis that compulsive buying represents a shoplifting gateway activity, Grant and Kim (2003) present the case of a compulsive shopper who fits the compulsive buying disorder characteristics outlined by Black. This case also supports the clinical notion that compulsive external, out-of-control-driven behavior leads to shoplifting.

3. The Atypical Shoplifter

Cupchik (1997), a respected shoplifting researcher, proffers a unique shoplifter category that he has termed the *atypical* shoplifter. This type of shoplifting is viewed in the simplest of terms as not motivated by personal economic gains. This notion of shoplifting as a noneconomically driven behavior is consistent with the case studies presented in Chapter 6. Another factor shared by the shoplifters in the cases presented here is that none of them had any idea why they engaged in theft but that it was certainly not because of money.

4. The Kleptomaniac

Kleptomaniacs also steal for no apparent reason. However, they represent only a small percentage of shoplifters, statistically not more than 5%. Kleptomaniacs are impulsive and often careless in their shoplifting approaches. They will often take clothing items that don't fit them or things they could never use in their everyday lives. When caught, many will admit they are kleptomaniacs and often use superficial excuses such as "I don't remember taking it," "How did that get in my purse?" and "There must be some mistake; that shouldn't have been in my shopping cart."

Not only is this classification relatively small in number, it is also the most psychologically controversial typology. In the current psychiatric diagnostic code, the *Diagnostic and Statistical Manual of Mental Disorders (2000) DSM–IV–TR* correctly lists kleptomania as an impulse-control disorder but states, "the stealing is not committed to express anger/vengeance." Most shoplifting researchers take exception to this classification. Most of the shoplifters I have diagnosed and treated have demonstrated pronounced feelings of anger or vengeance, and typically both; thus, those shoplifters do not fall into the *DSM–IV–TR* classification. A complete discussion of this poor diagnostic classification is presented in Chapter 2.

Psychosocially Motivated

5. The Thrill Seeker

The thrill seeker, viewed as a higher-risk shoplifter, steals on a dare or for the intrinsic excitement connected to stealing, and this group of shoplifters will often join with others and steal in groups. Many teenaged shoplifters fall into this category. The social/psychological payoff for thrill-seeking shoplifters is a quest for autonomy and individuation, perhaps from their parents or from society in general. Their goal for shoplifting is viewed as psychological overcompensation—that is, while these shoplifters may have a history of failure, shoplifting gives them a personal sense of autonomy that overcompensates by using upside-down reasoning. One thrill seeking shoplifter stated, "It was like the only thing I did pretty OK! Even though it was probably bad, I still felt good about it." This shoplifter typology has been expanded from Shulman's original definition.

6. The Trophy Collector

Recently, there have been more cases of shoplifters whom I have labeled *trophy collectors* reported from studies conducted by other investigators and by the news media. Shulman (2011) comments on what he has labeled "trophy shoppers" who "tend to need to have the best of everything; they seek out that perfect object, be it fashion, art, car, etc.—the more special, unique or rare, the better" (p 72). He does not, however, include shoplifting in his trophy shopper typology.

Many people have a penchant for collecting fine objects such as Ferraris, Rolex watches, fine paintings, or villas. These same people also derive personal ego satisfaction from the collection process, possession, and value of these items. A Ferrari, of course, can get you from point A to point B, but so can a Ford pickup truck! The differences between the two are level of prestige, perceived status, and retail value. Another difference between the legitimate collectors and the trophy-collector shoplifter is that the former has legitimately paid for these items and uses them in everyday life, and the latter does neither.

An increasing percentage of shoplifting cases I have treated in therapy involve out-of-control persons who steal valuable retail items or *objets d'art*. They do not personally use these stolen items but derive a measure of vicarious satisfaction or gratification from both possessing and in some instances surreptitiously viewing these objects often at a later date. Mrs. Daio (Chapter 6, Case 1) is representative of the trophy-collector shoplifter. She had shoplifted/collected more than 400 designer purses and placed them in a separate, secret room in her home, where periodically, and unbeknownst to her family members, she would admire them to get what she identified as a kind of "ego enhancement and substitutive sexual reinforcement." As is the case of the trophy-collector shoplifter, Mrs. Daio did not use these stolen and carefully collected items and almost never carried the purses in public. To a large extent and dissimilar from the other typologies, the trophy-collector shoplifter is motivated by possession of the expensive items. The issue of ownership sets trophy shoplifters apart from all of the other shoplifter typologies who play the shoplifting game solely based on psychological drivers pushing them further into the theft zone.

Another trophy shoplifter, Carmen, stole only expensive watches from several fine jewelry stores in Los Angeles. Similar to Mrs. Daio, Carmen surreptitiously arranged these watches on a designated jewelry tree in her home and derived pleasure from looking at them, holding them, and what she describes as almost caressing them. At times she said there was a kind of sexual bond between her and her beautiful and beloved watches. Mrs. Daio's and Carmen's shoplifting both fall into the trophy-collector typology.

There is a direct connection between the collector and the trophy shoplifter. Many news stories concern people who collect pets, for example, until the situation gets so out of hand that they have gathered dozens of stray animals they cannot properly care for. These people still collect, yet for very different psychological reasons compared with the trophy-collector shoplifter. In the end, though, they are both collectors. The collection process may be a component of shoplifting, or it can be differentiated from it. Psychologists Frost and Hartl (1996, pp. 341-350) differentiated compulsive shoplifting from collecting by identifying three features of collecting: (1) the acquisition of and failure to discard a large number of possessions that appear to be useless or of limited value; (2) maintaining living spaces that are sufficiently cluttered so as to preclude activities for which those spaces were designed; and (3) causing significant distress or functional impairment. Both the collector and the trophy-collector shoplifter may, in addition to being out of control, have other serious emotional deficits such as perceived loneliness, alienation, absence of outside attention, or lack of love.

In some cases, the trophy-collector shoplifter pattern has been associated with an underlying, defined sexual component. This sexual arousal usually occurs during the postexcitation phase (see Chapter 5). Women feeling genital arousal just after stealing expensive items have been noted by Fishbain, who "describes the case of a woman with a history of depression and kleptomania who masturbated while shoplifting. Fishbain felt that the patient's depression was a stimulus to risk-taking behavior which had an antidepressant effect" (as cited in Goldman, 1998, p. 82). Mrs. Daio, whom we will meet in Chapter 6, also reported sexual arousal as she viewed many of the hundreds of stolen designer purses in a secret room in her home.

Mrs. Daio's and Carmen's trophy-collecting shoplifting can, to a degree, be put into the context of a fetish defined as: "the intense sexually arousing fantasies, sexual urges or behaviors involving the use of non-living objects" (American Psychiatric Association (2000) DSM-IV-TR p. 256). Clearly, these women periodically used inanimate objects to achieve a type of substitutive sexual payoff.

Regardless of which shoplifter typology a person falls into, he or she inevitably will pass through a variety of not necessarily equally weighted psychological stages when entering the shoplifting zone. This creates a chain of behaviors culminating with a shoplifting episode. The trophy-collector shoplifter becomes trapped in the postexcitation stage and can see no route of escape (see Chapter 5).

7. The Binge-Spree Shoplifter

The binge-spree shoplifter is usually younger, similar to the provisional/delinquent shoplifter, and to some extent reflects weak impulses, but the primary motivational factors remain psychosocial. A few of the binge-influenced shoplifters do carry their shoplifting over into adulthood. These offenders are characterized by short, serial thefts, often including three or four incidents in a single day followed by long periods (up to a year) of abstinence, then an unaccounted for return to theft. Their intermittent behavior is similar in many respects to binge drinkers, from which the term is derived. They also share psychological similarities to binge shoppers.

This category may be socially influenced in that such stealing may be done with others to achieve the secondary gain of peer status and subcultural recognition similar to gang attention seeking. One binge shoplifter put it this way: "It was to see which one of us could get the most stuff in one day hitting the three stores, and not get caught!" Binge shoplifters engage in high-risk behavior, and for this reason they score high on the Rotter Locus of Control Scale, similar to the externalizer shoplifter (Typology 1). Binge shoplifters character- istically do develop a theft modus operandi as well as ways to avoid apprehension by either loss-prevention personnel or the police.

8. The Equalizer

During my many discussions with shoplifters, I often detected a sense of retaliatory justification as forming their motivation for stealing. In short, these shoplifters have long memories of past items (both perceived and real) that have been taken from them or life events that have not worked out as they would have liked. Mrs. Konvitz (Chapter 6, Case 2) expressed her equalization statement this way: "Why shouldn't I take things when so much has been taken from me and my family?"

Equalizers are often agitated and edgy, traveling through life with a good-size chip on their shoulders. They glance back at life seeking to rebalance a life tilted in a negative direction. In some cases, imagining situations in which they have been slighted now in order to get even, they attempt to make it right again. This shoplifter class is resistant to treatment because it comprises those who are on a self-imposed, single-direction mission in which retreat is usually not an option.

9. The Situational Shoplifter

Situational shoplifters engage in shoplifting for opportunistic reasons. They suddenly see an item that appeals to them—retail merchandise—and they are irresistibly drawn to it; they must have it, so they steal it. This process is almost unconscious. Often the stolen items are later judged to be of little or no real use to them, and they are discarded. This typology shares many descriptive dynamics with the compulsive shoplifter.

Economically Influenced

10. The Professional

Professional shoplifters are people who steal for profit or lifestyle enhancement. Professionals will try to steal high-end, expensive items. This group, if caught, will tend to resist arrest. When caught and detained, they will remain cool and calm, showing no remorse for their actions. Even though they steal high-end items for possible later resale, professional shoplifters are quite different from trophy shoplifters, whose theft preference may also lean toward costly items that later provide noticeable self-reinforcement and personal aggrandizement.

11. The Impoverished (Economically Disadvantaged) Shoplifter

Impoverished shoplifters are those who steal out of economic need. Typically, they will steal necessities such as food, diapers, toiletries, or children's clothing. If caught, they will usually show remorse but voice hostility against a "system" that for most of their lives has kept them down and thus impoverished. The nationwide "Occupy" groups, with their attention focused on the 1%, who they claim have all the money, have been reported engaging in prolonged "flash shoplifting" and when doing so, this particular theft, can be classified into this category.

Age-Determined

12. The Provisional/Delinquent Shoplifter

This shoplifter category is comprised of younger offenders who steal primarily during their teenage years. Their theft patterning coexists with the identity confusion usually associated with the "troubled teen" years and is characterized by intermittent thefts similar to the binge shoplifter. Most of these shoplifters are not apprehended, and eventually terminate their stealing behavior, not developing into chronic shoplifters. The psychophysiological drivers include rapid hormonal changes, acute identity crisis, and possible attention deficit hyperactivity disorder–type symptoms affecting their judgment and impulse control. When interviewed, provisional/delinquent shoplifters have stated that their thefts were centered around patterns of what can be termed *short-run hedonism*—that is, danger-seeking, fun, thrill-oriented actions, and simple frivolity in order to get a quick rush or cheap high at someone else's expense.

The concept of short-run hedonism as applied to this category of shoplifter derives from the delinquent-related research conducted by Cohen, who described short-run hedonism in these terms: "There is little interest in long-run goals, in planning activities and budgeting of time" (1955, p. 203). This concept is equally applicable to the short-run influenced shoplifter. The provisional/delinquent's shoplifting actions are marked by moments involving quick, tangible rewards without contemplation of the social and legal consequences attached to theft.

Alcohol and Substance Abuse–Connected

13. The Drug or Alcohol Addict

Shoplifters of this typology are clearly delineated from the others because they actively commit theft to support their addictions. In a sense, they could additionally be classified in the economically influenced category. To some extent, they are rather bold in their shoplifting modus operandi. For instance, they may enter a store in a shopping mall, steal whatever they can as quickly as possible, gathering as many items as they are able to carry, and quickly run out the door. The level of risk they are willing to take is extremely high. Moreover, both drug addicts and those addicted to alcohol or prescription medications have been shown to be highly external on the Rotter Locus of Control Scale (Brady, 1990). Their elevated external orientation influences them to take many unquantifiable risks when stealing. An almost complete lack of preplanning is typical of this group with a conspicuous lack of theft methodologies or escape routes.

Mentally or Medically Impaired

14. The Alzheimer's Suffer/Amnesiac

This shoplifter typology does not manifest the legal or the mental intent to steal—permanently depriving the victim of material goods. Because of their progressive memory and general cognitive impairment, these shoplifters more or less absentmindedly walk out of stores without paying for merchandise. In addition to not intending to steal, this group makes no attempt to hide items not paid for. Because of the rapidly aging population, this group may be the fastest-growing new shoplifter typology. When confronted, these shoplifters have no immediate recollection that they have stolen at all. This typology also includes those shoplifters with an IQ level below 50, who also lack legal intent to steal share and make little or no attempt to disguise their actions.

15. The Chemically Alcohol Driven Shoplifter

This typology is quite different from that connected with alcohol or substance abuse–connected typology. These shoplifters do not commit acts of theft to support their drug/alcohol habits; thus, they are not economically driven. Their offenses are underscored by their altered state of awareness (or, indeed, consciousness) contributing to their compromised judgment at the time of the theft. Their mental state typically involves such symptoms as confusion, psychomotor agitation, memory lapse, disorientation, nervousness, and perceptual disturbance, especially associated with those shoplifters experiencing "meth"or cocaine intoxication. When confronted by authorities, this group is the most belligerent and potentially dangerous of all shoplifter groups. Loss-prevention personnel and police have confirmed that this shoplifter typology presents the largest risk to public safety.

CHAPTER 3

No Identifiable Psychosocial Drivers

16. Inadvertent/Amateur

Everyone, including myself, has at times forgotten to pay for an item from a store. It might be as simple as not remembering that Snickers bar you picked up at K-Mart while selecting new tires for your car. Later, of course, when you noticed that you failed to pay for it, there are two decisions that can be made: (1) return to the store and pay for the forgotten candy or pay for it during your next visit to the same store; or (2) put it out of your mind entirely and chalk it up to "I just forgot." However, if the item is of a higher value (not that the Snickers bar was free), say between $10 and $50, and if you do not return to compensate the retailer, then it is well accepted that a shoplifting event has occurred. In these situations, the person's conscience must be the guide.

Postarrest Shoplifter Syndrome

Although many detailed descriptions exist of shoplifter behavior during and immediately after arrest, usually provided by the police or paramedics, I have found nothing in the literature that attempts to explain or interpret the bizarre behaviors exhibited by some shoplifters at the point of arrest. Furthermore, a review of the shoplifting literature does not indicate that attention has been directed to an interpretation of the shoplifter's behavioral symptoms immediately after his or her arrest.

The sixteen typologies listed above are both descriptive and explanatory as to why shoplifters engage in a specific type of theft patterning while shoplifting. Conversely, this section is devoted to an explanation of the shoplifter's mental status after the theft and during the arrest procedure. The theory of postarrest shoplifter syndrome (PASS) came about quite serendipitously and represents a unique contribution to shoplifting theory.

In some shoplifting cases, the shoplifters reported psychological symptoms mimicking the medically influenced symptomatology usually associated with a specific set of epileptic symptoms, the post-ictal state. Interestingly enough, the topic of these symptoms arose during conversations I had with several paramedics who had provided medical treatment to shoplifters who, attempting to avoid arrest, had chosen instead to flee the shoplifting scene in their cars, only to be arrested by the police shortly afterward. After arrest, these shoplifters began to manifest varied and peculiar psychological symptoms that appear similar to those induced by seizures.

In most shoplifting situations, the psychological drivers and moti-vational influences have been identified as being mainly passive and nonconfrontational, typically resulting in the shoplifter's on-site arrest either in a shopping mall or store where the theft occurred. But some-times the outcome for the shoplifter can be very different. Commonly in petty theft (shoplifting) cases, the first official the identified shop-lifter encounters subsequent to his or her in-store detection is the store's loss-prevention agent. The next link in the arrest chain is the request, often made by the store's management team, to call for law enforcement assistance to arrest the suspect. But the chain does not necessarily end at that point if the shoplifter attempts to escape.

A relatively small number (estimated at 1–%) of in-custody shoplifters exacerbate their already bad situation by making an ill-conceived decision to attempt to avoid police arrest, and the distinct possibility of going to jail, by trying to run from the scene of the shoplifting apprehension, usu-ally by racing to their cars and then trying to get away. Routinely, in these escape situations, a police chase follows. Mrs. Konvitz (Chapter 6, Case 2) was involved in this type of chase as she sped away from a delicatessen still holding the package of kosher corned beef she had stolen in one hand as she drove with the other. As she approached her stately home, she tossed the meat package from her car window and drove up her quarter-mile cir-cular driveway. The pursuing police officers stopped to retrieve the corned beef, later photographed it, and booked it into evidence, which was used as proof that Mrs. Konvitz had committed a shoplifting act. It is at this point that the third link in the apprehension chain is connected.

In these cases, upon being apprehended by the police many shop-lifters will, for immediately unknown psychological reasons, begin to exhibit strange behaviors. At this critical juncture, because the shop-lifter is behaving so erratically, for the safety of both the shoplifter and the police, the police will call for the assistance of paramedics. On arrival, the paramedics have a firsthand opportunity to reverify the shoplifter's constellation of counterproductive behaviors and decide what medical course of action is most beneficial.

To clarify what kinds of behavior shoplifters exhibited during this postarrest phase, I have interviewed a number of paramedics who on multiple occasions have responded to these difficult chase-and-catch sagas. Their direct reportage provided me with new and insightful information about the complexity of shoplifter psychodynamics that I had not previously conceptualized or, for that matter, read about.

For example, one paramedic with eighteen years of experience told me that over the course of his career he had been involved in innumerable police chase episodes in which identified shoplift-ers decided to run rather than face immediate arrest. Most of these police chases had originated from a mall in Capitola, California, where he had been assigned as an employee of the Central Fire District of Santa Cruz County (Dermott, 2012). Dermott's comments concern-ing the after-arrest behaviors of this special group of shoplifters were deemed important for inclusion here, leading to what I have termed postarrest shoplifter syndrome, or PASS.

The paramedic presented cogent descriptions of psychological symptomatology he had witnessed when arriving on the scene on numerous occasions when shoplifters were being arrested. When I pressed him for additional information, he quickly stated that in almost all of those shoplifting cases where a chase was involved, it seemed to him that, although he wasn't a doctor, "they acted as if they were experiencing some kind of altered state of consciousness, involving memory lapses, disorientation, mental confusion, head-aches, suspiciousness, anger, and even aggression." He then added the salient point that the shoplifters' symptoms also seemed to be medically consistent with the "postictal symptoms with patients hav-ing refractory partial epilepsy episodes." Going through my criminal case files—including police reports—on the shoplifters I had treated,

I reviewed the many statements referencing the perceived psychological symptoms the shoplifters were exhibiting immediately after arrest. After a review of these reported shoplifter symptoms, I found them to be, for the most part, identical to those reported by the postictal seizure patients described by the paramedic.

These identified postictal symptoms and the shoplifter's reported symptoms after their arrest are presented in Table 3.2.

Table 3.2. Postarrest Shoplifter Symptoms Compared with Postictal-Related Psychological Symptoms

Symptom Descriptors	
Postarrest Suspects	Postictal Patients
1. Out of control	1. Agitated
2. Psychological fugue symptoms	2. Dissociative symptoms
3. Confusion	3. Confusion
4. Anger	4. Hostility
5. Amnesia (Where am I?)	5. Memory deficits
6. Visual attention deficit	6. Nystagmus, rapid eye movements
7. Hypomanic behavior	7. Mania
8. Delusions, hallucinations	8. Psychotic-like symptoms
9. Childlike actions	9. Regressive behavior
10. Feelings as if "I can do anything"	10. Omnipotence

I discovered that these postictal psychological symptoms had been previously researched but not specifically with shoplifters. For example, Kanner, Soto, and Gross-Kanner (2004, pp.708-718) found the following postictal symptoms: "depression, psychotic symptoms, hypomanic symptoms, fatigue, anxiety, cognitive dysfunction, and neurovegetative symptoms." These medically described symptoms could also be applicable to the characterization of shoplifters after arrest. In an important psychological way, PASS symptoms are similar to the induced, psychogenic fugue state experienced by some shoplifters as described in Chapter 5 (The Shoplifting Zone).

Perhaps there is some type of "after arrest" biochemical crossover pattern between these postictal, physical etiological factors and the symptoms exhibited by some shoplifters. In fact, there may be some heretofore unknown physical causes contributing to the postarrest shoplifter syndrome that produce symptoms similar to the behavior described by the paramedics with postictal patients. At this time, we can only hypothesize that many of these shoplifter postarrest symptoms may be caused by certain biochemical reactions such as the following neurotransmitters and genetic factors:

- Decreased levels of serotonin cell site 5-HT2A.

- An increase in dopamine availability.

- Cerebral autoregulation dysfunction—a decrease in the correct flow of blood to various areas of the brain. This may account for shoplifter confusion and "fog states."

- Epinephrine increases linked to heightened anxiety levels and the fight-or-flight response.

- Rapid changes in cell site receptors such as the GABA receptors, the chief neurotransmitters for the central nervous system.

- Monoamine oxidase A (MAOA) factor (discussed below).

An intriguing new study has linked amount of credit card debt to a genetic enzyme, monoamine oxidase A:

People with one "low" MAOA gene and one "high" MAOA gene reported having credit card debt 7.8 percent more often than people with two "high" versions even when controlled for factors like education and socioeconomic status. For people with two "low" versions of the gene, that number jumped to 15.9 percent (Ross 2010).

Impulsivity is directly correlated to MAOA levels. The results of these studies may prove valuable when examining the role played by neurotransmitters in the maintenance of shoplifter recurrent fantasies after arrest.

Chapter 3 References

American Psychiatric Association (2000) Diagnostic and statistical manual of mental disorders (4th ed.,text rev.) Washington, DC: Author.

Berlin, P. (1996). Why do shoplifters steal...and why do so many continue to steal even after getting caught? Reprinted from The National Report on Shoplifting. Jericho, N.Y.: Shoplifters Alternative, pp. 3–4.

Black, D. W. (2007). A review of compulsive buying disorder. World Psychiatry, 2, p. 3.

Brady, J. C. (1990). Drug addicts: Are they out of control? San Mateo, CA: Western Book/Journal Press.

Cohen, A. K. (1955). Delinquent boys. New York: Free Press.

Cupchik, W. (1997) Why honest people shoplift or commit other acts of theft. Toronto: Tagami Communications.

Dermott, J. Personal Communication. (2012, December).

Fishbain, D. A. Cited by Goldman, M.J. Kleptomania: The compulsion to steal-

What can be done? Far Hills New Jersey: New Horizon Press, 1998. P. 82.

Frost, R. O. & Hartl, T. (1996). Hoarding, compulsive buying and reasons for saving, Behavioral Research Therapy, 34 (4), 341–350.

Grant, J. E. & Kim, S. W. (2003). Stop me because I can't stop myself: Taking control of impulsive behavior. New York: McGraw-Hill.

Hipp, T. (2010, December 27). Shoplifting and loss prevention: Do we need a fresh look? Ezine @rticles, p. 5.

Kanner, A. Soto, A. & Gross-Kanner, H. (2004, March 9). Prevalence and clinical characteristics of postictal psychiatric symptoms in partial epilepsy. Neurology 62, 708–713.

Ross, V. & De Neve, J. Born into debt: Gene linked to credit card—Card Balances, August,12, 2010 Scientific American. Retrieved January 15,2012, from http://www.scientificamerican.com/article.cfm?id=born-into-debt

Shulman, T. D. (2004). Something for nothing: Shoplifting addiction and recovery. West Conshohocken, PA: Infinity Publishing.

Shulman, T. D. (2011). Cluttered lives, empty souls—Compulsive stealing, spending and hoarding. West Conshohocken, PA: Infinity Publishing.

CHAPTER 4

LOCUS OF CONTROL: WHO'S THE BOSS?

Kleptomania means in principle to take possession of things which give the strength or the power to fight supposed dangers, especially, as before, supposed dangers of loss of self esteem.

—OTTO FENICHEL, M.D.,

The Psychoanalytic Theory of Neurosis, 1945

Am I Out of Control?

Perhaps Fenichel is right—shoplifting gives the actor power, at least for while. Many people, including shoplifters, have been characterized as being out of control of their lives. Every day we hear, "Well, he did it because he was out of control at the time." Being out of control is more than just a metaphor or a description of a mental state. In psychology, being out of control has a specific meaning that usually relates to the locus-of-control variable that constitutes the centerpiece of this work. Being out of control is a quantifiable psychological construct that can be used to measure a person's sense of control over his or her life or, conversely, a perceived absence of control.

The term *locus of control* was first introduced in the 1950s by psychologist J. B. Rotter (1966). It refers to a person's basic belief system about the influences that affect either positive or negative outcomes in one's life. Rotter provided the necessary social, psychological, and theoretical basis for locus of control in his social learning theory model. He conceptualized locus of control as a generalized expectancy of reinforcement based on prior experience and learning, and held it to be of major importance in relation to performance in diverse social learning situations. Rotter maintained that "consistent individual differences exist among individuals in the degree to which they are likely to attribute personal control to reward in the same situation" (1954, p.1), and succinctly defined locus of control as follows:

When a reinforcement is perceived by the subject as following some action of his own but not being entirely contingent upon his action, then, in our culture, it is typically perceived as the result of luck, chance, fate, as under the control of powerful others, or as unpredictable because of the great complexity of the forces surrounding him. When an event is interpreted in this way by an individual, we have labeled this a belief in external control. If the person perceives that the event is contingent upon his own behavior or his own relatively permanent characteristics, we have termed this a belief in internal control (Rotter, 1966, p.1).

Stated another way, locus of control pertains to the amount of perceived control individuals at any moment in time have over the events controlling their lives. Some people feel they have almost complete control over their destiny. These people have an *internal* locus of control. Other people feel they have very little control over their lives and are characterized as having an *external* locus of control. In an important way, locus of control relates to the personal power or control we believe we have to manage our lives or to manage our reactions to diverse social-psychological situations. The locus-of-control dimension has been related to such factors as autonomy; competence; beliefs about fate, chance, or luck; power; self-concept; self-confidence; and truthfulness (Strickland, 1989).

There are two very distinct classifications of people in this system: the internal locus-of-control person and the external locus-of-control person. It is generally accepted that the most successful people in society tend to be internally directed, while those with an external locus of control tend to be more negative about the world and their place in it, and in the end are less successful.

People with an internal locus of control believe that they are primarily responsible for the behavioral outcomes in their lives. These people tend to be self-reliant and believe that nothing can hold them back except themselves. Studies have shown that people with an internal locus of control tend to be more achievement-oriented because they believe they can work toward an identified life goal. Studies have also shown that as people become older, one result of the maturation process is that they become more internally focused.

Individuals with a well-defined external locus of control believe that forces outside of themselves affect their ability to succeed and advance in life. They tend to stake their futures on beliefs such as fate, luck, fortuitousness, God, society, or being in the right place at the right time. Because they believe they have very little personal stake in their future, those with an external locus-of-control orientation tend to put less effort forward on most projects they engage in. Studies show that "externals" are generally less successful in college and careers than those with an internal locus of control, or "internals."

It is often believed that those with an external locus of control are destined to be unhappy. There is no guarantee in life that those with an external locus of control are unable to be successful or that they are predestined to be unhappy. Many people with this external life script see their existence as a series of fated chance events that they can just as easily fall on the good side of. Some are able to find personal freedom in this concept and live happy lives in the process.

Locus-of-control research has shown that well-adjusted people in general are internal on this measure. For example, one study done by Williams and Nickels (1969) showed that internal people see themselves as clever, efficient, ambitious, assertive, dependable, organized, reasonable, and in control of their actions. On the other hand, external individuals indicated self-pitying and negative responses. External scorers were also seen as prone to more frequent accidents and had suicidal thoughts more often than did internal scorers. Tolor and Reznikoff (1967) concluded that external people showed a high tendency toward premature death, anxiety and unhappiness. Patterson (1966) related external locus of control to personal depression, a prevalent psychological factor identified with shoplifters and tested in this study.

Kelley, the author of a study on locus of control and shoplifters, using a sample of 196 subjects, concluded that "at-risk youth are more apt to develop an insecure, alienated belief system…where their fate is in the hands of outside circumstances and their world view or locus of control will tend to become more external" (Kelley, 1996, p. 2). The investigation of locus of control and shoplifters is an explanatory and useful theory concerning why people shoplift and their own lack of understanding about why they do so. The present study demonstrates that shoplifters reflect an external locus of control.

Shoplifter Locus of Control: Psychological Descriptors

Shoplifters, similar to the general population, reflect one of two locus-of-control orientations: internal or external. Considerable research

(Nowicki, 2012) indicates that there is evidence for many locus-of-control descriptors. The 20 descriptors listed in Table 4.1 represent a synthesis of hundreds of descriptive locus of control states that can apply to both internals and externals. These psychological descriptors are described in the work of Nowicki (2012) at Emory University, who has spent 35 years researching this dimension. My study finds that the preponderance of shoplifters manifest external descriptors. Because of the shoplifter's dependence on these external descriptors, behavioral change toward not stealing is resistant to therapeutic efforts. Many life scripts affect a person's choice to steal: self-doubt, personal alienation, existential crisis, and especially an external locus of control.

Table 4.1. Locus-of-Control Psychological Descriptors

Internal Dimensions	External Dimensions
1. Self-discipline	1. Lack of self-discipline
2. Accepts authority	2. Questions authority/trust
3. Self-directed	3. Other-directed
4. Rejects fate concept	4. Believes in fate
5. Not impulsive	5. Impulsive, pro–law violating
6. High self-concept/self-esteem	6. Low self-concept/self-esteem
7. Focused	7. Has minimal focus
8. Low-risk-seeking behavior	8. High–risk-seeking behavior
9. Trust	9. Suspiciousness, hypervigilance
10. Self-driven	10. Group-driven

11. Transparent self	11. Social masking, deceptive, afraid
12. Personal reliance	12. Joiner
13. Reserved	13. Social boldness, acting out, callous
14. Low physical risk taking	14. High physical risk taking
15. Positive emotions	15. Negative emotions
16. Outgoing	16. Shy, depressed
17. Relaxed	17. Tense, angry
18. Rejects luck, chance	18. Accepts luck, chance
19. Assertive, responsible	19. Withdrawn, suicidal
20. High energy level	20. Low energy level

Based on a behavioral analysis of locus of control, in their own way, each of the four shoplifters interpreted in this study evidenced many of these external locus-of-control descriptors, thus establishing their externality positions. Each case presented in Chapter 6 denotes a particular idiosyncratic set of external descriptors. The numbers of the external descriptors are given in parentheses in the case descriptions below when they apply to a particular case. For example, Mrs. Daio's external dimension of "social masking, deceptive" corresponds with external dimension 11 in table 4.1, "social masking, deceptive, afraid."

Identification of these patients with external locus-of-control descriptors is also inextricably tied to their co-occurring depressive states, and the results of this study confirming that the two psychological concepts are positively correlated.

Locus-of-Control Descriptors for Four Case Studies

Case 1. Mrs. Daio: A Place for Everything, and Everything in Its Place

Mrs. Daio's case is both psychologically complex and intriguing because she is the only shoplifter profiled here who stole, collected, and subsequently hoarded very expensive merchandise, usually designer purses. Because of this behavior, she was classified as a trophy-collector shoplifter (Chapter 3, Typology 6). Both depressed and suicidal, her theft patterning carried with it an additional secondary psychological reinforcer, sexual gratification. Mrs. Daio scored 17 on the Rotter Locus of Control Scale, which indicates a highly external locus of control. Her identified external dimensions are:

A. Impulsivity and an attitude that is pro–law violation attitude (5)

B. Social boldness (13)

C. Social masking, deceptiveness, fear (11)

D. Engages in high-risk-seeking actions; she stole high-end merchandise worth $400,000 (8)

E. Accepts that her life is influenced heavily by fate, luck, chance, and fortuitousness (4, 18)

F. Questions authority and those who may temper her behavior, creating an aura of distrust (2)

Case 2. Mrs. Konvitz: The Corned Beef Caper

Mrs. Konvitz's case is characterized by feelings of intense anger and frustration, and a large measure of survival guilt associated with the extermination of most of her family members during World War II at the hands of the Nazi SS. Her score of 18 on the Rotter Locus of Control Scale also indicates a highly external locus of control. Her case remains both enigmatic and tragic for her and her existing family, although she has elected to maintain a veil of secrecy related to her chronic shoplifting. Many of her more obvious psychological symptoms are in keeping with a diagnosis of narcissistic personality disorder. Mrs. Konvitz evidenced these external control descriptors:

A. Social masking, deceptiveness, fear (11)

B. Questions authority, has lack of trust, and is self-centered (narcissistic) (2)

C. Abundance of negative emotions, including anger-hostility patterning (15)

D. Tense, angry, high levels of suspiciousness (9)

Case 3. Mrs. Chow: When the Cradle Will Rock

Mrs. Chow's personal, psychological overcompensation pattern stemming from her inability to bear children took expression in the form of her indiscriminate and self-defeating shoplifting. Her secret motivation to steal children's clothing as a type of overcompensation was underscored by her feelings of not being in control of her life. She tested highly external on locus of control with a score of 19. The following descriptors are representative of her external locus of control:

A. Very low energy level (20)

B. Shy and withdrawn (16, 19)

C. Impulsive (5)

D. Social boldness, hypervigilance, and suspiciousness (13, 9)

Case 4. Mrs. Nelson: Blood, Sweat, and Tears

Mrs. Nelson's journey into the shoplifting zone included bizarre self-destructive acts involving exsanguination. This was done to mask her attempted suicide, attributing it to an untraceable medical etiology or perhaps to a neutral diagnosis such as pernicious anemia. She scored 18 on the Locus of Control Scale, and her external locus-of-control descriptors include:

A. Shy, depressed (16)

B. Tense and angry, not being relaxed (17)

C. Impulsive and pro–law violating (5)

D. Social masking, deceptiveness, and fear (11)

E. Very withdrawn, overt, suicidal gestures (19)

Each of these shoplifters has demonstrated evidence of these external descriptors as psychological factors predisposing them into the murky milieu of the shoplifting zone.

Measurement of Locus of Control with Shoplifters

The emergence of the locus-of-control variable almost 50 years ago represents an enduring addition to personality theory. This dimension enables psychologists to better understand and interpret the behavior and motivation of diverse groups, including—as it has been applied here—shoplifters. Rotter's pioneering work on this dimension, especially the development of the Rotter Internality-Externality (IE) Scale (Rotter, 1966), remains the definitive work on the subject. The Rotter IE Scale has been used extensively with many behavioral groups, including a number of shoplifting groups; thus, it was selected as the instrument in this investigation of shoplifters. Rotter and his colleagues developed the IE Scale to ascertain whether the controlling events of human behavior lie inside or outside the individual.

The first attempt to devise an IE scale was done by Phares in the mid-1950s. He studied the impact of chance, fate, and luck on personal perception of power (Phares, 1957). Phares's pioneering work was followed by revisions of the IE scale. Other psychologists have undertaken the broadening of this instrument through the construction of new subscales such as criminal thinking, achievement, affection, political attitudes, depression, and social alienation. This test determines whether the patient is driven by internal or external psychological factors. External locus of control has been connected to many malappropriate behaviors and psychological conditions associated with interpersonal conflict, including criminal behaviors such as car theft, sexual acting out, crimes against property, shoplifting, gambling, rape, domestic aggression, white-collar crime, substance/alcohol abuse, anxiety, anorexia and bulimia, and posttraumatic stress disorder. I have used the Rotter Locus of Control Scale for 30 years to evaluate criminals, drug addicts, alcoholics, and now shoplifters. Because so many shoplifters I saw had mentioned that they felt totally out of control when they stole, the inclusion of the IE Scale seemed clinically appropriate for this study as it was with other criminal populations with which I have used it successfully.

Sample Locus-of-Control Items

The final Rotter IE Scale used in this investigation comprises 29 forced-choice items, can be completed in 15 minutes, and requires a 6th-grade educational level. Two sample items reflecting externality are:

- Many times we might as well decide what to do by flipping a coin.

- Children get into trouble because their parents punish them too much.

The four shoplifter-patients presented in Chapter 6 were given a complete psychological test battery including the 29-item Rotter IE Scale. All four women reflected an external locus of control, scoring an average of 17.8. Thus, they were classified as shoplifting "externals." Moreover, they recorded an average of 11.5 external locus-of-control descriptors, thereby verifying their external status (see, Rotter Quick Score Analysis, Table 6.2, Chapter 6).

The Cases of Four Women Shoplifters

The four cases analyzed in Chapter 6 each involve women shoplifters who, in addition to reflecting externality, were depressed at the time of the assessment. Most of the shoplifters referred to me for assessment are women who have repeatedly engaged in theft.

A survey of the literature revealed that 77% of all reported cases of kleptomania or shoplifting involve women, a fact that is subject to various explanations. "Men with impulse control problems tend toward pyromania, pathological gambling and explosive behavior," notes Goldman (cited in Yagoda, 1994, p. 2). He continues:

Women tend toward kleptomania and trichotillomania [compulsive pulling of the hair]. But there are more male kleptomaniacs than there might seem. A guy who steals bicycles and trucks, and abandons them—he's in jail. He's not called a kleptomaniac, but he probably is one. On the other hand, a 61-year-old divorcee who repeatedly steals designer blouses from Neiman Marcus, and gets caught, is in treatment —not in San Quentin.

That more women than men have a predilection to shoplifting is suggested by additional shoplifting research. For example, Smith has stated:

While pinching a candy bar from a newsstand or eyeliner from a makeup counter is almost an adolescent rite of passage, most girls grow out of such behavior. But a minority of more vulnerable women develop an irresistible urge to continue because, according to experts, stealing provides a thrill and a subconscious way to compensate for deep psychological pain (2002, p. 220).

The four cases presented in Chapter 6 demonstrate the negative impact that an external locus of control can have on the lives of shoplifters. In fact, having an external locus of control is one reason they became shoplifters.

Chapter 4 References

Frankl, V. (1969). The will to meaning. New York: New American Library.

Kelley, T. M. (1996). At-risk youth and locus of control: Do they really see a choice? Juvenile and Family Court Journal, 47 (4), 39–54.

Nowicki, S. Personal communication. (June, 2012)

Patterson, C. H. (1966). Theories of counseling and psychotherapy. New York: Harper & Row.

Phares, E. J. (1957). Expectancy changes in skill and chance situations. Journal of Abnormal Social Psychology, 54, 339–342.

Rotter, J. B. (1954). Social learning and clinical psychology. Englewood Cliffs, NJ: Prentice-Hall.

Rotter, J. B. (1966). Generalized expectancies for internal versus external control of reinforcement. Psychological Monographs, 80 (entire no. 609), pp. 1-27.

Smith, R. S. (2002). Why women get the urge to steal. Cosmopolitan, 3 (3), p. 220.

Strickland, B. (1989). Internal-external control expectancies. American Psychologist, 44, 1–7.

Tolor, A. & Reznikoff, M. (1967). Relation between insight, repression-sensitization, internal-external control, and death anxiety. Journal of Abnormal Psychology, 72, 426–430.

Williams, C. B. & Nickels, J.B. (1969). Internal-external control as related to accident and suicide proneness. Journal of Consulting and Clinical Psychology, 33, 485–494.

Yagoda, B. (1994, February). Addicted to stealing. Self Magazine, p. 1-4.

CHAPTER 5

THE SHOPLIFTING ZONE: FOUR STAGES, OR HOW I GOT THERE

Curiosity is sibling to imagination. Before one soars, he must examine, test, prod, burrow and inquisitively inspect.

—MELVIN M. BELLI, *MODERN TRIALS,* 1963

In the Zone

An athlete who exhibits superior performance during a particular game is sometimes described as being "in the zone." The zone, of course, connotes a positive state of mental awareness combined with achievement, leading to a happy and productive ending. For example, the leader in the 2011 British Open golf classic, Tom Lewis, was quoted after setting a record low score, "I think I was totally in the golf zone today," to explain his historic performance (*San Jose Mercury News*, 2011).

Most of the many shoplifters I have treated engage in their illegal acts because of hidden, psychologically driven motivations or obscure triggers and not because they need the purloined merchandise or because they cannot afford it.

Even for those shoplifters who have demonstrated material gain as a prime motivation, their thinking has also been shown to reflect underlying negative psychological factors. These parallel factors highly influence the materially driven shoplifter who may be unaware of how he or she entered into the shoplifting zone. No matter what the apparent motivation—"Macy's won't care about a few purses"— both the psychologically motivated and the material-driven perform the same act: they first steal, then in most cases, struggle with why they have chosen this course of problematic behavior. Except for shoplifting, these people are highly resourceful, with full-time jobs or professional careers and families who love them; for the most part, they remain clueless as to why they crossed the line and committed the crime of shoplifting. The hidden etiologies supporting their shoplifting surface only after a long-term commitment to in-depth treatment and only at the moment in time when they are ready, along with me, to find out why.

The psychological research results presented in this chapter are subdivided into the four stages of the psychological shoplifting zone:

1. Anticipation/readiness

2. Neutralization—moral decision versus moral erosion

3. Action (the theft act)

4. Postexcitation/depression—two sides of the same coin

Stage 4 has, in turn, been bifurcated into postexcitation, identified by psychological symptoms, and the postdepression phase, characterized by other diagnosable symptoms.

The progression through these four confusing and painful stages results in what I have depicted as a *psychosocial reidentity stamping procedure*, in which the shoplifter surrenders his or her positive pre-shoplifting self-identity and mentally replaces it with a negative post-shoplifting identity. The majority of the shoplifters I have diagnosed and treated have no understanding of why they stole, although they have alluded to their perception that prior to, during, and after the shoplifting event, they felt as if they were in some kind of a negative mental zone, a fog, a trance, a disassociated or fugue state, this time without the happy sports ending. Shoplifters have described this sensation as being quasi-hypnotic. Recounting this zonal experience, sometimes shoplifters have little, if any, recollection of how they got to a certain shopping mall, what merchandise they stole, where they were, and how or when they returned home after a particular stealing episode.

Additionally, many shoplifters I have treated have become almost amnestic to the fact that they sometimes had driven long distances from their homes (more than 100 miles in one of the cases presented in Chapter 6) and committed grand or petty shoplifting theft offenses.

Mrs. Daio (see Chapter 6, case1), in her own words, typifies this zonal or hypnotic state:

A weird feeling I couldn't understand came over me prior to stealing, and suddenly, almost literally, I didn't know where I was or how I got there! It was very confusing, and I thought I was losing my mind. The next thing I remember is that I was arrested and taken to jail, and the police searched our home and found the purses I had stolen.

As stated in the preface to this book, a review of the literature on shoplifting behavior reveals almost no credible psychological explanation or research into the shoplifting experience itself. I hypothesize beginning, middle, and end stages for these people who ultimately elect to steal. Many vivid anecdotal descriptions have been provided to a wide variety of reporters and journalists chronicling the shoplifting scene, yet no direct studies have identified the progressive or sequential psychosocial stages that shoplifters experience that dramatically alter their life paths. Based on in-depth interviews with at least 100 shoplifters, I offer these four stages of shoplifting as constituting a shoplifting zone.

For the many people I have treated, shoplifting has been a devastating as well as life-altering process involving a clear personal morality shift—from honest, law-abiding citizen to law violator. The impact of the shoplifting experience also tends to dramatically modify the shoplifter's personal self-identity in that, once arrested, he or she is both privately ("I've been a bad person") and publicly stigmatized (his or her name appears in the newspaper, on television, and in police reports). The paparazzi track down celebrity shoplifters as if they were wild animals in an African game park. Witness the cases of Lindsay Lohan, Winona Ryder, Britney Spears and Peaches Geldof whose every move since they were accused of shoplifting has been dissected by many mean spirited writers.

As I moved progressively further into the real, not theoretical, world of the shoplifter, I discerned that the faulty reasoning shoplifters use to ex post facto explain their thefts often involved philosophical and ethical dilemmas that they have struggled with. To fully comprehend the social-psychological dynamics of shoplifting, it is essential to explain the stages the individual shoplifter succumbs to as well as the erosion (neutralization) of his or her moral reasoning and judgmental awareness at the time of the shoplifting offense. This psychological analysis helps explain how ordinarily law-abiding people abandon their core morality tenets, ethical beliefs, and adherence to society's laws and commit a criminal act.

Simple attribution to an impulse control disorder seems descriptive enough, but it falls far short of providing a comprehensive explanation of how a shoplifter gets to the point of walking into the downtown Macy's and then strolling out with a purse crammed full of stolen jewelry. After treating dozens of shoplifters, it became increasingly clear to me that there had to be a common or shared psychosocial pathway that shoplifters experience on the way to losing control over their lives, culminating in repeating their theft episodes.

Also of significance is the fact that, to date, no shoplifting investigators have conducted any reliable research analyses using a variety of validated instruments, nor have they presented any replicable data as to why shoplifters have such high rates of recidivism, or, in turn, why they are continuously resistant to most methods of psychological intervention. The fact remains that with a greater frequency than most other crimes, shoplifters do repeat their offenses, undeterred by arrest, conviction, or even by serving jail time. As has been reported by a number of shoplifters, apparently the positive reinforcement, perhaps attributable to the "high" attached to the shoplifting act, appreciably outweighs the negative reinforcement, the embarrassment of being arrested, or the possibility of losing their personal freedom by going to jail.

The psychological position advanced in this chapter is that shoplifters enter the shoplifting zone, where they become fixated or mentally frozen in one or more of the four regressive stages I have described. Once fixated, it is as if they have fallen into a deep crevasse of no return, from which they unable to extricate themselves back to pre-shoplifting freedom. The goal in this chapter is to describe as well as unlock these transient stages so shoplifters can slowly pull themselves out of this mental abyss and return to an identity not associated with stealing. Shoplifter recidivism, then, is seen as directly tied to being mentally trapped in the shoplifting zone.

To explain this pernicious shoplifting zone of influence, I first need to explicate the four stages that compose it. At the center of this new psychological terrain are two interrelated concepts:

1. An investigation into criminal and ethical choices made by shoplifters.

2. Identification of those mitigating factors of psychological neutralization.

Shoplifting can then be interpreted as a violation or breach of the shoplifter's ethical integrity, in many ways impacted by feelings of being out of control of his or her life at the time the shoplifter made the bad choice to commit a crime.

In almost every case, the decision to steal involves a compromise of personal ethics; the shoplifter is intentionally doing something that is both morally wrong and he or she knows is against the law. As shoplifters move through these four stages, they make additional moral compromises that hold them in the shoplifting zone, disallowing them from doing what they know is ethically right.

Zasky, the editor of *Failure* magazine, interviewed Bazerman and Tenbrunsel, who in their 2011 book *Blind Spots: Why We Fail to Do What's Right and What to Do About It*, discussed why most people overestimate their personal ability to do what's right and how they act sometimes without intentionality. Doing what is right versus making bad decisions is the story of the shoplifter's life. As Bazerman and Tenbrunsel point out (2011, p.5): If ethics—training is to actually change and improve ethical decision making, it needs to incorporate behavioral ethics, and specifically the subtle ways in which ethics are bounded."

These authors address one of the largest unethical crimes in U.S. history: the Ponzi scheme, perpetrated by Bernard Madoff that resulted in the outright swindling of $65 billion from hundreds, if not thousands of investors. Though on a lesser scale they could also be discussing the ethical boundary violations, as addressed by Bazerman andTenbrunsel, of the average shoplifter, who also must struggle with his or her own right versus wrong ethical dilemma.

Based on their research, Bazerman and Tenbrunsel additionally believe that some people behave unethically because they fail to recognize that the decisions they are about to make have ethical components to them. Germane to the world of the shoplifter, they opine, all of us have a tendency to overlook information that works against our best interest. Again and again, shoplifters demonstrate that many of their unethical decisions, especially those made during the neutralization shoplifting stage, are manifestly counterproductive and not in anyone's best interest.

The cases presented in Chapter 6 establish that shoplifters reach this critical theft threshold through a series of sequential steps or stages during which they progressively become more and more out of personal control over their lives, and that loss of control leads to their repeat thefts. In this view, each shoplifter's individual theft track incorporates a series of very real, overlapping moral, ethical, and behavioral judgments that cloud his or her reasoning capacity, triggering his or her almost inescapable theft actions. This psychological sequence becomes a ritualistic, recurring pattern performed time after time in preparation for, during, and after (postexcitation depression stage) the shoplifting event. These psychological stages help identify out-of-control shoplifters and often distinguish them from those driven alone by monetary gain, opportunistic thieves, or organized retail offenders. These progressive stages, always involving bad choices, contribute to shoplifters' initial paradoxical feelings of elation, "the rush," replaced later by equally intense feelings of guilt, sadness, and often acute and measureable depression. These four stages progressively prevent the shoplifter's ability to focus on morally correct, psychologically healthy, life coping strategies not involving theft episodes. The results, as we shall see, can be devastating.

The four shoplifting cases unfolded in Chapter 6 capture a personal, sometimes paralyzing, and commonly tragic mental slide into a more primitive developmental region in the shoplifter's personal growth. It is as if the shoplifter momentarily turns back his or her life clock, psychologically relocating into a more maladaptive and earlier fixated time in his or her life, reflective of early childhood, prior to the acquisition of a well-established adult moral compass. I have found that these regressive and important adaptational patterns that predispose a person to shoplifting are highly resistant to change and can only be reversed via intensive psychotherapy, group therapy, cognitive therapy, family therapy, or addiction-type shoplifting self-help therapy. Treatment with shoplifters is always an uphill struggle, regardless of which system of behavioral change is employed.

The Shoplifting Zone: The Four Stages

The clinical view expressed here, accounting for the stages comprising the shoplifting zone, relies on my experience both diagnosing and treating more than 100 shoplifters that clearly establishes shoplifters' slow progression through at least these four progressive psychological stages (see Table 5.1).

Table 5.1. The Shoplifting Zone: The Four Stages

STAGES	SHOPLIFTING PROGRESSION
1. Anticipation/Readiness	Initial
2. Neutralization—Moral Decision versus Moral Erosion	} Middle
3. Action/Theft	
4. Postexcitation/Depression	Late

These individual stages are delineated by initial-, middle-, and late-phase thoughts and theft behavior characteristics. These identified stages constitute an experiential resocialization for the shoplifter. They are not meant to be discrete and completely separate psychosocial entities unto themselves, and thus the behaviors indigenous to one stage may also be identified as occurring in one or more of the other stages.

In some cases, in addition to not being discretely different, each of these four stages forming the shoplifting zone is not totally sequential; some overlapping of behaviors has been identified. More important, however, the psychological movement into and progressively through these stages is almost never done on a conscious level. The shoplifter does not wake up one day and say, "This is a perfect day for me to begin stealing, ruin the rest of my life, greatly embarrass my family, and maybe go to jail." Many of the shoplifting cues or triggers remain relegated to the shoplifter's unconscious, where they reside perhaps for decades, as was the case with Mrs. Konvitz (Chapter 6, Case 2).

Mrs. Konvitz's stealing behaviors, for example, were traced back more than 60 years, directly to her vicarious "survival guilt syndrome" connected to the extermination of many of her family members in the Nazi-operated Bergen-Belsen concentration camp in 1944. She did not easily move through the four shoplifting stages, because during Stage 3, action/theft, she seemed to have become fixated, thereby reinforcing Mrs. Konvitz's extensive theft career. During therapy, when her negative unconscious, and historical antecedents were gradually introduced into her awareness, she was able to decondition herself from further shoplifting episodes, becoming a more contented person who was again able to be empathic and happy around other people, feelings she could not exhibit when she was stealing.

The four shoplifting stages commence with the aura or initial depression and attendant feelings of loss of personal control experienced by the potential as well as the seasoned shoplifter that serve as the impetus to the first anticipation/readiness stage. After the shoplifter sequentially progresses through the other three stages—neutralization, action/theft, and postexcitation/depression—he or she returns full circle to return invariably to the anticipation/readiness stage, where the stealing cycle begins anew. The shoplifter becomes inextricably trapped in this self-defeating negative psychological cycle, a shoplifting circle that he or she has little power to either prevent or escape from. This four-stage interdependent shoplifting cycle is illustrated In Figure 5.2.

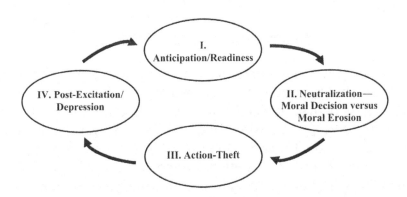

Figure 5.2. The Shoplifting Circle

At various times in their theft careers, shoplifters become vaguely cognizant of the fact that they are experiencing the signs and symptoms connected to one of these regressive stages in the shoplifting circle, yet they are unable to unhook from them, thus disallowing them the opportunity to restore their prior identity as a nonshoplifter. The shoplifters in this study have made innumerable references to their somewhat cloudy identification at a certain point in time with each of the four stages, not necessarily understanding how they got there or, for that matter, how to reconstitute themselves back to a law abiding self-identity. Consider these statements made by the four shoplifters investigated in this study about their mental states in relation to stealing:

1. "It sounds trite of me, but it was as if some outside force was acting on me." (Mrs. Daio, Case 1)

2. "I was depressed a lot, and, believe it or not, stealing made me feel better, at least for awhile." (Mrs. Chow, Case 3)

3. "Something, almost like a force, came over me. Why would I steal from a place where I go to shop for groceries three or four times a week?" (Mrs. Konvitz, Case 2)

4. "It [stealing] overtook me, and in the end, I felt okay about it. Maybe it relieved tension or something." (Mrs. Nelson, Case 4)

Stage 1: Anticipation/Readiness

During this initial aura stage in the shoplifting progression, the novitiate or repeat shoplifter begins to manifest troubling mental tension and restlessness, perhaps typified by racing, out-of-control, manic thoughts, becoming perceptibly anxious, angry, or hostile for no comprehensible conscious reason. Feelings of ennui, disorientation, and impending doom have also been identified. The person is totally consumed by imploding self-directed thoughts that "bad things are about to happen," and often this is an accurate prediction, because many negative events do lie ahead if the person elects to steal. He or she begins to generate one or more of the 10 negative self-descriptors outlined above. Many times self-destructive ideations have been reported. Feelings of loss of self-control combined with self-centeredness or narcissism have also been recorded by many shoplifters during Stage 1. This selfish or narcissistic bent may begin during the first stage; however, it is prominently manifested during Stage 4, postexcitation/depression, as commented on by one shoplifter: "Maybe I'm just a selfish "bitch" who deserves to get arrested?" (Mrs. Daio, Chapter 6, Case 1).

Many shoplifters have reported during this stage that they have intense feelings of dizziness; a sense of unreality, disconnectedness, and loneliness, and a general feeling of physical shakiness. Something unpleasant is overtaking them, yet they cannot quite identify or prevent it. Often shoplifters are bombarded with self-generated negative and confusing thoughts or self-sentences (messages they tell themselves) concerning the denigration of their personal worth as well as their existential, deep probing of what the meaning of their life is. These confusing thought patterns constitute the beginnings of their loss of control and segue into Stage 2, neutralization—moral decision versus moral erosion, during which major moral compromises including a series of bad judgments take place.

To cope with these random, uncontrolled, and perplexing thoughts and sensations of psychological ennui during stage 1, the shoplifter begins taking real mental steps to do something, act. Mrs. Daio described it this way: "I just had to get out of the house and do something. I wasn't exactly sure what it was, but I had to get going somewhere. Then for some reason I ended up at Saks Fifth Avenue and didn't know why I was there, and then I was arrested and wound up in county jail!" This stage is further depicted by the shoplifter's desperate, frenzied feelings of loneliness, detachment, and then isolation from the world as they know it. Winona Ryder put it perfectly when describing her alienation, withdrawal, and loneliness during an interview with Diane Sawyer on ABC News' 20-20: "I wish I had someone to talk to, a friend or someone, and I didn't" (Ryder, 1999).

From all accounts, Ms.Ryder is a successful movie star with everything going for her, except apparently she was quite alone and lonely, as she told Diane Sawyer. Perhaps Ms. Ryder overcompensated for this personal sense of alienation, exemplified during Stage 1, driving her deep into a self-defeating theft trajectory. It is my guess that even today, Ms. Ryder probably has no idea why she stole. The anticipation/readiness stage is often set in motion because of alienation and depression, and one by-product of shoplifting results in the decrease in depressive symptomatology, at least for a brief period after stealing (Stage 4, the postexcitation/depression phase).

This perception of being alien and cut off from others is emblematic of the moral neutralization process in Stage 2. The shoplifters are headed in an undesirable direction, but they do not know where they are going or how to stop from getting there. During Stage 1, their usually sound moral barriers against theft progressively begin to drift and then weaken appreciably. Rational cognitions not to steal are beginning to be replaced by irrational and deviant thought errors that promote the development of increasing theft cognitions, paving the way for entrance into the subsequent shoplifting stages.

The following thinking errors have been identified with deviant groups, including shoplifters. Once their cognitions get off track, leading to an initial theft, the probability significantly increases that shoplifters will continue down the slippery path of becoming career offenders. These and additional thought errors contribute in a direct way to a further erosion in the logical cognitive restraints against engaging in theft. When experiencing stressful feelings such as anxiety, mental confusion, depression, or loss of control, shoplifters respond irrationally using the following negative scripts:

- Jumping to the worst possible conclusion (catastrophizing).

- Predicting the future instead of waiting to see what happens (fortune-telling).

- Jumping to conclusions about what other people are thinking of oneself (mind-reading).

- Focusing on the negative and overlooking the positive (mental filtering).

- Discounting positive information or twisting a positive into a negative (disqualifying the positive).

- Putting oneself down as a failure, worthless, or useless (labeling oneself as a shoplifter).

- Listening too much to negative gut feelings (emotionally based) instead of looking at the objective facts (cognitive reasoning).

- Using words like should, must, ought, and have to to make rigid rules about oneself, the world, or other people (demanding) (Willson & Branch, 2010, p. 43).

These profound thought deficits pave the way for a shoplifter to later make self-destructive decisions, followed closely by bad consequences as indicative of Stage 2, neutralization. My research indicates that, in order to steal, shoplifters must make moral compromises in order to neutralize if not justify a series of bad decisions. Even though they are making poor and even self-destructive life decisions, shoplifters have told me that the act of theft lends a certain meaning to their lives.

Confirmation for their lives and their validation as persons has been chronically problematic for shoplifters. Mrs. Nelson (Chapter 6, Case 4) framed her personal search for meaning this way:

> I really felt like my life was going nowhere, and I was trying desperately to get somewhere. I was very unhappy with myself, and stealing was a big part of it, but I couldn't stop. There was little doubt that it was ruining my life. I really didn't know who I was anymore. In fact, and as dumb as it seems, the only real time I felt alive was when I stole.

The intrepretation of criminal behavior—including shoplifting, then, from the existential viewpoint—suggests that it is at its most seductive for individuals who generate their self-esteem from quick fixes, short-term projects with a rapid turnaround in which stimulation and instant gratification are the priorities; the clue is present in the language we use—"taking control of the moment." Projects of self-affirmation that can be sustained over a longer term can sidestep the technical transgression that is crime (Goudy, 2003, pp. 11–12).

Stage 2: Neutralization—Moral Decision versus Moral Erosion

The neutralization stage represents the first step in the middle phase of the shoplifting progression. The psychological neutralization stage, in my view, has proven to be the most important and the most complex of the four stages, directly affecting a person's later mental decision to shoplift. As explained earlier, I have found that a person's self-defeating decision to steal most frequently is not driven by economic incentives but by vague external control variables (such as external locus of control) that tend to vitiate a person's usually sound judgmental reasoning and contribute to his or her making inappropriate decisions which lead to the commission of a crime. It is this maladaptive decision process that results in the considerable counterproductive consequences for the shoplifter, quite possibly leading to the loss of his or her personal freedom.

To Steal or Not to Steal: Rational Choice?

During the past two decades, criminologists, psychologists, and behavioral economists have examined the criminal decision-making process, including the shoplifter's decision to offend. For instance, some behavioral economists view and interpret crime, including shoplifting, as a completely rational personal act occurring when individuals evaluate the relative gain of both criminal and noncriminal actions and then freely choose the alternative with the highest perceived net payoff (Becker, 1973).

In the field of criminology, advocates of rational choice theory have often linked it to such individual propensities as self-control (interpreted in this study as locus of control), poor impulse regulation, and low self-concept formation. The rational choice models of offending are recent theoretical frameworks, which first began to appear in the criminological literature around the 1980s. However, the investigation of these etiological theories of crime has increased in frequency during the past 20 years.

Attention to these individual propensities affecting rational choice has, according to Piquero and Tibbetts (2002), mainly focused on nonviolent crimes such as drunk driving and general theft as well as shoplifting. They found that the individual propensities of low self-control and faulty moral beliefs exert both direct and indirect effects on offending via the perception of shame and the rewards associated with perceived benefits of the act committed. Rational choice theory has been demarcated from other crime causation models, i.e., conflict and radical theory, control theory, strain theory and biological theory, to mention a few.

Rational choice theory directs attention to the act of engaging in criminal or deviant acts. According to this view, notes Siegel:

> Law-violating behavior should be viewed as an event that occurs when an offender decides to risk violating the law after considering his or her personal situation (need for money, personal values, learning experiences) and situational factors (how well a target is protected, how affluent the neighborhood is, how efficient the local police happen to be). Before choosing to commit a crime, the reasoning criminal evaluates the risk of apprehension, the seriousness of the expected punishment, and the value of the criminal enterprise ...(Siegel, 1992, p. 131).

Rational choice theory is, however, not without its critics. For example, Kahneman and Tversky's (1979) decision-making research, labeled "prospect theory" which is discussed at length later in this chapter, is at variance with the traditional rational models accounting for human decision making. Clearly there are issues with the applicability of rational models when an attempt is made to account for all criminal decisions. A first challenge that has been advanced concerns the implicit assumption that criminal behaviors such as shoplifting have as their intended outcome some form of cost-benefit calculus, such as, "If I successfully engage in this planned criminal act, then there shall be a clearly defined positive payoff for me." Given statistics showing that the shoplifter recidivism rate is somewhere between 70% and 90%, then one might ask, How can this be true?

A second direct challenge to the validity of the rational choice model has been advanced by Simpson, Piquero and Paternoster (2002), contend that the rational choice model is assailable in those situations under which human rationality may, for a variety of reasons, be compromised. The contention put forth here is that the four shoplifters described in Chapter 6 reflect severe deficits or compromise regarding their usually efficient reasoning capabilities.

A third challenge to the rational choice model, at least for shoplifters, is the belief among researchers that the model may not be universally applicable with all classes of offenders. For example, Jones (2001) has argued that at the behavioral level, rational choice theory may not be applicable. Based on this perspective, the model does not accurately capture or fully explain all social-psychologically driven criminal behaviors. Jones discusses what is termed "bounded" rational choice, which connotes the idea that human actors are no doubt goal driven and intentional, but their judgment is not fully operational in some situations. All four of the shoplifters in this study to varying degrees were afflicted with bounded or mitigated rationality. This supposition then, if representative, means that their reasoning capacity during Stage 2, neutralization, is inevitably less than perfect. Because their shoplifting involves a calculable risk and obvious uncertainty as to the outcome, offenders are rarely in a position to quantify all the salient variables in order to solve the costs-versus-benefits equation. This is why the offenders' decision making is characterized as rational, although in a mitigated way (Paternoster & Bancman, 2000).

Carroll (1978) has framed the moral decision issue in terms of the quantification of acceptable criminal risk. The individual must weigh the risk of apprehension against the desirable gain when deciding to commit a crime. However, if the probability of arrest and incarceration is high when taking into consideration the weight of the penalty, then crime reduction can be anticipated.

An alternative method, examining the criminal versus noncriminal decision-making process as tied to shoplifting, is provided by Brantigham and Brantigham (1993), who support the theory of rational choice or rational utility, as it relates to decision making related to criminal behavior. Their theory assumes that certain people develop a mental readiness to offend, steal. Concerning the mental readiness to steal, including shoplifting, they argue criminal thinking varies greatly from individual to individual. For example, background factors, emotional issues, and drugs or alcohol can influence a person's choice to steal. Readiness to commit a crime necessitates the potential offender to anticipate both value and utility in what he or she is about to do.

Brantigham and Brantigham's concept of "mental readiness to offend" is consistent with Stage 1, anticipation/readiness, that I have expressed as forming the primary theft basis, setting in motion the shoplifting cycle, and extends into Stage 2, neutralization—moral decision versus moral erosion.

The question arises: Are shoplifters so overwhelmed with external psychological forces and moral-ethical conflict that their free will has been compromised? There is compelling evidence from the cases I present that at times shoplifters are externally impacted by what can be labeled as irresistible impulses to do things (e.g. commit theft) against their will or at least against their self-interest. Some shoplifters have stated that they felt a total lack of free will when it came to resisting shoplifting. As Mrs. Konvitz (Chapter 6, Case 2) described her impulsive imperative to steal: "Not only didn't I have any personal control over my shoplifting, it was like I was somehow compelled to do it; I had little or no choice!" A body of research supports the position that many shoplifters lack or abdicate the principle of normative rationality. In my professional view, the shoplifters I have treated demonstrate restricted rational choice based on quantifiable factors such as external locus of control and clinical depression. Their ability to choose rationally becomes restricted, and they are not able to fully function.

The case studies in Chapter 6 demonstrate that the shoplifter's decision to steal is based on personal moral conflict. Thus, in many ways, the shoplifter's moral state is regressive and in concert with a primitive or more childlike decision state than that of a mature adult. Shoplifters may have developed a mature moral reasoning code at some time in their lives, yet for a variety of reasons, mostly psychological, they regress or slide back into an earlier and more dysfunctional moral decision stage.

Kohlberg (1981), developed a theory of moral development, has commented on this moral decision-making process and created a moral conflict theory by which people can be classified into one of six stages of moral development. The successful progression through the six stages of moral development culminates in the formation of a well-defined moral conscience ultimately encompassing adherence to social-legal rules and principles. The most primitive of these moral stages are Kohlberg's stages 1 and 2, characterized by a naively egoistic drive and orientation further suggesting a sense of moral relativism and a value system determined by certain external factors.

The shoplifter's moral compromise promoting the choice to steal is particularly relevant during Stage 2, neutralization, because similar to Kohlberg's moral external factor, the shoplifter, as this study's results have established, is highly influenced by an external locus of control. The more externality the shoplifter reflects, the higher the probability for moral erosion contributing to decreased restraint against the development of attitudes favorable to violation. In this psychological context, Kohlberg's stages 1 and 2, egotistic orientation directed by external happenings, seem to be highly correlated with Rotter's (1966) external locus-of-control construct that is positively connected with shoplifting behavior (see Chapter 4).

Moral Neutralization Factors

Specifically regarding shoplifting, these 7 identifiable factors are usually present during seven the neutralization stage:

1. Denial. The shoplifter denies that the offense ever happened or claims, "I've had so many losses in my life. It's not a big loss to Nordstrom."

2. Minimization. The shoplifter tries to either minimize the theft or the number of times he or she engaged in shoplifting.

3. Factual fabrication. The shoplifter invents idiosyncratic stories, going into great detail for the express purpose of covering up the shoplifting act: "I was just testing or verifying their security system to make sure it worked properly."

4. Sympathy strategy. The shoplifter displays what appears to be deep regret about the thefts and points out his or her own personal civic achievement: "I volunteer my free time at a local homeless shelter, so why should this be a big deal?"

5. Synthetic reasoning. Although this mental concept as I have defined here is closely related to factual fabrication, synthetic or deceptive shoplifter reasoning goes much deeper, forcing the shoplifter to do the impossible—impute logical meaning into a seemingly meaningless theft event. And dissimilar from factual fabrication in a second way, synthetic reasoning does not attempt to cover up the shoplifting event. It does entail supplying what appears to be an adequate, surface reason for the real, often unconscious one.

6. Condemnation of the condemners. The shoplifter maintains that those who condemn his or her behavior are doing so based on spite and misplaced blame: "They're probably worse people than me anyway."

7. Misrepresentation of consequences. The shoplifter tends to minimize the nature of the retailer's loss; "It's a big chain store; they won't miss a few CDs."

The presence of these self-eroding, neutralization factors further contributes to the shoplifter's loss of personal control and predisposes the person to Stage 3, action/theft, or the actual stealing phase.

Clinical studies of the rational bases for criminal actions such as shoplifting have historically provided only limited explanatory results.

The pragmatic utility theory of theft, the getting-something-for-nothing (as stated by Shulman and the title of his 2004 book) reasoning model of criminal theft, assumes that the prospective criminal shoplifter is rationally capable prior to and at the moment of the stealing, of collecting all the salient data and then processing it—that is, able to weigh the pros and cons, factors relevant to the objective probabilities for success of his or her anticipated action. These rational criminal models as applied to shoplifting have at best yielded very mixed results. The fact is that most shoplifters are not at all governed by a rational thought system or by desire for material gains. Rational models of shoplifting presuppose that the stealing has been committed based on a means-to-end reasoning paradigm—that is, the shoplifting act is a means to a predictable, logical goal or end the shoplifter had in mind at the time.

The position I advance looks at shoplifting from a different perspective, as being based on a process-reinforcement system. Most stealing done by rich women, is not specifically influenced by ends-oriented thinking or direct payoffs, particularly those of a material nature. This is to say, the most powerful reinforcement to the shoplifter takes place during the actual stealing (Stage 3), although additional psychological rewards do occur during the Stage 4 postexcitation/depression phase, when for example, depression is briefly ameliorated. It remains constant that it is the four stages of the shoplifting experience provide shoplifters with the emotional high that serves to perpetuate their stealing into the future. According to rational choice theorists, shoplifters may also not process information correctly.

This apparent shoplifter deficit in information processing is viewed as connected to the three-step traditional criminal decision paradigm as put forth by Johnson and Payne (1976, p.174), who categorize general criminal decision making into the following three propositions:

1. A set of actions or alternatives

2. A set of outcomes or payoffs—for example, being apprehended or departing undetected

3. The probability of the occurrence of each outcome of their action

Because of their external life orientations premised on the external determinants of luck, chance, and fate, shoplifters are unable to see the real possibility of viable action alternatives when faced with making the decision to steal or, conversely to conform their behavior to the requirements of the law and not steal.

Most important, however, is that historically rational choice theory has not accounted for the multiplicity of unquantified psychosocial variables that influence a person's decision to steal, nor does it help explain the steps he or she encounters during the shoplifting path; this notwithstanding the fact that a limited number of shoplifter typologies are indeed influenced by ends-driven material motivations (see the shoplifter typologies in Chapter 3). These include professional and impoverished shoplifters whose goals or ends are very different, centering on or highly influenced by economic or dollar-driven incentives. The shoplifters presented in Chapter 6 are not influenced by the constraints of rational utility maximization. Rather, they are highly influenced by a series of complex psychological and social variables such as an external locus of control and clinical depression, which compromise their rational information gathering and -processing abilities. Moreover, shoplifters become trapped in one or more of the shoplifter stages, which accounts for their criminal, counterproductive decision making process.

Negating the concept of personal rationality altogether, Kahneman, a psychologist who won the Nobel Prize in economics for his work on psychological assumptions and their impact on economic theory, has done extensive research into decision-making. Working with another psychologist, Tversky, in the 1970s and 1980s in "a collaboration that lasted 15 years and involved an extraordinary number of strange and inventive experiments, they had demonstrated how essentially irrational human beings can be" (as cited in Lewis, 2011, p. 145). Their combined behaviorally and economically determined decision making centers on capriciousness should be taken into consideration when attempting to impute logic into the shoplifter's seemingly illogical choice to steal:

The agent of economic theory is rational, selfish, and his tastes do change. I was astonished. My economic colleagues worked in the building next door, but I had not appreciated the profound difference between our intellectual worlds. To a psychologist, it is self-evident that people are neither fully rational nor completely selfish, and that their tastes are anything but stable (Lewis, 2011, p.145).

In many cases the shoplifter's subjective belief system concerning getting caught and punished prior to stealing may contain incomplete information and be highly influenced by seemingly inconsequential factors. Kahneman and Tversky (1979) developed the concept of "framing or prospect theory"—the idea that two almost identical choices when thought of marginally differently can result in very different and counterproductive outcomes. During the neutralization stage, the potential shoplifter contemplates innumerable subjective decision paths of whether or not to offend. Many times these probabilities of future behavior outcomes are inaccurate or become distorted. Kahneman and Tversky account for these perceptual distortions and contend that this mental confusion is primarily based on a person's problem with the determination and anticipation of the behavioral consequences directly affected by their general mood or affect state. The results presented in this study demonstrate that shoplifters' mood levels are highly impacted due to their not infrequent abdication of personal responsibility (reliance on external locus of control) and because of their depressed mood levels. Many shoplifters reflect apparent deficits related to the mental framing of their logical choices available to them just prior to the theft stage. The view advanced here is that their antisocial behaviors, appreciably impacted by exogenous variables, can be interpreted from the standpoint of poor information processing. This theory may help explain why the shoplifter recidivism rate is among the highest considering all offenses against property.

Later in this chapter (in the section titled "Perhaps They Are Just Selfish?") shoplifters' bad choices are seen as driven by both selfishness/narcissism and an external locus-of-control orientation. The interplay of these combined factors contributes to shoplifters making innumerable irresponsible and irrational decisions.

Stage 3: Action/Theft

Stage 3 is the final segment in the middle phase of the shoplifting progression. The action/theft stage is typically characterized by shoplifters feeling out of control or the perception that external factors such as fate, luck, chance, fortuitousness or control by outside "powerful forces" are now influencing them and irreversibly impacting their choices, contributing to a bad result—that is, stealing and thereby committing a crime. At this action/theft point, however, because of their cognitive thinking errors, shoplifters are led into making the malappropriate decision to steal, perhaps one of the most devastating decisions of their lives.

The shoplifter's perception of the theft act itself is frequently internalized and then conveniently objectivized as a defense mechanism: "It was as if I was watching someone else doing the stealing. It couldn't have been me. I couldn't be a thief!" This shift in perception from the first to the third person represents an unconscious mental deflection of personal responsibility and to avoid the consequences of their criminal actions. This perception shift has its genesis in Stage 2, neutralization—moral decision versus moral erosion. Projection of personal responsibility as a defense mechanism permeates the other shoplifting stages.

Shoplifting: Going Down a Lonely Road

Shoplifters typically drive alone and travel long distances from their homes to complete shoplifting acts. From many interviews with shoplifters, I have surmised that shoplifters take these trips, sometimes in a mental daze, surveilling large shopping malls. This stage involves a sequence of mostly confused, random, and seemingly purposeless behaviors, ultimately culminating in an act of theft. The action/theft stage is characterized by its solitary nature. Shoplifters are usually alone, lonely, alienated, confused, and depressed when they choose to steal. Out of control, depressed, lonely, shoplifters have reported driving for hours in and out of a variety of shopping malls, even at times becoming geographically lost even though their vehicle was equipped with a functioning GPS system. Many times shoplifters reported having problems finding their way back home after the realization that they had driven more than 100 miles in one direction, often to a city they had never previously visited.

Sometimes shoplifters allude to the sketchy recollection that, as one shoplifter put it, "It was just by accident I went to Union Square in San Francisco and stole those dresses and accessories." Of course, this is far from the truth. Shoplifting implies intentionality and a goal-directed mission: to steal. Another shoplifter told me, "I had to drive the 90 miles from L.A. to San Diego because I had to buy a gift for my daughter's wedding, because she was only registered at Macy's in San Diego's Fashion Valley, so I had to go there in order to buy what she wanted. At least that's what I thought at the time."

I have heard this type of faulty thinking, characterized by clouded thoughts, so often that I have termed it shoplifter's synthetic *reasoning* (see the section "Moral Neutralization Factors" earlier in this chapter). That is, shoplifters, when pressed to answer why they stole, provide what they believe on a conscious level to be a sound justification for, as an example, destination shopping; whereas the real reason is tied to their underlying need to steal something. Accordingly, this type of reasoning distortion can be explained using the cognitive explanation I developed—shoplifter's synthetic *reasoning*.

Confused, if not bewildered, by their repeated shoplifting on the surface, they supply what appears to them to be a good reason for their criminal actions rather than the real reason—they have begun to get caught up in the shoplifting zone. The formal process of shoplifter's synthetic reasoning prior to the theft event begins earlier during the Stage 2, neutralization phase, and persists throughout the remaining two shoplifting stages. Time after time, subsequent to being caught in the act, shoplifters deploy this self-deceptive, synthetic reasoning strategy, not only to lend a certain credence to their illegal behavior but, more important, to explain to themselves and possibly to others what, for the most part, remains inexplicable.

Why Do Shoplifters Get Lost and Become Disoriented?

A salient psychological factor tied into the action/theft stage is that frequently shoplifters have no recollection of how they arrived at a particular destination or what items they selected to steal. Often, when hearing these accounts, skeptical law enforcement officers just raise their eyebrows and believe the shoplifter who has been arrested is pretending to be disoriented, faking or making up a story concerning his or her alleged disorientation to justify stealing and still worse to explain getting arrested. When questioned about where they were when arrested, some shoplifters reportedly had to refer to police booking records to learn their correct locations. Because they usually drove to these malls, subsequent to their arrest, their vehicles were then secured by law enforcement. Several accused and disoriented shoplifter defendants who I have treated had their vehicles impounded. They then had to contact their spouse, other family members, or friends to retrieve their vehicles.

The problem was they did not know the location of their vehicle or sometimes even the city where it was located. Therefore, they could not provide any accurate directional information about where to go to get their vehicle. For many it was as if they were in a fog or cloud state involving disorientation, confusion, and momentary psychogenic amnesia. This state of psychological confusion or trancelike episode, in many important psychological respects, is consistent with the diagnostic criteria associated with dissociative fugue state in the *Diagnostic and Statistical Manual of Mental Disorders (2000)* (4th ed., text rev.) *DSM–IV–TR.*, 300.13). It is essential for the clinician, in cases where amnesia is suspected, to evaluate the shoplifter for fugue-state symptoms.

Amnesia—Is That It? Or Is It Psychological Fugue?

The *DSM–IV–TR* diagnostic criteria for dissociative fugue state include:

A. The predominant disturbance is sudden, unexpected travel away from home or one's customary place of work, with inability to recall one's past.

B. Confusion about personal identity or assumption of a new identity (partial or complete).

C. The disturbance does not occur exclusively during the course of Dissociative Identity Disorder and is not due to the direct physiological effects of a substance (e.g. a drug of abuse, a medication) or a general medical condition (e.g. temporal lobe epilepsy).

D. The symptoms cause clinically significant distress or impairment in social, occupational, or other important areas of functioning.

Criteria A, B, and D in this diagnostic classification are most consistent with the stories reported by several of the shoplifters presented in Chapter 6.

The shoplifter's psychological fugue state shares certain characteristics with what Katz (1988) terms "the sensual metaphysics of sneaky thrills." In his view, sensuality is associated with the shoplifting experience. He presents a compelling argument that shoplifters may indeed engage in metaphysical denial; although they know they are breaking the law, nonprofessional shoplifters and vandals commonly feel when they are arrested, an irresistible protest that "this can't be happening to me!" It is as if they lived the process of the crime like a character moving in a myth or a dream (Katz, 1988, p. 74).

Shoplifters perceive the experience similar to a somnambulant state when the boundaries between fantasy and reality remain sketchy. When considering the emotional impact and sensual dimension attached to the shoplifting event, they do seem to wander, as if in a dark cloud.

The action/theft stage necessitates a further cognitive examination of the shoplifter's mental clarity prior to making the irreversible decision to steal. The four shoplifting cases presented in this book represent people who have reported that for the balance of their adult lives, they ordinarily possess moral restraint against offending of any type; even running a stop sign would seem out of character for them. On the one hand, they know that theft is both morally and legally wrong; yet on the other, they still entered the shoplifting zone; that is, they held two competing, opposing, and illogical thoughts at once: "to steal or not to steal."

This produces a conflict state Festinger has termed *cognitive dissonance*. Festinger's theory of cognitive dissonance, his greatest contribution to individual decision making, is based on two main assumptions: the first is that people strive to find out if their opinions and judgments are correct; the second is that when objective means are unavailable, people evaluate their opinions and judgments by comparing them with those of others who are similar to themselves (Festinger, 1957).

When a person becomes committed to stealing something, cognitive dissonance is invariably created. This yields personal psychological discomfort and tension, and palpable psychological pressures will arise demanding reduction until the dissonance is eliminated—that is, resolution of the question to steal or not to steal. The person must make a decision. This process is also reminiscent of dynamics at work during Stage 2, the neutralization phase of shoplifting. If the potential shoplifter proceeds to make the fateful, irrevocable decision to steal, he or she may at that point supply various, inconsistent reasons why such an illogical and illegal choice was made. This was evidenced from the convoluted and sad case of Mrs. Nelson (Chapter 6, Case 4), who told me that she stole items from Bloomingdale's,

> because I felt like I didn't have the choice to buy any nice things for myself. All the money went to support my family, and I really felt sad about it. I know, in a way, I was only thinking about myself, and that's pretty selfish of me!

Mrs. Nelson not only felt sad and selfish, but was additionally impacted by a long history of suicidal ideations. Selfishness does play a contributing role for most shoplifters.

Perhaps They Are Just Selfish?

The issue of the shoplifter's volition or lack of rational choice during the action/theft stage referred to by Mrs. Nelson certainly demonstrates the existence of an external locus-of-control orientation as well as depression. And, in important ways, these psychological components are bound up with the shoplifter's self-centeredness, selfishness, and a life orientation that "it's always about me first" that may drive the person toward committing a shoplifting act. Psychological reliance on uncontrolled self-interest is perhaps largely responsible for how the shoplifter became psychologically dysfunctional in the first place. These self-centered feelings, I have noticed, come up all too frequently during Stage 3, the action/theft stage of shoplifting.

After an intensive analysis of the more than 100 shoplifters that I have treated, it became evident that their external locus of control negatively impacted their lives, pushing them ever so slowly farther into the shoplifting zone. Combined with this external control finding, it was also abundantly clear to me that shoplifters, as a rule, demonstrate an intense self-devotion, a close psychological relative to selfishness and even to diagnosable narcissism. This recurrent pattern of concentrated devotion only to self-interest at the expense of others was seen repeatedly in the therapy conversations I had with innumerable shoplifters. It was as if they lived on some uninhabited and isolated island where they were alone, distant, cut off, and detached from others. The shoplifters' personal lack of insight into their self-centeredness is without question an underlying factor motivating their theft actions, serving additionally as a shoplifting driver and contributing to their personal alienation.

This intense narcissistic desire to be the center of attention has pervasive roots in Stage 3, the action/theft stage of shoplifting. The action/theft stage which obviously requires a person to commit an illegal act—shoplifting. The illegal act of stealing requires the person to first form criminal intent and then engage in a shoplifting act, and, in turn, the intent relies on the person being able to weigh all the best options available at the time and only then make the choice whether or not to steal. Many times this choice selection is pervaded by intrusive, narcissistic thought intrusions, which further cloud the shoplifter's decision- making process.

Narcissism: Maybe It's Part of the Profile

Mrs. Nelson's statement, "I guess I was only thinking about myself," is particularly emblematic of the undercurrent of narcissism often recognized in shoplifters. Additionally, these self-centered shoplifters manifest a recognizable sense of personal entitlement that also connotes their narcissistic worldview: "Why shouldn't I have these things [the stolen items]? I deserve them." Mrs. Daio (Chapter 6, Case 1) told me that the justification for her outright theft of more than 400 expensive purses revolved around her sense of perceived personal entitlement at the time of her offenses. Because of Mrs. Daio's unswerving self-centeredness and feelings of entitlement, she no doubt would meet at least several of the nine *DSM–IV–TR*, (p.294) diagnostic criteria for narcissistic personality disorder (NPD). In fact, all four cases described in detail in Chapter 6, to some extent, meet the following diagnostic criteria for NPD. Each case reflected these NPD symptoms:

1. A sense of grandiosity and self-importance

2. Fantasies of unlimited success and power

3. Belief that they are special

4. Requiring admiration

5. Intense feelings of entitlement

"A pervasive pattern of grandiosity (in fantasy or behavior), need for admiration, and lack of empathy beginning by early adulthood and present in a variety of contexts" is also a defining characteristic of some shoplifters (*DSM-IV-TR* p.294).

For example, the four shoplifters described in Chapter 6 were to some degree all self-absorbed, personally obsessed and became devoid of thoughts or considerations for the important people in their lives. A shoplifter's quest for the next high or psychological rush derived from stealing trumps their thoughts of people around them. Their own needs dominate their existences, forcing them deeper into tragic isolation, similar to Winona Ryder's account of her life in the time period when a Beverly Hills shopping excursion devolved into shoplifting.

Each case outlined in Chapter 6 displays one or more of these NPD identifiers. In addition to the narcissistic statements made by Mrs. Nelson and Mrs. Daio that have already been mentioned, Mrs. Chow and Mrs. Konvitz both have made statements in keeping with the NPD diagnostic symptom listing. Many of these statements are also psychologically consistent with rationalizations or justifications in support of their narcissistic demands and represent multiple layers of psychological defense armor, making them resistant to treatment. Here are their narcissistic symptoms as described in their own words:

1. Mrs. Konvitz (Case 2), a well-to-do resident supposedly in good social standing in her Santa Barbara, California community, oddly enough went into her favorite upscale deli and secreted away one and a half pounds of corned beef, for which she was later arrested. When arrested Mrs. Konvitz flatly stated, "What the hell, I've seen lots of women do the same thing or worse, and at those prices, why shouldn't I do it too?" NPD Criterion 8, "is often envious of others," is particularly applicable here.

2. Mrs. Chow's (Case 3) shoplifting trigger to steal children's clothing was her overcompensation for not being a mother. After her arrest for grand theft, she was sentenced to six months of local jail time as well as two years of follow-up shoplifter- oriented treatment with me. She was also referred to an addiction-type shoplifting support group. During one therapy session, the conversation turned toward what reasons she had to support her original grand theft charge. Mrs. Chow stated, "Why shouldn't I have a child with [my husband]? We certainly deserve it. We are really good people, and to be denied a child, especially for us, is just stupid, makes no sense." Believing "that he or she is special and unique" is part of NPD Criterion 3. Mrs. Chow's statement, along with many other comments voiced during psychotherapy, are consistent with the "specialness" of her and her husband's situation.

Narcissistic shoplifters are not generally viewed as nefarious people (though perhaps a little inconsiderate of others), and they are qualitatively dissimilar from the many psychopathic offenders I have treated in the past; they apparently travel through life terribly out of focus, gazing mostly at reflections of themselves whenever and as often as possible. They see the world differently, putting themselves at the center of it.

In many ways, the narcissism attached to shoplifting during the action/theft stage mirrors the tenets of what is known in criminology as the theory of *short-run hedonism*. As explained in Chapter 3, typically the provisional/delinquent shoplifter, Typology 12, the shoplifter does not demonstrate a strong focus on long-term planning or goals that in most cases necessitates adherence to delayed gratification. Many people who demonstrate an external locus-of-control orientation also evidence patterns of short-run hedonism, especially characterized by delay of gratification deficit. To put it frankly, "they want what they want, and they want it all right now." Bleiberg has commented on short-run hedonism and narcissistic self-absorption as reflecting a primary self-pathology: "lack of vigor and aliveness, obvious depression, low self-esteem, lack of pleasure in the self and its activities, lack of enthusiasm and initiative, and lack of long-term investments in goals and ideals" (1987, p. 297).

Along with their self-centeredness, the shoplifters I have worked with have also developed a well-defined aura of chronic narcissistic anger and overt hostility. This anger or even rage deeply embedded in the shoplifters' personalities represents their regressive attempt to cope with some vague and ill-defined, lifelong sadness or a series of real or imagined disappointments in their lives. At times, the narcissistic personality demands the need for revenge strategies taking form as perhaps righting a perceived (or misperceived) wrong or undoing some past emotional trauma incurred in the shoplifter's life. The narcissistic element in shoplifting can further be interpreted as a representation of the subjective experience of superiority. As Mrs. Daio (Case 1) stated, "I thought the sky was the limit, and there wasn't anything I couldn't do." In reality, these feelings of grandiosity (Criterion 1 for NPD) provide only a self-deceptive and limited cover-up because shoplifters are constantly haunted by the real underlying possibility of being exposed as just ordinary, if not inferior and socially inadequate (Bleiberg, 1987).

In my view, the narcissistic shoplifter shares many psychological commonalities with the equalizer (Chapter 3, Typology 8). This is especially true because both are characterized by anger, aggression, self-centeredness, and ample measure of vindictiveness.

Bleiberg describes narcissism this way: "By virtue of their beauty and cleverness, some are able to secure quite a lot of admiration. But it's never enough. In fact, success only perpetuates an impossible dilemma: to feel good, external approval is needed" (1987, p. 299). This is certainly part of the shoplifter's locus-of-control problem—his or her life is constantly reinforced by psychological forces lying outside of their perceived control. This external orientation or focus on personal needs as directed and even required by others necessitates the narcissistic shoplifter to elevate his or her status far above the average person's as if playing with an entirely different set of societal rules. This is equally applicable both to the celebrity shoplifter and to the ordinary shoplifter negatively impacted by narcissistic undercurrents.

This is not to say that the shoplifters in this study knew exactly how or why they arrived at this precarious self-centered point in their lives. Being previously law-abiding, they suddenly became the object of their own admiration (like Narcissus), and then started to justify their stealing. Although the four cases in Chapter 6 clearly involved certain narcissistic-oriented value systems and meet the general criteria for NPD, these patients had no conscious idea why they set out on a narcissistic collision course that could ultimately destroy their lives and negatively impact the lives of their family members.

One manifest goal of psychological treatment with shoplifters is to strive to therapeutically unhook them from the many addictive triggers supporting their drive to steal. These triggers are mostly unavailable to the shoplifter's conscious awareness, so with insight through therapy they are able to surrender their narcissistic drives to commit theft and return to an adjusted, non-theft-driven lifestyle. In the end, almost all shoplifters manifest self-loathing for their stealing.

Prin, an addictions therapist and author of three books on addictive behaviors, approaches shoplifting from the standpoint of rule breaking, combining shoplifting with narcissistic behavior. He states, "...the number one personality disorder that I see regarding rule breaking is narcissism or narcissistic personality disorder—the idea that 'I'm the center of the world, and everyone's supposed to recognize that and appreciate it..." (as cited in Shulman, 2011a, p. 203). He also addresses the shoplifter entitlement concept that is central to the *DSM–IV–TR* diagnosis of narcissism.

In related research on narcissism, Egan (2010) also studied a sample of shoplifters who completed four questionnaires to measure personality, consumer ethical beliefs, and attitudes toward shoplifting and demographics. The study's results identified four personality dimensions seen in persons prone to engaging in shoplifting: unpleasant attitude, antisocial tendency, personal disorganization, and unreliability.

Egan's study sample was composed entirely of male shoplifters. Analysis of his data indicates that, in general, shoplifting is psychologically linked to a person's unpleasant personality type. Unpleasantness can, in fact, be linked directly to narcissistic personality features. For example, Mrs. Konvitz (Chapter 6, Case 2) had developed over the years an abrasive, hostile style of relating to people that could fit into Egan's unpleasant personality model, and can be included in Criterion 9 for NPD, "shows arrogance."

Criterion 5 for NPD in the *DSM–IV–TR* states that the narcissist "has a sense of entitlement, i.e. unreasonable expectations of especially favorable treatment or automatic compliance with his or her expectations." This entitlement subsequently increases the probability for shoplifters to place their needs before others including their family. Some shoplifters risk it all quite simply because they think in some illogical context that they deserve the merchandise they steal. This is especially the case regarding the trophy-collector shoplifter (see Chapter 3) who prefers stealing a Rolex to a Seiko. The trophy shoplifter's sense of narcissistic entitlement directs his or her attention toward those high-dollar, coveted items for both monetary and symbolic value, even at times providing a sexual payoff (see Chapter 6, Case 1, Mrs. Daio's fetish).

During the initial stages of psychotherapy with shoplifters, I have noticed that their speech patterns were continuously punctuated with references to themselves, and most discussions were absent any third-person references, as if they were the only ones living on the planet that mattered—and perhaps in their thoughts they were. The pervasive me-first attitude with these patients was persistent sometimes lingering for months during the treatment sessions; in some cases, it never completely disappeared from the conversation regardless of what type of therapeutic interventions were attempted.

The task of the therapist must be intensely focused on deconditioning the narcissism, rationalization, and defense armor supporting the shoplifter's underlying psychological drive to steal. The piercing of this defense armor is a necessary condition for the formation of shoplifter definitions—that is, how he or she defines his or her life—that are antithetical to the commission of additional thefts down the road. Another psychotherapeutic goal is to facilitate a reduction in the shoplifter's misplaced adherence to feelings of omnipotence and grandiosity, also seen as woven into his or her narcissistic personality.

As a clinical entity, narcissism may not explain all shoplifters' acts of theft, but I have found that it is a valuable psychological descriptor that must be addressed in the therapeutic process.

Tools of the Trade for Stage 3 Shoplifting

Whether shoplifting is driven by a narcissistic motivation or by other maladaptive psychological traits (e.g., external locus of control or depression), after talking with many shoplifters, it became evident that they all had to learn and use some type of practical shoplifter methodology or technique (tools of the trade, so to speak) to achieve even a modicum of success with their stealing. Stage 3 requires that the person actually commit a crime; therefore, this shoplifting stage necessitates the deployment of some practical methods to be effective at evading detection.

Even the rich shoplifters I have seen have developed some type of an idiosyncratic system to facilitate their thefts that in turn, increased their probability for success and decreased the chance of their detection and arrest. The development of specific theft methods or techniques does not support the position that shoplifters are hardened criminals in the sense that bank robbers are. Loss-prevention reports chronicling shoplifters' in-store activities have, over the years, helped create a type of potential shoplifter identification checklist (or profile) that loss-prevention personnel should use to identify a would-be shoplifter.

Examples are the false-bottom box, loose-fitting clothing, or seasonably inappropriate clothing (a baggy winter coat worn in the summer, carrying an umbrella during fair weather conditions), bringing with them the store's own shopping bags with the logo clearly visible, price tag switching, or attempting to exchange stolen merchandise for cash or credit. Placing store merchandise in a baby carriage or stroller is an often-used method to literally roll out of the store with the items stolen covered with blankets, toys, and even the cute baby. "Crotch-walking" has been identified as a common technique used by women wearing full skirts who simply wedge the stolen items between their thighs and stroll out the door. Even a newspaper can provide cover for shoplifted items.

These red flags are used on a regular basis to increase the surveillance of an identified shopper as a potential shoplifting candidate. In addition to these more obvious physical cues, loss-prevention personnel have also been taught to evaluate subtle behavior characteristics such as nervousness, furtiveness, swiveling, or eyes continuously focusing and refocusing throughout a particular store's department—similar in some ways to the closed-circuit surveillance camera they quite probably are attempting to elude.

To a certain degree, all shoplifters, including the many celebrities who come to our attention, must demonstrate at least elementary proficiency, including a set of skills and resources, in order to be successful at stealing or they will be quickly detected, caught, and arrested. Shoplifting always becomes a strategic endeavor, a kind of cat-and-mouse game, for those who have progressed through Stage 2, neutralization, and are now committed to the critical Stage 3, action/theft. Even though a person may have morally compromised his or her resistance to stealing, a crime has not been committed until the potential shoplifter acts—that is, walks out the door without paying for merchandise.

According to Carroll and Weaver (1986), who have conducted extensive shoplifting studies, some offenders will match themselves to a potential target in terms of the resources required for a successful crime. They posit in one study (using admitted expert shoplifters) that experienced shoplifters were much more efficient as well as strategic in their shoplifting methods, soliciting appropriate items by size—larger items appeared to be less attractive because of concealment factors—as well as working out pragmatic solutions to overcome obstacles such as store security officers and surveillance devices.

Most of shoplifters that I have seen have been very successful at the completion of their thefts, mostly going undetected for a number of years. These shoplifters report an average of 50 shoplifting episodes prior to their first arrest. In these terms, they have been successful at least to the extent that they have avoided being arrested for a number of years.

In some situations, a store's security staff's job is made easy by overt or clumsy shoplifter error. Consider the news reports of Winona Ryder's theft spree, vividly filmed on closed circuit TV at Saks Fifth Avenue in Beverly Hills. I reviewed the videotape footage, and there is clear evidence that during her shopping-turned-shoplifting visit to the store, she placed $6,000 worth of clothing underneath garment bags or placed items under her own clothing. Subsequently, she exited the store without paying for them, as if, in the end, she unconsciously wanted to be apprehended—and maybe she did. The media has labeled this type of shoplifting as a "crime of fashion." It is not clear whether Ryder perhaps unconsciously desired to get caught, but her poorly improvised theft technique was indeed inadequate. It is also painfully clear from my analysis that her theft was probably related directly to some unknown psychological factors or other issues quite possibly beyond her control at the time she was arrested. Later Ms. Ryder acknowledged that, at the time she was arrested at Saks Fifth Avenue, she had been overprescribed "pain medication" that resulted in her being confused, disoriented, and quite probably in a fog state, which was previously noted as characteristic of Stage 1, anticipation/readiness, shoplifting.

However, bad theft techniques have not been the problem with most of the shoplifters I have seen for psychological assessment and treatment. Their specific shoplifting techniques are interpreted as an integral component of a psychological ritual used repeatedly by people when they decide to steal and be successful at it. It then becomes an essential element of Stage 3, the action/theft. For example, Mrs. Daio (Chapter 6, Case 1) developed a technique to circumvent the electronic sensors when they were even present at major department stores, including the same Beverly Hills Saks Fifth Avenue where Winona Ryder was arrested.

In her long-term quest to steal expensive designer handbags (estimated at a total value between $400,000 and $500,000) Ms. Daio devised the unique method of holding a purse in her hand, then elevating the stolen merchandise above the twin-pole radio frequency system (RFS) sensors (when used at all), placed at the height of five feet, to avoid detection as she casually walked out of many of the stores. She also had evaded sensor detection by simply passing the stolen purses outside of the RFS between the store entrance wall and the five-foot poles. Though not very ingenious, for her purposes, it was pragmatic enough. Mrs. Daio told me that she had successfully used this simple yet effective methodology more times than she cared to remember until she was finally caught on December 18, 2009, and promptly arrested for theft. She also reported that many stores she stole from had no security detection devices at all.

Mrs. Nelson's (Chapter 6, Case 4) shoplifting arrest involved the use of a utility tool to systematically remove antitheft sensors from items she selected, leaving them behind in dressing rooms. Mrs. Nelson reported she was always in possession of this handy tool just in case she "felt the need, urge or impulse to steal something." Already depressed when she shoplifted, afterward during the postexcitation/depression phase, she would extract her own blood because she felt guilty for her theft act and wanted to die. She especially did not want her mother to know she was a thief and castigate her further as being "a bad girl and a failure in life."

These ritualistic theft strategies and shoplifting techniques may appear on the surface to be perfectly rational and even thoughtfully premeditated. A more in-depth analysis, however, reveals that often the rituals associated with shoplifting are directly impacted and influenced by unexplained psychosocial variables shoplifters have been unaware of for years. These variables become wrapped into their motivation to steal. It is difficult to argue that because shoplifters have developed specialized theft strategies as illustrated in the cases presented here, the seemingly illogical choice to commit these crimes in fact was de facto based on rationally supported criminal choices. This was explained as occurring during Stage 2, the neutralization—moral decision versus moral erosion stage.

In many ways, the shoplifter's reduced rational judgment is similar to the psychological doctrine of diminished capacity, widely used in California courts for years. The California state legislature repealed the diminished capacity doctrine, which was applicable when a defendant had a psychiatric disorder, mental disease, or other condition that directly affected his or her state of mind as it related to the commission of a crime. All crimes require that the offender knowingly and purposefully, and with intent, perform some criminal act. If there is a diagnosable psychological condition, and if such condition interferes with knowing and execution of purposeful behavior, then psychological evidence is presented at trial for consideration in the determination of guilty or not-guilty verdicts. The shoplifters presented here are people whose ability to rationally appreciate their actions or form specific criminal intent has been drastically compromised.

Stage 4: Postexcitation/Depression—
Two Sides of the Same Coin

Stage 4 represents the final step in the shoplifting progression and is distinguished by both excitation and then depression. The single commonality shared by both the postexcitation and depression phases in Stage 4 is that they occur in a sequence after the stealing phase has been completed. Stage 4 is comprised of two subphases:

1. The postexcitation or exhilaration phase is characterized by highly charged anxiety features and manic psychological symptoms. It is also typified by uncontrolled or runaway mood-elevating thoughts that momentarily increase the shoplifter's sense of perceived well being which perhaps can reduce depression.

2. The depression phase characterized by innumerable depressive ideations, including, at times, suicidal thoughts and actions (see Mrs. Nelson, case 4, Chapter 6).

The onset of the postexcitation/depression phase typically begins when the shoplifter first begins to bombard him- or herself with self-denigration statements similar to what Amen (1998) has termed "automatic negative thoughts", discussed later in this chapter.

The Postexcitation Phase

Typically, the postexcitation/depression phases surface during the last segment of the action/theft Stage 3. During the postexcitation segment of Stage 4, increased feelings of exhilaration and euphoria are abundantly manifested. As a result of their thefts, shoplifters achieve a short-term positive payoff or reinforcement in the form of temporarily feeling good or better about themselves. However, this postexcitation state of mind, including feelings of manic euphoria and physical and mental excitement, continues, however, for only a short period of time after the theft incident and then leads to the depression phase. The intense feelings generated during Stage 4's postexcitation phase have been described as similar to a runner's high. As one writer who could have been describing this phase has stated, "The intense excitement from shoplifting produces a chemical reaction that is described as an incredible high feeling" (Hipp, 2010, p. 4). Mrs. Daio described the intensity of her postexcitation phase in the extreme as simulating an orgasm. A complete description of this case is presented in Chapter 6, Case 1, including an analysis of the sexual component associated with her shoplifting syndrome, which is indigenous to the Stage 4, postexcitation phase.

Mrs. Daio's repressed sexual component can be explained using a pure psychoanalytical interpretation of shoplifting and sexual arousal posited by Freudian-oriented researchers. For example, one of Sigmund Freud's converts and staunch, lifelong defender of psychoanalysis, Otto Fenichel, regarded by Freud as a brilliant psychoanalyst, also connected a sexual component to acts of female theft: "A woman of forty, who constantly reverted to thievery, reported that she was sexually excited whenever she stole, and that she even experienced orgasm at the moment she accomplished her theft…while masturbating, she would imagine that she was stealing" (Fenichel, 1945, p. 371).

Shteir (2011), the author of a recent and popular book chronicling the history of shoplifting, has discussed a shoplifting case including an identified sexual component presented by Austrian psychoanalyst Stekel. Stekel, a second generation, Freudian-style psychoanalyst, was an early proponent of the notion that shoplifting was associated with a sexual component including a sexual drive reduction theory:

> As early as 1906, Stekel was reading French case studies on department store kleptomania for a paper he was working on about the subject. In one case, a former seamstress became sexually aroused by stealing silk blouses and was unable to remember what she does with the silk at home. Another silkaholic who was also an ether addict described the 'amazing and voluptuous spasm' shoplifting the fabric gave her and ended this confession with a "shiver" (Shteir, 2011, p. 44).

Stekel further proposed that, "… kleptomania, whether it sub-stitutes for a primal sexual urge or expresses an infantile desire for revenge, is all about the repressed id. 'The root' of kleptomania is 'ungratified sexual instinct'" (Shteir, 2011, p. 44).

Once a loyal Freudian follower and a member of the prestigious inner European circle, Freud abruptly announced in November 1911 that "… Stekel is going his own way…there had been an attempt to stifle the liberty of the mind. He is an unbearable human being" (Gay, 1988, p. 232). Freud had previously praised Stekel for his steadfast defense of psychoanalytical practices, then vehemently disagreed with Stekel's newly adopted therapy practices, including abandoning the traditional therapeutic couch technique in favor of directly facing his patients across a desk while providing them with the unheard of: practical counsel and suggestions for amelioration of their psycho-logical conflicts, be they sexual or of another nature.

Shteir, an associate professor of dramaturgy, writes, "By the 1970s, the rise of pharmacology and the sexual revolution made attributing kleptomania to repression obsolete. Shedding its sexual reputation, shoplifting was reborn as a political action" (Shteir, 2011, p. 45).

Shteir apparently discounts out of hand the important possibility that for both men and women, the modern act of shoplifting contin-ues in most cases to manifest hidden or unconscious components, including those highly indicative of sexual ennui as well as overcom-pensatory hidden sexuality features that may be difficult for some nonclinicians to comprehend. Yet for many patients, including Mrs. Daio, these troubling sexual elements tied to theft are very real and remain confusing.

During my professional career as a forensic psychologist, hav-ing diagnosed and treated more than 100 shoplifters, many of them women, I have found that almost none of them had any conscious comprehension as to why they stole; in some cases, they did not even have any reliable recollection of their stealing episodes. At best they had only a vague idea that they had done something wrong. Because they did not know the psychological mainsprings of their stealing transgressions, and assuming they were not engaging in lying, faking, impression management or conscious malingering, then there is the obvious psychological possibility that unconscious drivers, including occasional sexual undercurrents, may have played an important role as an etiological factor in their stealing.

The pseudo-radical social justice focus pushed in the 1970s that I was exposed to as a graduate student at the University of California–Berkeley did present observable evidence of acting out; criminal street theft, perhaps masked as shoplifting, and an almost complete and wanton disregard for the property rights of the so-called capitalists. I fail to see how this anachronistic view made popular by 1960s and 1970s radical sociologists can accurately help explain why politically nonradicalized, upper-middle-class class and wealthy women in today's society steal.

This is not to conjecture that there are not people in society whose stealing is representative of some type of a political protest carrying with it a kind of self-serving moral justification and a social justice bent. I just haven't personally encountered any of them in my practice. Tomorrow, however, could bring another story.

Shoplifting Is Erotic

Shoplifting can also be viewed as an erotically charged form of deviant behavior bringing with it a seductive sexual theme or, as Katz (1988) a professor at UCLA, has stated from his in-depth interviews taken from 122 self-reports from his criminology students: "an element of seduction turning into irrational compulsion." In many of the accounts of shoplifting,

> there is an experience of seduction turning into irrational compulsion, a rush of excitement as contact is made with the item and another as it is guided across personal boundaries and inserted into a private place, then a physical process of movement in which the body is guided to a point of climax (p. 71).

One of Katz's students put it this way:

Every time I would drop something into my bag, my heart would be pounding, and I could feel this tremendous excitement, a sort of rush go through me. The experience was almost orgasmic for me. There was a build-up of tension as I contemplated the danger of a forbidden act, then a rush of excitement at the moment of committing the crime, and finally a delicious sense of release (p. 71).

Katz also quotes a necklace thief: "It's really funny being 23 years old now and in writing this, I can't stop feeling how thrilling it was, certainly a feeling much like the anticipation of sex" (p. 71).

The theft episode as described by Katz carries with it all the identified elements of a sexual act, including a heightened rush or flush of excitement at the moment of stealing, followed almost immediately by a symbolic climax associated with avoiding detection. This erotic-like game is symbolically much the same as the sexual mating ritual exhibited during the male-female courting process. Shoplifter participant accounts of their attraction to a particular object, according to one of Katz's students, "often suggest the image of lovers catching the other's eyes across a crowded room and entering into an illicit conspiracy…I'm not sure why I must have it, but I must" (Katz, 1988, p. 55).

Mrs. Daio told me that she had her most revered purses, considering them her favorites, stopping just short of naming them. The bottom line for her is that she spent an inordinate amount of time in the presence of these objects, which for her served as a source of comfort, stimulation, and ersatz sexual pleasure as well as ascribing humanlike characteristics to her beloved new friends.

Ascribing human characteristics to stolen items, one transcendent component of shoplifting, is typified when examining Mrs. Daio's motivational theft patterning. This underinvestigated area, not well understood by previous researchers, has been commented on by Katz (1988), who argues that some shoplifters engage in a variant of psychological anthropomorphizing. Nauert (2010) provides an acceptable definition of the term: "Giving human characteristics to animals, inanimate objects or natural phenomena" (p.1). Although Nauert does not specifically focus on shoplifters' specific emotional attachment to nonhuman objects, there is ample evidence that certain shoplifters do anthropomorphize, and Mrs. Daio is a representative example.

When a person shoplifting engages in anthropomorphizing, he or she begins to ascribe humanlike traits to nonhuman objects—in this case, the items that have been stolen. We all know people who sometimes use terms of endearment when referring to their pets or even as they make a reference to a special collector car: "Isn't *she* a beauty?" This tendency to anthropomorphize for nonshoplifters and shoplifters alike tends to increase proportionately as an individual becomes increasingly devoid of or lacking in human connectivity. Today's social networking craze provides us with innumerable operational examples of this commitment to "hook up" electronically, thus magnifying social alienation. For instance, people may perceive a sense of belonging to the extent they are loosely and vicariously tied to others via the Internet, to hundreds if not thousands of sometimes strangers, but when there are demands made on them for real face-to-face interaction, they are at a loss.

A recent social media study of 205 adults found that the motivational attraction to electronic communication was more powerful than an addiction to either cigarettes or alcohol (Goessl, 2012 p.1). The author relates that, according to the study, the "desires for media may be comparatively harder to resist because of their high availability and also because it feels like it does not 'cost much' to engage in these activities, even though one wants to resist." The real danger is not only the lost opportunity—time cost in lieu of spending time with family and friends—but also that the social media addict is slavishly drawn into synthetically manufactured relationships. There is no question that people might profit more from the acquisition and practices necessary to maintain productive human relationships. I have seen many shoplifters who for unknown psychological reasons have drifted away from mutually rewarding human interactions in favor of transcendent affinities for objects. Especially for the trophy-collector shoplifter like Mrs. Daio, possession of the stolen object represents what Katz (1988) calls "sneaky thrills" yielded from the act of theft itself.

Katz further comments on this attachment to inanimate objects for shoplifters: "To specify further how the would-be shoplifters endow the inanimate with a real power to move her, we might consider why the initial stage of magical provocation is part of the project of sneaky thrills"(Katz, 1988, p. 57). The tendency to anthropomorphize is directly connected to an individual's perceptions of being cut off, alien, and then ultimately disconnected from other people, disallowing him- or herself the chance to develop adequate social skills.

Thus, shoplifting represents a psychological conundrum for many shoplifters and not, per se, some type of rebellious political act, because, in today's terms, some greedy Wall Street executives at Goldman Sachs or American International Group, AIG, who themselves may have been stealing, are paid far too much and in the end have avoided jail time they probably deserve.

In addition to this overt sexual component as described by Fenichel, Stekel, and Katz, the present study, patients' direct anecdotal accounts suggest that the postexcitation phase represents the ultimate mental stimulation for them, with or without the sexual interpretation or the doubtful political bent.

Quite paradoxically, there are some shoplifting researchers whose findings lend support to the idea that the postexcitation phase of Stage 4 may serve as a type of substitute antidepressant, inoculating the shoplifter from immediate depressive thoughts, relieving at least for a moment additional negative, depressive considerations. In this view, shoplifting may represent, via the shoplifting-induced high, a replacement for psychiatric medication to combat depression or other feelings of negative self-worth and personal denigration. This odd equation—the unanticipated finding that the more frequent the shoplifting the less frequent, the depressive symptoms—has been looked at by Fishbain (as cited in Yagoda, 1994) who observed regarding his shoplifting patient, Kate, that "it appears that the act of stealing has antidepressant properties. The postulation is that perhaps these people are doing it to self-treat their depression" (as quoted in Yagoda, 1994, p. 2). What appears to confirm Fishbain's hypothesis is the fact that when he treated Kate with antidepressant drugs, she stopped stealing. When the medication was halted, she started again.

The postexcitation shoplifter phase of Stage 4 is additionally typified by these varied reported psychological symptoms: distractibility, grandiosity, a drug-like rush, mental agitation, mania, exaggerated startle response, hyperarousal, dizziness, irritability, shortness of breath, uncontrollable thoughts, unwarranted optimism and feelings of invincibility. In truth, it is quite the opposite; shoplifters in this phase are beginning to experience many unidentifiable intrusive negative psychological symptoms disguised instead as euphoric in nature. This process is called symptom substitution, and most of these psychological symptoms are underscored by personal feelings of clinical depression and lack of control of their lives.

Both of these mental states have been confirmed from the psychological test results in the present study. These and other manic-type symptoms have frequently been reported by shoplifters during and immediately after the action/theft of Stage 3, yet they are clearly identified again in Stage 4, postexcitation. Some shoplifting researchers have commented on the intense psychological stimulation experienced during and shortly after completion of the shoplifting act. Another researcher, McElroy (1994), has published an intensive study of 20 shoplifters. It was noted that some of the subjects reported feelings such as a "rush," a "thrill," a "high," feeling "euphoric," or feeling "manic" (as quoted in Yagoda, 1994).

A false feeling of omnipotence that suddenly pervades the shoplifter's emotional state—"I can do anything I want, and I guess that includes shoplifting"—is often experienced during this phase. This omnipotent mental component begins during late Stage 3, the action/theft stage, in the selfishness phase. This omnipotence is often accompanied with a sense of personal grandiosity similar to a cocaine rush reported by drug addicts I have treated, as the shoplifters feel they have limitless boundaries, new vistas to reach, and are able to get away with anything they desire, including the illegal act of stealing. Mrs. Daio stated, "When I got all of these things home, I felt the sky was the limit, and then I had a big letdown and felt terrible, but for a little while, I felt pretty good."

Another description of the shoplifter's post-theft high is described in these terms: "When trolling along aisles of especially alluring merchandise, active sufferers report feeling ripples of tension and often an exhilarating release, when they duck out of the store with the goods" (Carey, 2001, p. 1).

The Depression Phase

The second definitive phase of Stage 4 is depression and is characterized as having a noticeable, attendant mental let down period, which is not psychologically rewarding to the shoplifter when compared to the reinforcement provided during the postexcitation phase. The shoplifter's initial feelings of the rush and exhilaration experienced during the postexcitation phase have now dissipated and are almost immediately replaced by intense and disturbing feelings of despondence, despair, and personal guilt. Low self-esteem, depression, self-loathing, and external locus-of-control factors are revisited.

As Mrs. Daio put it, "I felt on top of the world for a little while after shoplifting, then I felt terrible about what I had done. I realize that I shouldn't do this, but at the time, I just felt I had no other good choices available to me!" This statement reflects the ultimate external locus-of-control position: externality or the intrinsic belief that people have no control over their lives. And, for the most part, shoplifters who feel this are correct. Again, the results of this research study confirm that shoplifters have very limited control over their lives especially at the exact moment they choose to steal. Other common depression-phase symptoms include suicidal ideations (Mrs. Nelson, Chapter 6, Case 4), shame, sadness, feelings of failure, and a sense of emptiness, similar to Winona Ryder's personal account of how she perceived her life as lonely and distant immediately prior to shoplifting. As, Mrs. Nelson recalls, she certainly felt a feeling of "crisis of willpower": "I really didn't want to do this because I know it's wrong, but I just couldn't stop myself and now I'm ruining my life as well as the lives of my family."

CBS News' *The Early Show (2004)* reported on just such an out of control and depressed shoplifting patient during an interview with Sandra, a Michigan shoplifter and grandmother:

Sandra, now 59, has been shoplifting for more than 40 years. Sandra first shoplifted when she was just barely a teen. It was her way to deal with a painful childhood. She married Tom, a happy time, yet Sandra stole on her honeymoon. "I had a wonderful husband who loved me no matter what. How could I do this to him?

This depression phase for the shoplifter is often accompanied by a stream of self-blaming and critical appraisals: "Will I ever be able to control myself again?" Sandra's case is fairly typical of the depression phase, during which she makes a number of negative, self-denigrating, references.

The depression phase can produce equally intense negative feelings of psychological and physical withdrawal. Increased heart rate, perspiration, headaches, sensations of being smothered, choking, dizziness, paresthesias, numbness and tingling sensations, chills or hot flashes, and a fear of losing total control have been reported by the four patients in the cases described in Chapter 6. These marked physical symptoms are similar to the symptoms reported by drug users experiencing detoxification and acute chemical withdrawal. Many shoplifters have stated that during the depression phase, they vomit, experience an increase in their temperature and blood pressure, and need to relieve themselves in the bathroom.

During the depression phase of Stage 4, many shoplifters report having bombarded themselves with self-deprecating statements that they are worthless as people and maybe deserve to be punished, or, worse, die, as was the case with Mrs. Nelson. These statements are in keeping with what Amen (1998, p. 97) has labeled *automatic negative thoughts* (ANTs). It is apparent to me that these ANTs share common psychological properties with the depression phase of Stage 4, including the negative self-statements generated by shoplifters. Examples of these negative self-directed statements that occur during this phase include:

- "I'm unworthy."
- "I'm a bad person."
- "I can't be trusted."
- "No one likes me."
- "I'm reckless."
- "No one will trust me again."

Subtly, this constant menu of negative self-messages serves to identify, label, and then stamp the shoplifter, in his or her own view, as a type of a deviant person, if not a societal outcast. The ultimate and most devastating label, of course, is applied when the shoplifter is finally arrested and his or her case is then adjudicated publicly in the criminal justice system, often coming to the attention of the hungry and unforgiving media. This deviant labeling occurs mostly during the depression phase of Stage 4.

Commenting on the general theory of deviant labeling perspective, Becker(1963) has aptly stated:

One of the most crucial steps in the process of building a stable pattern of deviant behavior is likely to be the experience of being caught and publicly labeled as a deviant…he may brand himself as a deviant because of what he has done and punish himself in one way or another for his behavior (p.31).

The most important consequence for the shoplifter after arrest is the drastic self-image alteration involving a clear downgrading of his or her public, peer, and societal identity. The process of being caught committing an improper, embarrassing, and illegal act ascribes a new and negative status to the shoplifter. This after-arrest status feeds the production of new negative self-messages similar to the ANTs. An example of this labeling process—now attracting the attention of the public—has been commented on at length by Shulman as he details his life-altering personal labeling after his first shoplifting arrest at age 21:

> I had stolen some cassettes from the store before and nothing happened. But this time the electronic gate went "beep, beep, beep." I knew I'd been caught. I stood there, frozen. A woman came running toward me. I tried to get rid of the cassette, but it fell to the floor, and she saw it. She pulled me to the back of the store and went to a nearby room to call the police ... I was terrified and ashamed (2004, p.13).

The bottom line here for Shulman, as well as for thousands of other first-time arrestees, is that their shoplifting acts heretofore focused as a private matter have now been made public, and the label may forever be stamped on them: "He's a shoplifter! He can't be trusted by anyone, anymore!" The direct application of this label contributes to the shoplifter's self-fulfilling prophesy :"I've done bad things; therefore, I must be a bad person, and now everyone knows about it. So, why should I stop?" The ultimate psychological impact of this public labeling dilemma is the shoplifter's insidious surrender of his or her positive self-identity as well as the reconstitution of a negative self-image as a bad person not deserving trust or respect from others.

The Scarlet Letter Syndrome

Whether it is shoplifting or another form of social deviance, such as alcoholism, delinquency, drug use, gambling, or mental illness, once the pejorative label has been applied by significant others such as the police, the court, society at large, or the media, the label tends to become internalized by the actor and then becomes part of his or her future identity and negatively tainting one's self-concept. This shift in identity has been well documented by researchers. Hamlin (2011), for example, comments on this labeling as applied to shoplifter social deviance:

> The persons who are considered deviant are actually victims "more sinned against than sinning." Persons are not inherently deviant

nor is deviance inherent in any particular behavior as noted by Erikson in his "notes on deviance" and again the introduction to *Wayward Puritans*, stressing the point that the social audience confers the label deviance on behavior. This social audience could be the community in general or particular agents of social control, e.g. the police (or teachers). In other words, behavior is not inherently deviant or normal but is defined and labeled that way by people in charge of defining and labeling (p. 2).

Hamlin continues on to reflect on the work of Erikson, a key deviance-labeling theorist, who has applied this labeling perspective to shoplifting:

> For example, in order for someone to be labeled a shoplifter, there must be a norm against shoplifting. If private property did not exist, shoplifting would not exist and neither could the deviant label of shoplifter. Just because a norm does exist does not mean everybody labeled shoplifter has actually violated the norm. There is a basic difference between rule breakers/rule breaking behavior and deviants/deviant behavior (p. 2).

Shulman's reported negative labeling experience is in concert with both Hamlin's (2011) and Erikson's (1966) viewpoints, unraveling of the road to becoming a deviant, for example, a shoplifter. Erikson (1966, pp. 11, 15, 16) described this identity shift from good to bad as necessitating a type of formal and very public ceremony characterized by three social psychological phases:

1. A formal confrontation between the deviant suspect (in this case the shoplifter) and community officials—the loss-prevention staff, police, sheriff, or news media.

2. A judgment including a ceremony about the suspect is formalized, then publicly announced, and finds its way into the news media—for example, "Ms. Winona Ryder, a famous movie star, arrested for shoplifting!" Whether, in fact, she was guilty as charged, the fact that she was publicly arrested, then stigmatized, becomes symbolically her Scarlet Letter Syndrome.

In fact, her public branding has been perpetuated by many not well intentioned journalists, whom, it seems have made careers telling the fate of this woman who admittedly did make a mistake but does not need to be constantly dragged through the dirt for the rest of her life. The question these so-called reporters might ask themselves is whether this type of edgy reportage betters the plight of the shoplifter or, for that matter, society? My answer is a definite no.

Erikson's work on the stigmatizing of witches in Puritan New England writes at length on the public labeling of deviants:

> The deviant is a person whose activities have moved outside the margins of the group, and when the community calls him to account for that vagrancy, it is making a statement about the nature and placement of its boundaries. It is declaring how much variability and diversity can be tolerated within the group before it begins to lose its destructive shape, its unique identity (1966, p.11).

Regrettably, as a society, it appears we have not moved very far beyond the public seventeenth-century labeling ritual, because we continue to especially stigmatize present-day public figures who may have strayed only for a brief moment from one of society's norms. Ryder's mistreatment is a good example of bad media behavior. The act of present-day stigmatizing of deviants is reminiscent of the Puritan practice of confining the accused, yet not convicted in stocks in the village square for all to see and publicly castigated as deviants and societal outsiders. More than 10 years ago, Ryder was publicly faulted, if not symbolically pilloried, mostly by the unfavorable coverage in the news media portraying her as a kind of societal outcast, with no proof to the contrary but nevertheless leaving her public and film reputation in tatters.

3. Social-psychological stigmatizing, including assignment to a public deviant role. Winona Ryder is arrested; therefore, as the

tautology goes, she must be guilty because lots of shoplifters are celebrities. Almost without exception, the labeling of the deviant shoplifter, like Ryder, must be done in some type of public venue:

> Whether these confrontations take the form of criminal trials, excommunication hearings, courts-martial, or even psychiatric case conferences, they act as boundary-maintaining devices in the sense that they demonstrate to whatever audience is concerned where the line is drawn between behavior that belongs in the special universe of the group and behavior that does not (Erikson, 1966, p. 11).

Unfortunately, one way shoplifters often choose to deal with this personal shift of identity is not to cognitively resist it but in some cases capitulate to it; accepting their new deviant role as having meaning in their own lives, and in fact acceptance of their new status, may serve to influence and redirect their future theft behavior.

A second example of this public labeling or social psychological stigmatizing process can be seen in the case of Mrs. Konvitz (Chapter 6, Case 2), who was charged with shoplifting from an upscale deli, Cyd's, and if convicted could have been sentenced up to a year in local jail. Her initial reaction to her impending legal problems during our first diagnostic session seemed to me to be a little off target. She stated, "Now everyone at Cyd's thinks I'm a thief, so it's going to be real hard for me not being able to go back there and shop for specialty food items. For God's sake, I know everybody in that store, and they all know me. I'll just have to go and shop somewhere else, I guess!"

The more I analyzed her obtuse, self-centered, and perhaps narcissistic comments, especially the fact that she was less focused on her considerable legal issues, than the real possibility of going to jail, the more I interpreted her statement in terms of the public label that had been placed on her, which confirmed her status as a social deviant in her community, as typified by the Stage 4 depression phase, the Scarlet Letter Syndrome.

Equally important, her story brought to light the reality that when the shoplifter begins to internalize the meaning of his or her newly applied public label or stigma during Stage 4 depression as a deviant, myriad different and more serious psychological symptoms have an increased probability of emerging. For instance, personal alienation and social isolation are key symptoms verified by the four shoplifters I treated and whose cases are presented in Chapter 6. Sometimes shoplifters like Mrs. Konvitz or Ms. Ryder see themselves as misunderstood, weak victims as opposed to wanton perpetrators of a crime.

From time to time, shoplifters have reported dissociated mental states in which in order to protect themselves from further psychological damage and end the pain connected to being pilloried they unconsciously strive to mentally escape via withdrawal or deploy other effective defense mechanisms such as denial, rationalization, or projection. Self-mutilation, cutting, substance/alcohol abuse, hoarding and anorexia have been reported by some shoplifters after the public labeling process became internalized. After the theft stigma has been realized and then accepted, an additional self-fulfilling prophecy emerges: "Call me the name, and I'll play the game." In other words, "If you want me to steal, that's exactly what I'll do." The label itself serves as a secondary gateway promoting more criminal acting out—that is, an escalation of their shoplifting into more serious types of criminal acts such as grand theft offenses, an easy step beyond simple shoplifting.

After their labeling, shoplifters at this point may have given up entirely on the reversal of the newly applied stigma or label and then begin to act in a manner or behavioral direction consistent with their assigned deviant status—that is, they act out in conformity with the applied and subsequently self-accepted label. As Mrs. Nelson (Chapter 6, Case 4) has stated, "So I had it in the back of my mind—Why do I do this? I didn't even know why I was doing this stealing. It was like I was trying to wreck my entire life and end up in jail. It was like what's the big deal? I did it again. What more did I have to lose? Nobody cares about me anyway!"

During this depression phase, it is not uncommon for shoplifters to report feeling a sense of adaptation to their new public shoplifting status. There is also evidence of their personal internalized accommodation: "They said it about me, so it must be true, and that's how I'll act." Acceptance of the deviant label carries with it a permanent type of negative status; people will never look at the person again in the same way, as honest, trustworthy, and responsible. This is certainly true of celebrities like Ms. Ryder who, even when only accused but not yet convicted in court for shoplifting, was labeled as a deviant and symbolically tried for her mistake in the media.

Once negatively labeled as a shoplifter, the individual then becomes what Gusfield has described as a *cynical deviant* who,

> hopes to get away with it, and he has cynical attitudes toward the norms of society, or at least toward those which he has violated (although he wants protection lest these same norms be violated when he or someone closely associated with him is chosen as victim). The cynical deviant knows that the norms are right, that he has violated them, and that when he is apprehended, his punishment is deserved, much as he would like to escape it (as quoted in Sagarin, 1975, p. 320).

Once the unique self-accepted label has been successfully applied during this phase, the shoplifter, according to Gusfield, often becomes hardened and cynical and acts in a manner consistent with the label, contributing to more serious pathological stealing that follows.

Another viewpoint concerning this cynical identity labeling has been proffered by Cloward (1968). This reidentity or branding is characterized as similar to the prisoner accommodation syndrome: "Having engaged in an act of conspicuous defiance, he [the offender, in this case the shoplifter] is redefined by both peers and officials" (Cloward, 1968, p. 99). At that point, the shoplifter may come to accept "a conception of himself as a criminal" using an elaborate set of supporting justifications for their deviance. The offender "internalizes the social rejection implicit with the new status and suffers the pains of lowered self esteem and self rejection" (Wheeler, 1968, p. 172). Defining down one's self-concept is therefore characteristic of the depression phase.

The psychological evidence presented here demonstrates that most shoplifters almost inadvertently choose to engage in an illegal activity, not so much for money but instead because of later identifiable psychological drivers or factors that in some instances have remained buried in their unconscious for years. This is certainly true of the four shoplifting cases I present later in Chapter 6. These four women could easily have afforded many times over to pay for the merchandise they instead elected to steal. Each of these women entered the shoplifting zone and became trapped in one or more of the four shoplifting stages. At the time of their thefts, of course, they were not cognizant of exactly why they chose to steal or which of the four shoplifting stages most reinforced their illegal behaviors. One or more of these sequential stages had become psychologically more salient in the maintenance of shoplifting deviance.

In Chapter 6, I have tried to specifically isolate which of the four stages played the most significant motivational role contributing to each of these four women's stealing patterns. For example, for Mrs. Nelson (Case 4), because of her suicidal depression, it was Stage 4—the postexcitation phase—that seemed to most reinforce her shoplifting behavior. As expressed in her words, "I felt high, excited, and it was as if I could do anything I wanted, including shoplifting." For Mrs. Daio (Case 1), on the other hand, the importance of Stage 1, anticipation/readiness, cannot be underestimated. During one therapy session she commented, "Just before stealing all those purses, I was confused, and I didn't feel I was worthwhile as a person. Strange feelings got a hold of me. I wanted to or had to do something, and I guess shoplifting was it!" These are key reminiscences tied to Stage 1, anticipation/readiness, that later set her shoplifting behavior into motion during Stage 3, action/theft.

In my personal interview with Shulman (2011,b), he summed up his intense feelings of being out of control when he first entered the shoplifting zone:

Naturally I knew the difference between right and wrong, but I had my own self-interest in mind. I just was not thinking of others. I desperately attempted to get back or replace those things in

134

my life that, interestingly enough, I felt had been stolen from me. This included the pain resulting from being rejected, and because of my father's death, I was placed in the uncomfortable role as a "super hero" for my family. I was depressed and scared and I had no way to vent these feelings. Shoplifting served as a channel to try and feel better about myself.

Shulman's personal description of what drove him into the world of theft is consistent with external loss of control. He perceived that exogenous variables were pushing him into behaviors (thefts) he knew were wrong, but he nevertheless compromised his moral judgment and shoplifted anyway. This moral compromise begins in Stage 2, neutralization, in the shoplifting zone.

Personality Transformation

Shulman's reference to getting things back that "had been stolen from me" fits precisely into the equalizer shoplifting typology proposed in Chapter 3 (Typology 8). The absence of self-trust as expressed by Mrs. Konvitz (Chapter 6, Case 2) forms the key foundation for her reformulation and acceptance of a shoplifter identity. This personality reformalization or self-reconstitution process has been previously studied in the scholarly works of Sarbin and Adler (1971) at the University of California Berkeley. They approach the reconstitution of the self from the theoretical standpoint of self-conversion:

> A set of concepts has proved useful in our attempts to account for the kinds of changes referred to variously as the process of conversion, reconstitution of the self, transvaluation of social identity, and profound conduct reorganization. This set of concepts deals with the source of information from which persons make decisions regarding action (Sarbin and Adler, 1971, p. 603).

This identity switch or conversion to the status of a shoplifter from a nonshoplifter status represents a self-perception shift similar to Erikson's (1960) process of becoming deviant. The shoplifter's self, once reconstituted during both phases in Stage 4, forces him or her to pose a number of critical questions concerning his or her life, such as: "What has happened to me?" "How did I get here?" There is also the existential question: "Who am I?" After being labeled as a shoplifter, many times a person feels relegated into the status of nonperson. He or she feels that part of the self has symbolically died and no longer exists.

Sarbin and Adler also suggest that certain commonalities lead to the reconstitution of the self, which can be applied to shoplifters. Several of these commonalities or themes that contribute to profound changes in conduct are viewed as particularly germane to the psychodynamics of becoming a career shoplifter. The initial common theme most frequently involves the symbolic surrender or death of oneself and the subsequent rebirth, depicted as follows:

> The death-rebirth theme in this context may be viewed, then, as the death or loss or relinquishment of one social identity and the rebirth or formation of another. The point of death, to use a metaphor of the social sciences, is when the individual becomes a "nonperson." The individual is treated by relevant others as not being able to meet minimal cultural expectations; he is perceived as not being able to perform actions to make good the occupancy of the undifferentiated, granted social roles (Sarbin & Adler, 1971, p. 607).

The shoplifters presented in Chapter 6 have made innumerable personal statements to me related to their changes in self-assessment subsequent to their initial choice to steal and especially after they had been arrested and then publicly stigmatized. Again, they felt that after commencing shoplifting, their personalities were split, fractured, broken, cracked, or in some additional aspects no longer whole. To a large extent, they adopted self-descriptions connoting they were less than human, "being a nonperson…is as if he/she were dead" (Sarbin & Adler,1971 p.607). This symbolic death process is characterized by a mounting arousal level and cognitive strain (Sarbin & Adler, 1971). In many ways, this process is the same as Festinger's notion of cognitive dissonance reported as occurring during Stages 1 and 3.

The rise in a person's cognitive strain in large measure contributes to and helps impel the nonshoplifter's choice to steal as marked by thoughts during the first shoplifting stage, anticipation-readiness. Shoplifter statements such as, "I really don't know what came over me," "it's not like me to steal," and "My whole life until now I never broke any laws, even traffic laws" are reflective of the shoplifter's slow yet insidious erosion of the self.

A second common theme in this shoplifter self-reconstitution shift is the emphasis placed on the adaptation of newly acquired ritualistic behaviors. In addition to seeing him- or herself from the viewpoint of "damaged goods," each shoplifter I have treated has engaged in self-defining ritualistic behaviors connected to and comprising an integral part of his or her shoplifting identities. In a certain sense, the person becomes driven into the shoplifting mode becoming progressively more alone and isolated from the outside world.

Sarbin & Adler (1971) comment on this form of ritualization as can be applied to shoplifters:

> In most systems of conduct reorganization we have encountered, the use of ritual has been to allow for the smooth transition from old to new lives. Such acts as staring, closing the eyes, praying, singing, dancing, jumping, regulating the breath, and other methods are used in the various systems to limit the convert's span of attention (p. 612).

These examples of idiosyncratic, ritualistic behaviors deployed by the shoplifters are represented in Chapter 6:

1. Mrs. Daio's (Case 1) placing and fastidious arrangement of hundreds of stolen, expensive purses in a certain order in her secret hiding room. Additionally, Mrs. Daio's ritualistic behavior pattern was marked by periods of posttheft amnesia. As she told me, "I would drive to L.A., find a mall, and shoplift. Sometimes I didn't even know where I was or how I got there or why I got home so late. When I looked at the clock, I couldn't believe how much time I lost track of."

2. Mrs. Chow's (Case 3) theft of children's clothing (she did not have children) beginning with infant items and progressively stealing more appropriate clothing suitable for teenagers as if she was in reality raising and dressing an actual child.

3. Mrs. Konvitz's (Case 2) praying prior to and after her multiple thefts. She did not pray not to get caught but instead as a way to expiate her guilt for having done something she knew was both morally offensive and illegal yet somehow she could not stop, and in the end, her prayers were not answered.

4. No doubt the most bizarre ritual was performed by Shari Nelson (Case 4), who, after stealing from multiple department stores, would begin to extract her own blood using a large-gauge needle (she was a nurse). This ritualistic "suicide on the installment plan" was done because of fears that her mother would label her a "bad girl" if she discovered her daughter was common thief, thereby confirming what her mother had always believed—Shari was a miserable failure in life.

During the depression phase, the shoplifter begins to impose troubling thoughts connected to self-distrust: "If I steal, then I can't be trusted ever again by others." This sense of personal self-loathing marked with self-distrust is then internalized, turned around, and redirected outward. As Mrs. Konvitz put it, "If I can't trust myself [to not steal things], then I can't trust other people's motivations and intentions either. Maybe in the end, other people are no better than me." This internal feeling of distrust and self-loathing can at times approximate a paranoid delusional dimension.

Shoplifters not only distrust themselves during shoplifting but also become suspicious of others, and even when not engaging in shoplifting behavior, their suspicions endure. This ill-founded system of suspicion becomes fixed and then gradually generalizes to every-one the shoplifter interacts with, leading many times to the destruc-tion of the family and their relationships with coworkers and friends. This paranoid facet of the depression phase serves as an additional, significant barrier to the shoplifting recovery process: "If I can't trust anymore, why should I trust a doctor to help me?"

Certain shoplifters have reported deriving more reward or actual reinforcement during one particular stage more than others. Ironically, although the shoplifter does complete the theft episode during Stage 3, action/theft, he or she may become hooked into or fixated on the reinforcements derived from one of the other stages; thus, all stages are seen as inextricably bound together. It is usually the case that even though the total shoplifting experience in the main yields negative outcomes, some shoplifters are more stimulated, though not in a positive way, by one stage than by the other three.

For example, Mrs. Nelson (Case 4), desperately attempting to alleviate her depressive state, felt her depression lifted during her actual stealing process in Stage 3. She told me:

During the shoplifting part in the stores, I felt not only kind of falsely justified in what I was doing but I also felt a lot less depressed and sad about my life. Of course, the depression came right back later on, just like it always does.

For Mrs. Nelson, it appears that she became fixated at the stealing stage, which produced for her a small paradoxical reward: "I felt less depressed about my life!" Her attachment at Stage 3 lent some existential meaning to what she felt as an otherwise empty life, as she also stated, "I somehow felt, even though it was wrong, I was finally doing things for myself. I was tired of taking care of everyone else and getting nowhere in the process."

Hopefully the analysis of these four essential stages of shoplifting comprising the shoplifting zone has cast additional light onto the decision-making process the shoplifter experiences prior to, during, and then after a shoplifting episode. An important part of what the forensic psychologist does is to help shoplifters uncover and interpret for themselves these critical four stages so they are able to move on with their lives in a more positive and noncriminal direction.

Chapter 5 References

ABC. 20/20. Interview Part 1 with Winona Ryder by Dianne Sawyer. [YouTube video]. Retrieved, December 1, 2009, from www.youtube.com/watch?V=ZogBCYILm3A

Amen, D. G. (1998). Change your brain, change your life. New York: Three Rivers Press.

American Psychiatric Association. (2000) Diagnostic and statistical manual of mental disorders (4th edition, text rev.) Washington, DC: Author.

Bazerman,M.H. & Tenhunsel, A.E. (2011). Blind spots. New Jersey: Princeton University Press.

Becker, G. S. (1973). Crime and punishment: An economic approach. Journal of Political Economy,76, 169–217.

Becker, H. S. (1963). Outsiders. New York: Free Press.

Berlin,P. Why do shoplifters steal...and why do so many continue to steal even after getting caught? Reprinted from The National Report on Shoplifting. Jericho, N.Y.: Shoplifters Alternative, pp. 3-4.

Bleiberg, E. (1987). Narcissistic disorders in children: Clinical and developmental characteristics. In J. D. Noshpitz (Ed.), Basic handbook of child psychiatry, volume 5. New York: Basic Books.

Brantigham, P. L. & Brantigham, P.J. (1993). Environmental criminology, Prospect Heights, IL: Waveland Press.

Carey, B. (2001, December 27). Famous and unlikely thieves: The thrill of kleptomania. Los Angeles Times. Retrieved ,June 15, 2012, from http://www.community.seattletimes.nwsource.com

Carroll, J. S. (1978). A psychological approach to deterrence: The evaluation of crime opportunities. Journal of Personality and Social Psychology, 36 (12), 1512-1520.

Carroll, J. & Weaver, F. (1986). "Shoplifters' perceptions of crime opportunities: A process-tracing study." In D.B. Cornish & R. V. Clarke (Eds), The reasoning criminal. New, York: Springer-Verlag.

CBS News. (2004, October 22). Experts increasingly believe shoplifting can become an addiction. The Early Show. Retrieved ,March 05, 2012, from http://www.cbsnews.com/stories/2004/10/21/earlyshow

Cloward, R. A. (1968). Social control in the prison. In L. Hazelrigg (Ed.), Prison within society. Garden City, N.Y.: Doubleday.

Egan, V. (2010). Shoplifting linked to unpleasant personality. Personality and Individual Differences, 48 (8), 878. doi:10.1016/j.paid.2010.02.014

Erikson, K. T. (1960). Notes on the sociology of deviance. Paper presented to the American Sociological Meeting, New York.

Erikson, K. T. (1966). Wayward puritans. New York: John Wiley.

Fenichel, O. (1945). The psychoanalytic theory of neurosis. New York: W. W. Norton.

Festinger, L. (1957). A theory of cognitive dissonance. Stanford, CA: Stanford University Press.

Gay, P. (1988). Freud—A life for our time. New York: Penguin Books.

Goessl, L. (2012, February 4). Study: Social media more addictive than cigarettes or alcohol. Health Magazine. Retrieved ,11-23-2012, from http://www.digitaljournal.com/article/319011

Gowdy, G. (2003). Existential criminal. A Middlesex University Resource. Retrieved, April 15, 2012, from http://www.studymore.org.uk/xgoudy.ht

Hamlin, J. (2011). Labelling theory (societal reaction theory). Department of Sociology and Anthropology, University of Minnesota, Duluth. Retrieved, Februrary 10, 2012, from http://www.dumn.edu/cia/faculty/hamlin/2311/labelingoftheory

Hipp, T. (2010, December 27). Shoplifting and loss prevention: Do we need a fresh look? Ezine @rticles. Retrieved, May 15, 2012 , from http://ezinearticles.com/shoplifting-and-lossprevention:do-we-need-a-fresh-look

Janis, I. L.(1983). Group-think, 2nd edition, revised. New York: Houghton-Mifflin.

Johnson, E.J. & Payne, J.W. (1986). The decision to commit a crime: An information processing analysis. In D. Cornish & R. Clares (Eds.), The reasoning criminal: Rational choice perspectives of offending. New York: Springer-Verlag.

Jones, B. D. (2001). Politics and architecture of choice: Bounded rationality and governance. Chicago: University of Chicago Press.

Kahneman, D. & Tversky, A. (1979). Prospect theory: An analysis of decisions under risk. Econometrica, 47, 263–291.

Katz, J. (1988). Seductions of crime. New York: Basic Books.

Keel, R. D. (2005, July 14). Rational choice and deterrence theory. Retrieved, April 4, 2009, from http://www.umsl.edu.keel.005

Kohlberg, L. (1981). Essays on moral development, volume I: The philosophy of moral development. San Francisco: Harper & Row.

The Legal View (2011). Retrieved December 14, 2012, from http://www.legalview.info/legal-dictionarydiminishedcapacity.html

Lewis, M. (2011, December). The king of human error: Interview with Daniel Kahneman. Vanity Fair, 616, p. 138, 144-146, 153-154.

Nauert, R. (2010). Why do we anthropomorphize? Retrieved May 24, 2010, from http://psychcentral.com/news/2010/03/01/why-do-we-anthropomorphize/11766.html

Paternoster, R. & Bancman, R. (2000). Explaining criminals and crime. Los Angeles: Roxbury Publishing.

Payne, J. W. (1976). Task complexity and contingent processing in decision making: An information search and protocol analysis. Organizational Behavior and Human Performance, 16, 366–387.

Piquero, A. R. & Tibbetts, S. G. (2002). Rational choice and criminal behavior: recent research and future challenges. New York: Routledge.

Prin,J. (2011) Rule breaking/Risk taking. Cited by Shulman T.D.,Cluttered Lives,empty souls. West Conshohocken, PA: Infinity Publishing, 2011a. P.203.

Rotter, J. B. (1966). Generalized expectancies for internal versus external control of reinforcement. Psychological Monographs, 80, pp. 1-27.

Sagarin, E. (1975). Deviants and deviance. New York: Praeger Publishers.

Sarbin, T.R. & Adler, N. (1971). Self-reconstitution processes: A preliminary report. Psychological Review, 57 (4), 600-616.

Shteir, R. (2011). The steal: A cultural history of shoplifting. New York: Penguin Press.

Shulman, T. D. (2004). Something for nothing : Shoplifting addiction and recovery. West Conshohocken, PA: Infinity Publishing.

Shulman, T.D. (2011). Cluttered lives, empty souls. West Conshohocken, PA: Infinity Publishing.

Shulman, T. D. Personal communication. (August 10, 2011b.)

Siegel, L. (1992). Criminology, 4th edition. St. Paul: West Publishing.

Simpson, S., Piquero, N. L. & Paternoster, R. (2002). Rationality and corporate offending decisions. In A. Piquero and S. G. Tibbetts (Eds.), Rational choice and criminal behavior: Recent research and future challenges. New York: Routledge.

Smith, R.S. (2000, September). Why women get the urge to steal. Cosmopolitan. Retrieved June 10, 2012, from http://www.shopliftingprevention.org/whatnaspoffers/nrc

Sports Staff Writer. (2011, July 15). The Zone. San Jose Mercury News.

Wheeler, S. (1968). Socialization in correctional communities. In L. Hazelrigg (Ed.), Prison within society. Garden City, N.Y.: Doubleday.

Willson, R., & Branch, R. (2010). Cognitive behavioural therapy for dummies. Chichester, West Sussex, England: John Wiley.

Yagoda, B. (1994, February). Addicted to stealing—Interviews with Fishbain and McElroy. Self Magazine. Retrieved November 20, 2012 , from http://www.shopliftingprevention.org/whatnaspoffers/nrc/articlestored/addicted-to-stealing

Zasky, J. (2011, April). Ethical blind spots—Why you're not as ethical as you think you are. An Interview with M. H. Bazerman and A. E. Tenbrunsel. Failure Magazine. Retrieved June 18, 2012 ,from http://failuremag.com/index/php/feature/article/ethicalblind-spots

CHAPTER 6

CASE STUDIES: NOT DEPRIVED AND DEFINITELY NOT HAPPY CAMPERS!

So we beat on, boats against the current, borne back ceaselessly into the past.

—F. Scott Fitzgerald, The Great Gatsby, 1925

Not Deprived

During the past 25 years, I have been called upon to diagnose and subsequently provide outpatient treatment (sometimes court-ordered) for at least 100 shoplifters as well as many people charged with other offenses. Most of the shoplifters had been charged with either grand or petty theft. The majority of these shoplifters were fairly well to do, holding high-level, responsible positions, some even had a net worth over $2 million! Generally, those who are well off financially and for ill-defined and complex reasons begin to shoplift do not elicit much sympathy from the public. This is especially the case with celebrity shoplifters such as Winona Ryder as well as ordinary people who become thieves. Uncovering the underlying psychological drivers that negatively impact the shoplifter can provide additional insight as to why economically well-off people decide to steal and repeat their crimes until, at some point, arrest and perhaps jail time occur.

The four cases highlighted in this chapter were referred directly to me by defense attorneys or by superior court judges throughout California for psychological assessment and treatment subsequent to the defendants being arrested for a criminal theft charge. The initial aspect of every psychological evaluation I conducted was to determine whether there were any identifiable psychological variables that could serve as mitigators in evidence. In the shoplifting cases analyzed here, some involve the theft of high-end items, and others involved the theft of seemingly meaningless, low-price merchandise such as doughnuts, pantyhose, toothpaste, lipstick, chewing gum, nail clippers, canned goods, greeting cards, and cough drops. For example, in Case 2, Mrs. Konvitz stole one and a half pounds of corned beef from an upscale deli in a wealthy Santa Barbara suburb. A pervasive feeling of being out of control and sadness are commonalities psychologically linking these four cases.

The four shoplifters profiled here had, on average, $65,000 in savings or checking accounts as well as several credit cards in their possession when they were arrested, some with limits up to $100,000 and near-zero balances. Additionally, they had substantial pocket cash, $200 or more, with them at the time of their arrests. Thus, merely having ready cash available, or access to it via checks, ATM withdrawals, or credit cards does not in itself appear to be a theft deterrent.

These shoplifters were never motivated by material or financial gain. Far from it, they were well off financially with lots of material trappings, including four or more closets literally stuffed with a expensive jewelry and legitimately purchased clothing, in addition to racks of purloined merchandise they never used or wore in public. So why did they do it? Over the years, nonclinical interpretations have been put forth that perhaps the well-heeled in society simply cannot squeeze enough material goods into their lives. Their rapacious materialistic drive cannot be satisfied even as they acquire more and more stuff to further complicate their already cluttered lives. It is as if they were affected by some type of yet-to-be-defined, vague over consumption syndrome.

Notwithstanding the present psychological investigation into why well-off women steal and a few previous studies scattered as far back as 50 years, little solid research has been devoted to the topic. Two important questions arise: Why do rich people steal? And why are most of them women?

Addressing the first question, Shteir stated, "The few studies gauging the connection between shoplifting and income reveal counterintuitive results. In the 1960s, one landmark paper showed that shoplifters who looked affluent were detained less frequently than those who looked scruffy. Joshua Barnfield argues that wealthy shoplifters are statistically underrepresented. 'Every few months Harrods arrests a millionaire shoplifter'" (Shteir 2011, p. 88).

Subsequent to reporting a study claiming that "Americans with incomes of $70,000 shoplift 30% more than those earning up to $20,000 a year," Shteir concludes, "Having some money arouses desire more than having little" (2011, p. 88).

Based on my clinical experience as a forensic psychologist, and the diagnosis and treatment of shoplifters, I have verified that few of them were afflicted with some variant of a "material overcompensation complex." This research study demonstrates that the primary drivers underlying theft patterning behaviors for the shoplifters in my sample were clearly associated with identifiable and measurable psychological factors. The notion of getting more material things just to have more, as a kind of naive shoplifting envy syndrome, was never a conscious factor motivating their stealing. Quite the opposite was true. The mainly upper-middle-class shoplifters I treated remained clueless as to why they engaged in a type of social deviance that, uncontrolled, could lead to jail, prison confinement, or at the very least personal humiliation and reputation destruction. This viewpoint may appear as supporting a masochistic interpretation of shoplifting, yet for most shoplifters, the theft experience is identified as a repeating self-punishment regime from which they cannot escape in order to functionally rebalance their lives as nonshoplifters.

The answer to the second question—why more women than men shoplift—is predicated by the simple fact that more women are arrested throughout California, where my practice is based, for this crime, and subsequently more women than men are referred to me for psychological assessment to help their attorneys prepare an adequate defense. This is not to conclude that I have not seen men who were also arrested for this offense and needed professional help to determine why they shoplifted. In fact, most of the time they, too, were impulsively driven into theft, usually by the same motivations as their female counterparts.

In the course of my forensic practice, I have found these cases to be perplexing, intriguing, and psychologically complex. I quickly discovered that theft for personal gain was not the primary reason these specific offenders shoplifted. Because of a recent plethora of cases of rich people turned thieves, there has been a renewed research interest in the motivational patterns as well as the psychological correlates associated with the shoplifting dynamic. This is especially true regarding those shoplifters who apparently do not need the stolen items or who forget about or discard them after the shoplifting act. In these cases, in addition to being out of control, the shoplifters engaged in theft as a convoluted method of compensating for some unidentified perceived losses in their lives. For instance, the cases of Mrs. Daio, Mrs. Konvitz, and Mrs. Chow presented in this chapter all share this element of shoplifting as a substitute for a perceived, personal loss. Cupchik has described a "loss substitution by shoplifting hypothesis," and states his position on the substitution-loss theory thus:

> Individuals may attempt to replace or substitute for an unfair (as perceived), actual or anticipated loss of a significant person, place, or object by unfairly taking another object, usually without any conscious awareness of the psychological relationship between the perceived (as unfair) loss and the (unfairly obtained) acquisition (Cupchik, 1997, p. 66).

Although the substitution-loss hypothesis has been supported by some researchers, not all investigators agree with the theoretical concept advanced by Cupchik. For example, Grant and Kim (2003) have stated: "Although kleptomania has long been thought to occur secondary to emotional loss, there is no systematic evidence that notable events give rise to uncontrollable stealing" (p. 49). Even though Grant and Kim reject the substitution-loss hypothesis, their selected population may have differed from Cupchik's because their study population was diagnosed with kleptomania. Evidence is presented here that lends support to the theory that certain shoplifters steal as a way to compensate for a perceived loss in their lives. Specifically, Case 2, "The Corned Beef Caper," is clinically representative of the substitution-loss hypothesis. Mrs. Konvitz had no idea what sinister spirits had been chasing her for years, driving her to steal inconsequential store items.

Treatments Used

These four cases have been treated with varied degrees of success. None of the women has recidivated for shoplifting for a one-year follow-up period, using these modalities:

1. Twelve-step AA-type intervention adapted for use with shoplifters

2. Family therapy model

3. Variants of rational emotive behavioral therapy, REBT

4. Self-help and group therapy. In some cases, these treatments were combined with individual therapy, although in most cases individual treatment alone, similar to medication management, is not recommended.

These women shoplifters were provided with outpatient counseling sessions chosen from these four categories of treatment. This book is not directed toward the concept of treatment. Therefore, only a limited description of the therapy progress is presented here. In my forthcoming my books, *Treatment for Rich Women Who Shoplift* and *Klepto-Bismo* (both to be published in January, 2014), a more in-depth analysis of shoplifter treatment is addressed.

Case Diagnoses: The DSM-IV-TR

Each psychiatric diagnosis made in the shoplifting cases presented here relied on a multiaxial system of diagnostic coding as referenced in the American Psychiatric Association (2000) *Diagnostic and Statistical Manual of Mental Disorders* (4th ed., text rev.), *DSM–IV–TR*. The multiaxial classification system described below involved assessment on five separate axes, each of which refers to a different domain of information that can help the clinician plan treatment and predict therapeutic outcome.

The Multiaxial System

The use of the multiaxial system facilitates comprehensive, systematic evaluation of all patients, including shoplifters, with attention to the various mental disorders and general medical conditions, psychosocial and environmental problems, and level of functioning of each referred case. Axes are labeled with standard numeric codes that indicate specific presenting mental conditions. This multiaxial system is presented in Table 6.1.

Table 6.1. Five *DSM–IV–TR* Axes

Axis I	Clinical Disorders
	Other Conditions That May Be a Focus of Clinical Attention
Axis II	Personality Disorders
	Mental Retardation
Axis III	General Medical Conditions
Axis IV	Psychosocial and Environmental Problems
Axis V	Global Assessment of Functioning

The Global Assessment of Functioning (GAF) evaluates the patient's highest overall level of functioning on a scale of 0 (danger of severely hurting self or others) to 100 (superior functioning in all life spheres).

All subsequent references to the *DSM–IV–TR* diagnoses with the four shoplifters refer back to the multiaxial system shown in Table 6.1.

The women's cases presented here have not been diagnosed with kleptomania because they do not match the relatively narrow criteria associated with that diagnosis in the *DSM–IV–TR*. The problems associated with the inadequacy of the specific five diagnostic criteria for kleptomania presently contained in the *DSM–IV–TR* are detailed in Chapter 2.

Psychological Tests Presented
Each of the four women shoplifters were given these psychological instruments:

1. Rotter Locus of Control Scale (LOC)

2. Carlson Psychological Survey (CPS)

3. Beck Depression Inventory II (BDI-II)

The investigation of locus of control was the central variable germane to this study. Each shoplifter described here was presented with the Rotter Locus of Control Scale and each scored in the high or external range (between 16 and 23).

For reference, a quick scale table is presented here as table 6.2.

Table 6.2. Rotter Quick Score Analysis

2–5	6–10	10–16	16–23
High Internal	Mild Internal	Mild External	High External
This means you are:			
In Control	Mostly in Control	Fate Plays a Small Role	Generally Chance, Fate, and Luck Run Your Life

Clinical Cases: Are They Out of Control?

Case 1. Mrs. Daio: A Place for Everything and Everything ITS PLACE

Case Introduction

Mrs. Daio's case presents a psychologically intriguing mixture of shoplifting behavior and a trophy-collection syndrome focused on the stealing of expensive merchandise, as well as a hidden sexual component. Furthermore, her specific case dynamics are representative of the trophy-collector shoplifter as presented in Chapter 3, Typology 6.

Her secret urge to steal and collect high-priced items (usually purses, and hundreds of them) was underscored by her intense feeling of being out of control of her life. Obviously, this was not her first shoplifting episode, but she told me that she was convinced it would be her last. She was driven to maintain a chronic shoplifting ritual that included designating a secret room in her spacious fifteen-room home—a home so large and with so many rooms that neither her husband nor her two children knew about this secret room. A few times over the years when her husband inquired as to what was in the room, Mrs. Daio responded curtly, "This is a storage area, for my personal things." Additionally, she had the only key to it. Over 10 years she stored hundreds of stolen items, mostly expensive designer purses, in the room. In a sense, this room became a symbolic temple or shrine for her, where she often secretly visited when feeling alone and depressed. She then viewed the precious items, and almost magically felt her depression lift.

Then, at least in her opinion, she "was now somebody who was important for a while." Her newly self-ascribed status represented a real, yet short-term, high for her and was consistent with the Stage 4 postexcitation phase of the shoplifting zone described in Chapter 5. She rapidly progressed through all four shoplifting stages, becoming more depressed, suicidal, and out of control. Her out-of-control behavior was evidenced by an elevated external locus-of-control score; she, like the other three cases, is seen as an externalizer shoplifter.

Mrs. Daio was seen for initial psychodiagnostic sessions subsequent to her theft and arrest for shoplifting at Saks Fifth Avenue in Los Angeles on December 18, 2009. This included in-depth psychological testing to determine whether there were any measurable psychological causes for her recent shoplifting behavior. Mrs. Daio's defense attorney referred her to me for a comprehensive shoplifter assessment, having seen via the Internet that I conduct shoplifter evaluations. The attorney wanted the test results along with a written report for submission to superior court.

Mrs. Daio completed the three psychological tests I use to assess shoplifters, and was very cooperative. She understood the nature and importance of the evaluation and that a confidential report would be forwarded to her attorney's office as requested prior to her next court date.

Mrs. Daio was depressed, sad, and at times expressed hopeless-ness during these initial interviews. However, she was extremely con-trite concerning her theft and arrest at Saks Fifth Avenue and stated that she would "never do this again. I don't want to go to jail and ruin my life forever! It's just not worth it. I can't for the life of me figure out why I'm doing this."

Mrs. Daio's Identifying Information

Dates of Testing: December 2009

Client's Name: Mrs. Mailing Daio

Birthplace: Mainland China

Age: 32

Place of Examination: The Rational Counseling Center, 2980 Wilshire Boulevard, Los Angeles, California

Date of Report to Mrs. Daio's Attorney: December 2009

Prior Arrests: None known to this examiner

Criminal Charges: Grand theft, California Penal Code Section 484/488.

Prior Psychiatric Treatment: Treatment with Dr. Singh, psychiatrist, since 2004 for medication management and two prior counsel-ing sessions for her depression.

DSM–IV–TR Diagnoses	
Axis I:	300.40 Clinical depression, dysthymic reaction
Axis II:	301.81 Narcissistic personality disorder
Axis III:	None; no confounding general medical issues

Axis IV:	Psychosocial including family issues, legal concerns, occupational—underemployment, resentment
Axis V:	Global Assessment Functioning = 50–60; past suicidal ideations, shoplifting, depression, occupational concerns, shoplifting compulsion still evident, family issues, possible collecting/hoarding symptoms

Mrs. Daio's Personal History

Mrs. Mailing Daio, age 32, was born in Taichi, China, and moved to California in 1997. Although Chinese is her first language, she communicates well in English.

Mrs. Daio is Catholic and has remained religious. She attended a Catholic college in China, where she attained her advanced electrical engineering degree. She has experienced the overt pangs of guilt associated with her stealing. Mrs. Daio denies that she had any childhood or adolescent behavioral problems, although she told me that while growing up she missed her father, who died when she was quite young. There is no indication that she engaged in shoplifting as a younger woman.

Presently, Mrs. Daio is employed at a Southern California electronics company as a lead electrical engineer. Previously, she worked as an engineer for two years at IBM. Mrs. Daio has been married since 1996 and considers that she has a happy marriage with a loving, supportive husband. Her husband, who is also well educated, is a prominent Southern California heart surgeon with a successful medical practice. He was unaware of his wife's shoplifting. Their combined incomes approximate $850,000 annually. The Daios have a five-year-old daughter and a 16-month-old son. Mrs. Daio told me repeatedly that she had not been previously arrested for crimes against property, despite presenting a long history of stealing from shopping malls. Mrs. Daio has been depressed at a moderate level for several years. Her depression has been judged to be chronic, extending back at least 10 years.

She has been prescribed Celexa by Dr. Singh in moderate doses during the past four years. Her medication management has not been followed up with conventional talk-therapy treatment or targeted shoplifter treatment, though Dr. Singh did provide two therapy sessions for her. Though, her doctor's choice of medication, Celexa, a selective serotonin reuptake inhibitor, or SSRI, may at times alleviate her depression to some extent, it has not decreased the mental fantasy drive and reinforcement that is tied to her shoplifting. There is clinical evidence suggesting that the use of this class of drugs with shoplifters can worsen an already bad theft situation. This clinical use of SSRI-type drugs to treat shoplifters has a propensity to foster and, in fact, increase out-of-control manic behaviors for some shoplifters. Medication is not seen as an answer.

Mrs. Daio told me that she has not abused drugs or alcohol, including prescription medication, although she does use alcohol occasionally to induce sleep when her anxiety level increases. She feels guilty and upset because of her recent arrest and does not ever want to shoplift again.

Mrs. Daio has made some bad decisions in her life leading to her arrest for shoplifting (petty theft) and grand theft. Her careless theft episode at Saks Fifth Avenue has embarrassed both her and her family. This offense, as well as her previous thefts, was obviously not driven by economic or material gain, because Mrs. Daio never used the stolen merchandise. Rather, she sequestered all of it in a specially designated room the size of a huge master bedroom suite in her home.

The special room was off-limits to other family members. It was kept locked, and Mrs. Daio had the only key. Because monetary gain was not the chief driver underlying her theft, an alternative explanation for her shoplifting action had to be explored. Based on her Locus of Control score (highly external at 18), she has been clinically characterized as both an externalizer and trophy-collector shoplifter (she only stole expensive designer purses and had about 400 of them). Instead of using them, she instead viewed, admired, and even fondled the purses as surrogate sex objects, even deriving sexual pleasure from them.

During our initial few interviews, Mrs. Daio remained for the most part sad, tearful, and depressed. She stated, "I've been depressed a lot lately. I guess, thinking back, I've been depressed for a long time." Her mood during our sessions was dysphoric and depressed; her speech was clear yet pressured and at times disconnected. She remained alert, and her thoughts were organized with no loose associations, nor delusional material evidenced. She did not reflect any hallucinations, and her memory for recent, intermediate, and remote events fell within normal limits. She showed some problematic concentration issues that might derive from her depression. Serious psychopathology, organic brain disorder, and psychotic behavioral features were ruled out based on the results of her psychological testing. As a product of psychotherapy Mrs. Daio is, step by step, developing insight into the reasons for her long theft history.

Psychological Test Results

Why would this well-educated and highly compensated ($153,000 per year) engineer engage in repeated self-destructive acts of shoplifting? Of import to her present case, she told me about a similar incident on the day preceding her arrest. On that day she went to a different large shopping mall and engaged in the same type of theft, stealing seven expensive purses from four upscale stores. She was not caught on that occasion. After her successful theft on that day, she took the stolen purses home and stored them in her treasure room. After her arrest, Mrs. Daio's home was carefully searched by two local police officers accompanied by at least three Saks Fifth Avenue loss-prevention representatives.

The quantity and nature of the stolen merchandise left even the experienced police officers and loss-prevention agents shaking their heads. Hundreds of stolen items were found secreted in her home. All the designer purses were carefully photographed, to be used later, as evidence in court against Mrs. Daio. When I showed these police photos of the stolen property to my wife whom, at the time, was the jewelry manager at Nordstrom, she said, "this is unbelievable, because this merchandise has to be worth hundreds of thousands of

dollars." Her valuation was quite close to what the store's loss prevention records verified.

Mrs. Daio's stealing dynamics do not meet the specific diagnostic
criteria of the *DSM–IV–TR* classification for kleptomania. Mrs. Daio told
me that at the time of the crime she was "confused, angry, upset, and
mad." Criterion D for kleptomania states - "the stealing is not committed to express anger or vengeance" (American Psychiatric Association,
2000). Thus, the diagnosis of kleptomania is ruled out in Mrs. Daio's
case.

Mrs. Daio, for most of her life, has been a responsible person who
comprehends the difference between right and wrong and usually
has a sound moral compass. This information was later confirmed
in a telephone conversation with her husband, who was shocked
that his wife had shoplifted and by the fact that she had carefully
arranged her stolen treasures in the secret room, more or less right
under his nose. He had been convinced that the room was used for
legitimate storage purposes. In a sense, the room was used to store
things, but not the types of items that Dr. Daio had in mind. Dr. Daio
was at home when the police and loss-prevention representatives
arrived to execute a search warrant. That was when the secret room
was entered and the discovery of several hundred meticulously
arranged, expensive, stolen handbags was made. The police photographs of Mrs. Daio's stolen treasures documented the shoplifted
purses. Most of these still had the store security tags in place, along
with the price tags, almost as if she were setting up a retail display
in her special room.

Her Carlson Psychological Survey, CPA, scores strongly support
that she was depressed at the time she stole at Saks Fifth Avenue.
There were no other psychological indicators suggesting additional
serious psychopathology or criminal trends in Mrs. Daio's personality.
Her antisocial tendency scale, for example, associated with criminal
motivation on the CPS, was not consistent with a criminal offender's
and fell within normal limits, with a percentile score equal to 48, far
below the threshold of an identified offender's at the 75th to 99th
percentile (see Graph 1). Additionally, her scores on the CPS were not

reflective of the Carlson Type 3 property theft offender. It appeared that Mrs. Daio did not steal hundreds of pricey purses based on measurable criminogenic factors in her personality.

Based on the results of the psychological testing, Mrs. Daio was clinically diagnosed with dysthymic disorder (clinical depression), DSM-IV-TR, 300.40.

The diagnostic impression was supported from the BDI-II and the CPS self-depreciation test results. Mrs. Daio was also diagnosed with narcissistic personality disorder, DSM-IV-TR, 301.81. Her NPD descriptors are presented in Chapter 4.

Mrs. Daio's psychological condition is judged to be chronic and moderate in degree based on her many depressive mood fluctuations during the past 10 years. A bipolar diagnosis has not been ruled out. She is not presently suicidal but has had many suicidal ideations in the past tied to her shoplifting. Her potential for suicidal ideations has increased since her arrest at Saks Fifth Avenue. Major depression as a diagnosis has not been ruled out, and after her arrest she was placed in custody on a suicide watch in the county jail.

Mrs. Daio's depression, as she described her symptoms, was characterized by chronic feelings of pessimism and hopelessness. She continues to think of herself as unworthy and inadequate as a person. Mrs. Daio also describes herself as "feeling hopelessness, very sad, down and out."

Mrs. Daio has had continuous, chronic feelings of hopelessness, overt anger, and unworthiness for at least 10 years. This pervasive depression was well evidenced on the psychological test results. For example, on the BDI-II, she endorsed these sample depressive statements:

- I'm sad most of the time.

- I have had thoughts of killing myself.

Mrs. Daio's depression scale on the CPS (elevated to 88%) suggests pervasive clinical depression and feelings of almost no self-esteem. Her depression negatively impacts on her concentration level. Her low self-esteem is tied to her depression and was also demonstrated on the Locus of Control test results, where she tested highly external. She demonstrated an orientation toward external control; thus she is viewed as an externalizer shoplifter (Chapter 3, Typology 1). Mrs. Daio endorsed the following external locus-of-control items that reflect her depression and out-of-control status:

- Getting a good job depends mainly on being in the right place at the right time (Her endorsement of this statement connects to her stealing pathology).

- It is not always wise to plan too far ahead because many things turn out to be a matter of good or bad fortune anyhow.

She told me that during her recent theft episode she felt a flood of feelings, including excitement, exhilaration, pleasure, and gratification. Later she experienced additional feelings of heightened sexual arousal when she fondled her purses. These are specific and driving symptoms associated with an out-of-control shoplifter.

Mrs. Daio's depressive syndrome certainly negatively impacts on all spheres of her life, but it specifically potentiates her thefts. In combination with the prescribed antidepressant medication, which increased her direction toward mania, she also tended to self-stimulate via her theft episodes. In some situations, the simple act of stealing items, then later returning them to stores, relieved her mounting stress and momentarily helped to alleviate her perceived depression level. After a theft episode, Mrs. Daio's depression recurred, and the cycle begins again. This shoplifting circle is represented in Chapter 5.

I asked Mrs. Daio to rate her subjective depression levels on a scale of 1 to 10 (10 being the highest level) prior to shoplifting, during, and then after the theft events. Quite paradoxically, she verified that during and after her shoplifting, her subjective depression level had decreased. This is consistent with shoplifting Stage 4, the post-excitation phase (see Chapter 5), demonstrating that the shoplifter's depression dissipated after shoplifting, but only for a short period of time.

Mr. Daio had seven valid credit cards and two ATM cards in her possession when she was arrested. She could easily have purchased the purses that she instead stole from Saks Fifth Avenue, a criminal act for which she knows she will now be punished. However, it is theorized that her unconscious awareness that a theft episode could make her feel less depressed or better about herself, and that this outweighed her conscious moral compass telling her not to steal. At the time of this theft, and no doubt on all theft occasions, Mrs. Daio's moral conscience demands were subordinated to the emotional satisfaction or lift she anticipated she would derive from stealing. That is, she felt an emergent high. She stated:

> I was beginning to get depressed, a strange feeling came over me just prior to stealing. Then I would, for no apparent reason, drive to L.A., find a mall, and you know the rest of the story. Sometimes I didn't even know where I was, what city I was in, how I got there, or why I got home so late. It was all very confusing to me, and I thought I was losing my mind. The next thing I remember is that I was arrested and heading to jail. My husband, who is a very trusting man, even thought that maybe I was having an affair, and in some strange way, shoplifting for me was an affair of sorts, because, believe it or not, it made me feel better.

What mental events triggered her depression and resultant entrance into the shoplifting cycle? My clinical experience with shoplifters has provided ample evidence that a theft occurence is usually preceded by some emotional, antecedent psychological event. What was Mrs. Daio's precipitating psychological event, or was there an identifiable event at all?

I asked Mrs. Daio if there had been any recent, traumatic event in her life that may have contributed to her depression and motivated her stealing. She told me that recently she has been seriously and acutely depressed because she was passed over for a significant management promotion at the electronics company where she is employed. Her anger surrounding not getting a career promotion was loud and clear. She expressed it as follows:

> The job advancement was given to a colleague with only half of my experience, education, and other qualifications. When I got all of those things [purses], I felt the sky was the limit for me, and then later when I thought about it, I had a big letdown and felt terrible for what I had done. But the manager at my company was just stupid not to promote me to that position. I don't know if I hate him or not, now! Because of this stealing, now people will probably think I'm a common criminal.

Mrs. Daio's reformulation of herself as a criminal is typical of Stage 4, the Scarlet Letter Syndrome, outlined in Chapter 5. Her description of what precipitated her most recent theft reflects her identity shift evident during the neutralization stage (Stage 2) of shoplifting. She had to somehow neutralize her moral reasoning or best judgment, which told her not to steal, then quickly replace it with self-statements against her moral values that allowed her to move ahead and commit a criminal act. During the early stages of treatment, Mrs. Daio did not fully comprehend the psychological connection between her theft behavior and her need for constant emotional stimulation to reduce her depression, which led to her abdication of personal control over her actions as well as her acceptance of pro–law violation self-sentences. "I'm a bad person, and guess what, it's OK for a bad person like me to steal!"

Mrs. Daio's theft represents her unconscious belief that she could compensate for her failure to attain a major professional goal through a symbolic yet negative gain—shoplifted items. She told me that during the physical act of stealing, she feels very excited, even sexually aroused at times. Her depression is lifted during the shoplifting episode but reemerges during Stage 4, depression. Using her flawed reasoning, she is justified by at least coming away with something for her efforts—stolen items. In her mind, she held the false belief that she may not have really gotten exactly what she desired as a goal (career advancement), but at least for the moment she had achieved a small prize for her effort, although acquired illegally. Therefore, her psychological drive to steal became almost irresistible, and she could not stop or break the shoplifting cycle.

There is some discussion in Chapter 5 that the condition of shoplifting may have nonvolitional aspects that can mirror an irresistible impulse system. This present discussion does not directly address shoplifters' free will, but it is clear that in many instances, shoplifters compromise the choices available to them prior to stealing. It seems to them that their free will has been abrogated. Shoplifters neutralize their usually effective moral code to not steal, allowing them to engage in a criminal act. This act constitutes a pro–law violation position predicated on the shoplifters' shifting or eroding moral code. In making this moral shift, they greatly increase the procriminal definitions they hold that pervade their reasoning, paving the way for them to steal from others. Mrs. Daio was able to neutralize her better judgment against the commission of many crimes. She shoplifted based on a newly modified value system that provided incentives to commit crimes.

Mrs. Daio's repeated urges to steal coincided directly with her depressive and out-of-control states and occurred in unpredictable, periodic waves usually lasting from several days to a week. She disclosed to me that the day prior to her arrest for shoplifting at the Saks Fifth Avenue store, she had engaged in a similar theft act at another mall, though she did not recall exactly which one. It is believed that at that time she was also negatively influenced by her depression and rejection at losing a valued job promotion. Therefore, her need to steal is interpreted as a direct expression of psychological overcompensation for a perceived loss in her life.

The Saks Fifth Avenue Security Apprehension Report lists and includes photographs of at least 100 stolen items—including but not limited to the 80 to 100 expensive designer-label purses that she was charged with stealing from that store. When Mrs. Daio came to meet me for her initial interview after referral from her lawyer, she was carrying an attractive Coco Chanel handbag, which I noticed because of the distinctive logo that my wife taught me to recognize in case I planned a visit to the local mall. After I mentioned what a nice bag it was, she stated, "Oh, Dr. Brady, I didn't steal this one. I bought it, and I can prove it! Trust me, I don't steal everything I own! I'm not always a thief! Most of the time I pay for these." I registered her comment and moved the conversation to a discussion of her shoplifting history.

After each of her hundreds of thefts, Mrs. Daio then stockpiled the merchandise in her home, leading to another question: Why did she accumulate this huge treasure trove of illegally obtained items when she could have easily afforded to buy them, especially when theft brought the risk of arrest and a jail sentence?

The answer to the question seems to be that by stealing, collecting and hoarding, this large cache of apparel items in her home she felt momentarily empowered and significant as a person as opposed to being "small, nothing, a nobody, or just a loser who could not get the job promotion" she so coveted. Because she had previously gotten away with multiple thefts, she felt invincible and emotionally powerful, thereby repressing her real, out-of-control, depressive self-concept as someone who was perhaps in the final analysis "an inadequate failure." Because of her psychologically counterproductive shoplifting drive, her personal moral world had turned upside down. Engaging in negative behavior (theft) was for her suddenly positive because, after all, she felt better emotionally after stealing, even though doing something wrong was seemingly out of character. She had created a downward spiral of theft in which, at least in her thoughts, the ends psychologically justified the means.

Mrs. Daio's long history of shoplifting has been clinically tied to a trophy-collection pattern. This descriptive trophy-collecting syndrome played a significant and determining role in Mrs. Daio's chronic theft behaviors. Collecting, as she did, hundreds of designer-label purses is characteristic of the trophy-collector shoplifter type described in Chapter 3 (Typology 6). Mrs. Daio's trophy-collection behavior represents a very selective shoplifting act. She shoplifted and collected only those expensive purses that she was attracted to, because possession of them yielded a sense of power, fulfillment, meaning, and a momentary achievement that helped reduce both the intensity and the duration of her depression. Later, when she viewed her "trophies" in her hidden room crammed full of purses, she felt psychologically and sometimes physically or sexually stimulated, falsely secure in the special environment she had created in her home. Surrounding herself with expensive items, illegitimately acquired, afforded her the transient opportunity to achieve personal, albeit false, emotional security.

Mrs. Daio had amassed this treasure trove of expensive objects that only she could enjoy. At times Mrs. Daio also reported experiencing feelings of heightened sexual excitement when she looked at and occasionally fondled her ill-gotten treasures. She described a long history of holding, touching, and even caressing these inanimate objects as a surrogate method to perhaps both give and receive missed affection in her life, including the production of sexual arousal patterning.

The psychological trigger that was identified as setting in motion Mrs. Daio's Stage 1 anticipation shoplifting—an aura sensation—centered on her need to shoplift and then collect high-priced retail items. Possession, viewing, and later touching these highly valued items provided her with an identifiable secondary gain—her chronic depression was momentarily abated; yet, unfortunately for her, it almost immediately recurred. Mrs. Daio's reported sexual arousal subsequent to her shoplifting events and the stocking of her special room is a unique component that has historically influenced her theft patterning. Her locus-of-control test scores established that she is an externalizer shoplifter (Chapter 3, Typology 1). Proof of this is the fact that surrounding herself with these external material objects reinforced her need for outside or external stimulation, which contributes to her personal validation as a nonloser.

Mrs. Daio has repeatedly stated that she strongly wants to terminate her stealing. She stated, "I didn't want this problem to totally ruin my life or the lives of my family, maybe for the first time in my life. I know I need help." The results of her mental status examination indicated that there was no major psychosis or evidence of brain damage present that could account for her out-of-control shoplifting episodes.

Mrs. Daio's psychological tests were examined for preexisting criminal tendencies on the CPS antisocial (AT) scale. Her CPS psychological profile is not consistent with that of a criminal offender. In particular, her CPS AT subscale score is not consistent with that of a property offender. She is also not diagnosable as a kleptomaniac using the *DSM–IV–TR* classification. The negative results on the CPS AT scale suggest that Mrs. Daio's theft behavior is not motivated by measurable criminal tendencies. That type of offender lacks a conscience, is consistently irresponsible, and is incapable of learning from past mistakes. Mrs. Daio does not fit that description. She strongly desires to change the self-defeating theft cycle that has kept her for so many years dependent on shoplifting as a method to deal with her depression.

Mrs. Daio is not directed toward theft for economic gain, but is motivated by psychological, out-of-control factors she cannot comprehend or prevent. She has demonstrated a deep sense of remorse and guilt for her actions and for the embarrassment her stealing has caused for herself and her family. Clearly, the results of this assessment establish that her theft behavior is directly related to her depression and her overcompensatory need for achievement and status. She is committed to regaining personal control over her life.

It is difficult to comprehend why Mrs. Daio has not been previously arrested for any other shoplifting crimes, since she has admittedly engaged in at least 200 shoplifting offenses throughout Southern California. Her lengthy string of successes may be attributable to a well-polished theft technique or, less plausibly, to simple luck. Her engineering background may have aided her in working out a method for defeating the store security sensors.

In my written report to the court, I stated that:

> For this vulnerable, depressed, and confused woman at this point in her life, a prison sentence would seem to serve no useful purpose other than that of pure retribution. She is a psychologically very troubled and fragile person in need of intense treatment, not prison confinement as a criminal. She presents a favorable prognosis for behavioral change, because at this point she is coming to

understand the multiple reasons for her self-defeating theft and trophy-collecting behaviors.

It is apparent from this analysis that her theft behavior at Saks Fifth Avenue was not in any sense motivated by economic gain; rather, her drive to steal is psychologically connected to her overcompensation for loss pattern; the loss representing her not getting a significant career promotion she thought she deserved. She was personally and predictably devastated when the promotion was given to someone she felt was clearly inferior to her and who therefore did not deserve it. Mrs. Daio's flawed reasoning led her to believe that because she lost this major goal, she could substitute a minor goal, theft of purses, to compensate. Naturally, this represents a kind of convoluted logic. Most shoplifters I have treated evidence some type of distorted reasoning contributing to their theft careers.[1]

Mrs. Daio's reported sexual arousal response to her shoplifting is analogous to Lorand's (1950) analysis of the symbolic sexual component with the shoplifters he treated. One patient he diagnosed had never stolen before, and Lorand reported that this theft involved an element of sexual dysfunctionality quite similar to Mrs. Daio's. A confused sexual identity patterning was suspected with his patient, "which proves that sexual disturbance (or arousal) and stealing may go hand in hand, and such symptomatic stealing may have the fundamental aim of pleasure-stealing" (Lorand,1950, p.19). This depiction is similar to Mrs. Daio's reported post-shoplifting sexual arousal feelings. Her thefts can be labeled, at least in part, as a type of "sexual pleasure-stealing." Because of the increased frequency of these types of shoplifters, later research could confirm sexual pleasure stealing as an additional shoplifter typology for inclusion under the shoplifter typologies explained in Chapter 3.

Notwithstanding this sexual element, it is readily apparent that Mrs. Daio felt exhilaration and stimulation as well as a lifting of depres-

---

1   Psychological report submitted to the Los Angeles Superior Court on behalf of Mrs. Daio. The results of this report are a matter of public record.

sion both during her actual stealing and then later, after completing her acts of shoplifting.

For Mrs. Daio, her attraction to high-end designer purses was driven by her need not only to possess these coveted items but to satisfy an idiosyncratic fetishistic need, as she revealed during treatment. She consistently demonstrated that her need to steal expensive purses carried with it a certain implicit seductiveness. Commenting on shoplifters' seduction to their preferential objects, Katz (1988,p.55) has stated that:

> The would-be thief manages to bring the particular charm of an object into existence before she possesses it. Seduction is experienced as an influence emanating from a particular necklace, compact or Chapstick, even though the particular object one is drawn to may not be distinguishable from numerous others near it. In some accounts, the experience of seduction suggests a romantic encounter. Objects sometimes have the capacity to trigger "love at first sight."

Paradoxically for Mrs. Daio, the chief psychological payoff and reinforcement for her shoplifting derived from an ex post facto motivation— that is, her symbolic, romantic, and sexually charged odyssey did not precede her stealing but instead it closely followed it. In this sense, the interpretation of her individual psychodynamics differs from Katz's sociological analysis of his shoplifter example.

During therapy, Mrs. Daio recalled the first theft episode where she began to identify her sexually aroused state as triggered immediately after stealing:

> There was something very strange that happened to me, I guess, about five years ago after I went to Saks and took what I remember was a very nice and for sure expensive handbag that I think cost about $1,200. After I got home that evening, I went straight to a large, unused bedroom on the third floor in our house where, from time to time, I had put other purses I'd taken before. At some point along the way, I began to use this room for personal storage,

and then for some reason, I started to put all of the purses I'd stolen there so my husband and children wouldn't find out that I
was stealing. I always kept the room locked, and I had the only
key. That particular night when I started to arrange the purses
on the bed and on several side tables, I noticed what I thought
at first was a kind of "hot flash" experience, but as it turned out,
this was very different from the "hot flashes" I had during the past
few years. Then, all of a sudden and for no apparent reason that I
could figure out, I became sexually excited, and I was at a loss to
explain what was happening to me. Here I was completely alone
in this large room; just myself and those dumb purses. It is kind of
eerie now to think about it and how this must sound to you. It was
confusing and painful to me then, and it still is now, but one thing
that I clearly remember is that there was something very sexual
happening to me. I was very embarrassed and frightened about
it, but the feelings were real, and they were there. I have never
mentioned this to my husband. And, this may seem pretty crazy
to you, especially because I felt that the more expensive purses
seemed to really excite me more than some of the less expensive
ones I had taken from Kohl's [a moderately priced chain store] in
the past.

It is possible that the erotic stimulus value (Mrs. Daio's perceived
level of sexual arousal and satisfaction) derived from her stolen purses
was directly proportionate to the value or the retail price of the stolen items. Otherwise, she might have switched her modus operandi
and only stolen cheaper merchandise from Walmart or Kohl's and not
from Saks Fifth Avenue. These are identifiable characteristics of Stage
4, the postexcitation phase, in the shoplifting process.

During her therapy, Mrs. Daio has begun to focus on more effective ways to increase her self-esteem and reduce her depression. She
also needs to establish the connection between her depression and
her unconscious need to trophy-steal expensive items, which she later
views, as a way to vicariously feel powerful and significant as a person.
After serving a three-month local jail sentence, she committed herself
to a long-term counseling plan. Mrs. Daio has also been attending a
shoplifter-modified 12-step program that she began during her jail

term. If she follows through with her therapy plan, it is thought likely that she will present little threat to recidivate. During therapy, Mrs. Daio has terminated her psychological dependence on Celexa.

Mrs. Daio spent a considerable amount of time in Stage 2, neutralization. "I guess looking back it took me a long time to begin taking things from stores. I must have given it a lot of thought first. I really changed as a person, and not for the better. My thinking just got off track. I don't want to be that person again."

Case Disposition

Although she was initially charged with grand theft, the superior court judge sentenced Mrs. Daio to six months in local jail followed by three years of supervised probation, including verification that she was staying in treatment. Her maximum exposure to the California Department of Corrections and Rehabilitation (CDCR) was seven years. She remains in treatment and has identified a number of her shoplifting triggers. She maintains a positive outlook for a future without stealing and collecting. The secret treasure trove room has been dismantled and redesignated "for family storage only." The police and loss-prevention agents were able to identify, catalog, and return a total of 387 purses, with the sensors and price tags attached, to most of the stores from which they were taken. The net retail value amounted to $367,685. Thus, this case ended with good prospects for her future.

Case 2. Mrs. Konvitz: The Corned Beef Caper

Case Introduction

Severe masochism, depression, anger, intense anxiety, and World War II concentration camp survival guilt are some of the identifiable triggers that contributed to Mrs. Konvitz's twisting path into the shoplifting zone. As a result, she has had multiple theft arrests. How does a wealthy older woman living in one of the most upscale regions of the country, Santa Barbara, California, get arrested for shoplifting one and a half pounds of kosher corned beef? If Mrs. Konvitz's shoplifting experience was not so personally tragic for her and her family, it might be viewed humorously. Mrs. Konvitz entered Cyd's, an exclusive Southern California deli, took the corned beef, exited the store, and sped away from the shoplifting scene in a new Mercedes Benz. As the alert security guard from Cyd's pursued her, he saw Mrs. Konvitz toss the purloined meat out of the window of her car as she sped up her driveway.

Subsequently, the major emotional issue for Mrs. Konvitz was not that she had committed a crime but that everyone at the deli had known her for years, and now they also knew her as a thief. It was impossible for her to argue that she didn't do it. After all, she was seen stealing the corned beef and then making her getaway. But why did she do it, and why did she run?

The antecedent conditions leading to Mrs. Konvitz's arrest for petty theft have historical psychological tendrils extending back to the diabolical events of 1940s Nazi Germany, and the Holocaust experience of many of her family members who were murdered in gas chambers. Through cognitive behavioral therapy, Mrs. Konvitz was able to directly link her present out-of-control symptoms, including her shoplifting, to these past family horrors. She constructed an emotional bridge to the past to help explain her present maladaptive shoplifting. Her bridge to the painful past used a cognitive chain of events to revivify the past.

Of the four shoplifters profiled in this chapter, Mrs. Konvitz was initially by far the most recalcitrant, angry, negative, and defensive. Her family history contained good justification for these bitter, negative feelings, which, unfortunately, in large measure account for her present theft pathology. As I spoke with her during the initial session, Mrs. Konvitz's displaced hostility and overt anger flared out in all directions. But she did not know why she was exhibiting this mountain of negativity. Ultimately, when she was able to make the nexus, past to present, she did see that she needed to change. Like other shoplifters I have treated, she desperately wanted an opportunity for moral redemption.

Mrs. Konvitz's Identifying Information

Dates of Testing: October 2010

Client's Name: Mrs. Janine Konvitz

Birthplace: Jerusalem, Israel

Age: 65

Dates of Examination: October and November 2010

Place of Examination: Santa Barbara Therapy Institute, 1685 Del Tomaso Drive, Santa Barbara, CA.

Date of Report: November 2010

Prior Arrests: Four petty theft arrests and one prior conviction for theft

Criminal Charges: Petty theft

Prior Psychiatric Treatment: Medication management for stress/depression, prescribed Paxil.

DSM–IV–TR Diagnoses	
Axis I:	300.40 Clinical depression, dysthymic reaction, feelings of being out of control
Axis II:	301.81 Narcissistic personality disorder
Axis III:	None; no confounding general medical issues
Axis IV:	Psychosocial including family issues, legal concerns
Axis V:	Global Assessment Functioning = 65; past suicidal ideations, shoplifting, depression, denial, anger, fear of disclosure, death ideations, self-aggrandizement

CHAPTER 6

Mrs. Konvitz's Personal History

Mrs. Konvitz is an angry 65-year-old woman of German-Israeli extraction who was referred by her defense attorney subsequent to her arrest for petty theft, shoplifting. The information provided in the police report established that Mrs. Konvitz was indeed arrested, amazingly enough, for stealing one and a half pounds of corned beef at Cyd's, a tony deli near her ocean view home in Montecito, California. When an attempt was made to apprehend her, she reportedly rapidly fled the shoplifting scene at Cyd's driving a deluxe model 2009 Mercedes with a personalized license plate, Konvitz II. Konvitz I was her husband's car, also a new Mercedes. At the time of her arrest, the police verified that Mrs. Konvitz had five credit cards with her as well as $160 in cash, which was booked into evidence by the arresting officer. After her arrest, Mrs. Konvitz was referred to me by her attorney. She was very interested in the overall results of her psychological testing, and she knew that this assessment would be used as part of her defense preparation in her pending and somewhat embarrassing court case.

Subsequent to her arrest, she made a very self-revealing comment to the arresting officer: "All of those people at Cyd's have known me for years, and now I've made a public fool out of myself by stealing something as dumb as a little corned beef. Now I won't be able to go back there and shop because of what they'll think of me. It's so humiliating for me. If my family and friends find out about this, they also will be humiliated and feel the same way I do. I think this was one big mistake, and maybe I'm the one who should take legal action!" Mrs. Konvitz's emotionally charged statements are characteristic of her deeply held denial system and her displaced anger and depression, not uncommon reactions for shoplifters.

It would take a considerable amount of time in treatment to break through Mrs. Konvitz's well-protected defense/denial system. Her statement to the police demonstrates her distorted sense of proportionality. In her mind, the severity of her shoplifting offense, although minor, was less significant than her egotistical personal feelings of public shame and her possible inability to return to Cyd's to shop for groceries. At the time she was arrested, she said she felt out of control when she stole and added, "This stealing just isn't like me. It is as if an entirely different person did this." This perceptible shift in reference from the first to the third person is a typical symptom of Stage 3, action/theft stage in the shoplifting zone (see Chapter 5). It also is psychologically deeply woven into the shoplifter's sense of self-absorption and incipient narcissism, which for some adaptational reasons serves to protect the fragility of the perpetrator of a crime. The immediacy of the self-absorption in many respects comes at the expense of anyone else in the shoplifter's life. Refusing to accept personal responsibility for the theft act, which is typical of shoplifters, was well represented in Mrs. Konvitz's many statements deflecting her culpability for having, without excuses, engaged in an act of petty theft. For Mrs. Konvitz, personal moral redemption required much time and much therapy.

As odd as it might seem, there are apparently many cases in which people are accused of stealing meat from stores. For example, a recent news story from the *Pittsburgh Tribune Review* details a shoplifting incident where two suspects stole filet mignon steaks from a large grocery store and ran out the front door. Once outside, they dropped the steaks. This modus operandi is similar to Mrs. Konvitz's theft behavior and arrest. Later, "the two suspects stated that they stole (and felt justified) because weeks earlier they felt they had been cheated at the store" (Peirce, 2010). Mrs. Konvitz also, but in a different way, felt that she had been cheated out of something in her life.

Mrs. Konvitz's background and personal history are more unusual, complex, and far more psychologically traumatic than the other cases profiled in this book. Her parents and both of their families were raised in and had lived in Obersaltz, Germany, a small suburb 20 miles from Bonn. She and her family were Jewish, and in early 1943, members of her family were beginning to be taken from their German village to be transported to the Bergen-Belsen death camp in Lower Saxony. A few months later, all of her family members, except her parents, were exterminated by the Nazis in gas chambers. This included her grandparents, aunts, uncles, cousins, and her three older siblings. Like many Jewish families living under Nazi occupation, Mrs. Konvitz's family offered little or no physical resistance to the transportation and relocation process. In the years since the events of World War II, Mrs. Konvitz had heard many startling accounts of the atrocities associated with the unspeakable, murderous cruelty that took place at Bergen-Belsen.

She was particularly struck by the horrendous fact that 70,000 Jewish people had been exterminated in the gas chambers there, including most of her relatives, who had done nothing, except practice a religion that was forbidden by the Nazi regime. Fortunately, her parents were able to escape from the camp in 1944. Shortly thereafter, they became involved in a different and perhaps more humane relocation program that was to send them to Brevitzburg, a labor work setting located in Bavaria. They were again able to escape and were never transported to Bergen-Belsen. Instead, they were sent to a newly opened relocation camp just as the war was winding down. The same fate was not to be for the remaining members of Mrs. Konvitz's family, who were murdered at the hands of the Nazi SS. Mrs. Konvitz's parents, near the end of the war, connected with a freedom relocation program (Macht-frei), and when they had the opportunity, they immigrated to Israel, leaving behind the long, dark penumbra of the fate of her entire family, save her parents.

Mrs. Konvitz was born in Betselva, a small village outside of Jerusalem, in 1946 and remained there until she and her parents again immigrated in 1955, this time to the United States. They chose Southern California as a destination because of the Mediterranean-like climate, similar to Israel's, as well as for a real chance at freedom and job advancement. Mrs. Konvitz attended primary and secondary school and college in the Los Angeles area and earned a degree in fine arts and interior design. For many years, she has been a sought-after interior designer for the wealthy residents in and around Santa Barbara. As she tells it, "We know just about everyone in the Montecito area, including a few movie stars. I designed home interiors for them. But it looks like those days might be over until I get out of this."

Mrs. Konvitz's husband has been a successful patent attorney in Santa Barbara for more than 35 years. He had been fairly oblivious to his wife's pattern of shoplifting, he was also not aware of the psychological pain she experienced connected to her Jewish past in Germany during the holocaust. For her own personal reasons, Mrs. Konvitz had chosen to remain silent about the devastating loss of her relatives at the hands of the Nazis. She has also suppressed the present pain connected to this shoplifting episode from her anxiety-filled life.

The Konvitzes have three grown children, like Mr. Konvitz, they knew nothing about their mother's chronic stealing. Mrs. Konvitz has seen a psychiatrist for her depression and was prescribed Paxil for her episodic depressive symptoms, but she told me, "the medication didn't help my stealing to end. It only made me feel tired and confused most of the time." Mrs. Konvitz does not use alcohol or drugs other than the single antidepressant. She stated:

> I can't really remember a time when or if I was really very happy, and that's especially true of my childhood. Maybe I'm just a depressed and sad person, and that's my fate. I guess I was born that way and maybe, that's how I'll die.

I asked her what made her so sad, and she had no direct answer. "I've had a bad attitude for a long time, and search me as to why," was her response.

Psychological Test Results

Mrs. Konvitz has been psychologically out of control for years, reflecting an external locus-of-control orientation. She is considered an externalizer shoplifter. When she was first interviewed she appeared angry, hostile, visibly upset, rebellious, and initially somewhat hard to approach. It was as if stealing and arrest were for her personal and social impositions rather than serious events that could change her life forever. In short, she viewed her current arrest as a temporary social status setback in the community where she had previously enjoyed a high level of prominence.

Her mental status test results did not indicate she was experiencing or had experienced any psychotic disorders, nor was she experiencing any delusional symptoms that might explain her theft actions. Mrs. Konvitz was tearful during several interviews, especially when discussing her extensive theft history. Nevertheless, she again stated, "It's not fair for me to be treated like this." An attempt was made to determine whether there was a direct causal nexus between her identified psychological factors, including her overt depression, loss of control, and theft patterning, including the most recent incident at Cyd's.

During subsequent counseling sessions, she was a little more open, forthcoming, and considerably less defensive and hostile concerning her many prior theft offenses. Mrs. Konvitz slowly began to manifest a modicum of guilt and to take responsibility for her actions, including the corned beef theft at Cyd's, now cognizant of the fact that her humiliation was due to her own poor judgment. As therapy entered the fifth month, she slowly began to loosen her iron grip on the defensive positions she had previously employed as justification for her stealing. In fact, later in counseling she readily admitted that she had shoplifted in Southern California for many years, although she still did not know why she became a shoplifter in the first place.

A perceived therapeutic breakthrough came when I suggested that she should attend a Shoplifters Anonymous group. There she would meet and interact with other people who shared her problem. She said if it would help her not steal in the future and if she could avoid jail, she would do it. Mrs. Konvitz is now sorry for her stealing behavior and is committed not shoplift in the future.

Mrs. Konvitz's test results on the Beck Depression Inventory established that her score falls into the high range of depression, including her history of suicidal tendencies. She presented with a diagnosable mental condition under the *DSM–IV–TR*, dysthymic disorder (depression), 300.40. For example, her depression on the BDI-II was represented by endorsement of these depressive statements:

- I feel I am being punished.

- I am disappointed in myself and sometimes want to die.

Mrs. Konvitz's CPS depression scale results are in general agreement with the BDI-II results, indicating that she has been clinically depressed (depression elevated to 90%), lacks almost any measure of self-confidence, and has deep-seated anger issues. There is no indication that she has ever abused either illegal or prescribed drugs or alcohol before or during her shoplifting episodes; thus, chemical dependence as a shoplifting etiology has been ruled out. However, at the time of her assessment, a diagnosis of narcissistic personality disorder was made in addition to her depressive diagnosis.

The results of Mrs. Konvitz's psychological assessment do not reveal any other serious psychopathological conditions. Additionally, she does not reflect any key indicators or psychological factors associated with the Carlson Type 3 property offense typology. Of equal importance, her CPS antisocial tendency subscale score fell within normal limits at the 39th percentile (see graph 1, Chapter 1). However, her CPS test results do mirror those psychological factors connected to the Carlson victim profile, in which the person feels controlled by outside forces and sees him- or herself as being somehow unfairly treated and rejected by society. Progressively, as Mrs. Konvitz made steady therapeutic progress, she began to surrender her rigid defensive, victim status, developing more rationally based explanations for her stealing.

The Locus of Control Scale measured the degree to which Mrs. Konvitz felt controlled by internal forces (signs of an internal person) or, conversely, external forces such as luck, chance, fate, and fortuitousness (signs of an external person). She tested as being highly external on this measure. External psychological factors have been positively correlated with a shoplifting profile, as is established with the four shoplifting cases described in this book. Her external score of 18 on the Locus of Control Scale strongly suggested that most of her life she has felt as if external forces combined with guilt have driven her into a negative life trajectory. Hence, Mrs. Konvitz's feelings of being a societal victim have pervaded her thinking, remaining with her for many years. Her locus-of-control test results are clinically consistent with the externalizer shoplifter profile (see Chapter 3, Typology 1). This externalizer orientation was demonstrated by her endorsement of these statements:

- Many times we might just as well decide what to do by flipping a coin.

- Most people don't realize the extent to which their lives are controlled by accidental happenings.

- It is hard to know whether or not a person really likes you.

Mrs. Konvitz is typical of external shoplifters, feeling pressured by factors lying outside of themselves.

Mrs. Konvitz, in the course of treatment, was provided with rational emotive behavioral therapy. She slowly began to connect her history of self-defeating theft behaviors to her underlying chronic depressive reaction and a revivified sense of her family loss so many years ago in Bergen-Belsen. There is no doubt that her stealing can be psychologically tied directly to her feelings of despondence being out of control, and to overcompensation for past family losses. As she stated:

Before I got into counseling with you, I really felt I could do whatever I wanted to and at any time I wanted. After all, I didn't feel I was hurting anyone, but I guess in the end I was really hurting myself most of all. I didn't think of other people. I felt what I did was somehow justified.

This comment points out the underlying selfishness or self-centeredness demonstrated by many shoplifters and connects to the concept of narcissism, a condition that is tied to shoplifting behavior.

In fact, after a careful analysis of her self-centeredness, Mrs. Konvitz met the diagnostic criteria for narcissistic personality disorder. Criterion 1 for NPD, "a sense of grandiosity and self-importance," captures her pre-therapeutic attitude. The narcissistic person must meet his or her own needs irrespective of the needs of others, including family members. Mrs. Konvitz's uncontrolled ego-driven attitude was an excellent issue to focus on during her continued therapy. During the course of psychotherapy, she has become noticeably less depressed, and logically it follows that the less depressed she is, the less her motivation will be to overcompensate for her traumatic past losses via stealing.

During her later therapy sessions, Mrs. Konvitz also began to slowly make the *psychological* connection between the devastating fate of her family at the hands of the Nazis and her own history of overcompensation resulting in her serial theft behaviors. Many months later in a therapy session, she made another breakthrough as was indicated by her saying:

Thinking of what happened to my family during the war makes me furious, sad, and when I think about it, I get mentally exhausted. But the worst part is that I feel guilty. It's like somehow I want to be punished or something just like my family was.

She then acknowledged the fact that she was living and reliving in her mind the devastating survivor's guilt connected to her parents' survival as opposed to the demise of most of her family members.

Adverse psychological reactions to survival guilt, including Mrs. Konvitz's survival guilt related to World War II atrocities, have been present since the advent of war itself. Because Mrs. Konvitz's survival guilt is based on past traumatic events that she has revivified while also fantasizing about them, her guilt has been labeled latent or vicarious survivor guilt. Victor Frankl (1962, p.87), an influential psychoanalyst and himself a survivor of the Holocaust, wrote extensively about what he called existential or vicarious survivor guilt in his 1962 book, *Man's Search for Meaning*. Describing his personal reaction to liberation, he reflected generally on the survivors who had very mixed reactions to both their confinement and newfound freedom. Many of the newly liberated prisoners from Dachau and other death camps initially anticipated reconnecting with their loved ones left behind as well as returning to their former homes in European cities, villages, and farms. But the positive thoughts they had dreamed about while incarcerated were quickly replaced by guilt and negative thoughts due to the death of family and peers at the hands of the Nazis. They asked themselves why they had survived while so many others had died. Frankl comments on his own release from Dachau:

CHAPTER 6

Timidly, we looked around and glanced at each other questioningly. Then we ventured a few steps out of the camp. This time no orders were shouted at us, nor was there any need to duck quickly to avoid a blow or a kick. "Freedom," we repeated to ourselves, and yet we could not grasp it. We had said this word so often during all the years we dreamed about it, that it had lost its meaning (p.82).

In many ways, Mrs. Konvitz could not grasp the gravity of the circumstances that her innocent relatives had to face so many years ago. Despite the fact that she was born much later, and in Israel rather than Germany, her vicarious guilt patterning struggled to the surface and sought expression in her overcompensatory and anger-filled theft acts: "I take whatever I want. I deserve it." Paradoxically, because she and her parents survived, she unconsciously desired punishment for long-ago events that she had no power to control. On a purely psychological level, Mrs. Konvitz wanted to be apprehended and punished for, as she termed it, the "very dumb act of stealing corned beef." Her reaction to these events was quite real, though unconscious. The self-punishment regimen she had accommodated to became actualized over the years in her string of petty thefts. This masochistic pattern of out-of-control behavior characterizes Mrs. Konvitz's long history of shoplifting and subsequent painful arrests. The difference this time, of course, was the real possibility of receiving significant punishment from the legal system, including going to jail.

Based on her test results, Mrs. Konvitz was clinically diagnosed as experiencing dysthymic disorder (DSM-IV TR 300.40) and narcissistic personality disorder, NPD (DSM-IV-TR 301.81). Dissociative fugue state (DSM-IV TR, 300.13) cannot be ruled out at this time. Her depression fits all *DSM–IV–TR* criteria *for 300.4 Dysthymic Disorder.*

Her responses on the CPS depression scale indicated depression that is elevated significantly above normal. She is not presently seen as a suicide risk but states that she has had a number of self-destructive ideations dating back at least five years. An important factor in her case is that she had no clue why she was so miserable, upset, depressed, and angry most of the time. She commented: "You know, it's been years since I really smiled at another person, and I know I'm not a real treat to be around, mostly because I probably make other people miserable too." Mrs. Konvitz's depression score supports the view that she maintains a low self-worth and has a very low energy level. Her depression was addressed continuously during therapy. At times during these sessions, she stated that, although making progress in treatment, she still feels totally overwrought and confused by her repetitive stealing.

She was excluded from a diagnosis of kleptomania because, for this diagnosis, Criterion D states, "the stealing is not committed to express anger or vengeance." Mrs. Konvitz, on the contrary, was both angry and vengeful during her reported shoplifting acts. She stated, for example, "I was sort of trying to get back at people, and I guess at the same time trying to punish myself. In the end, I'm the big loser for getting to this low point in my life."

Mrs. Konvitz is cognizant of the fact that her repeated theft behaviors have progressively become more self-defeating and humiliating. Her collective psychological test results and her many statements during treatment verified that she feels extremely guilty and remorseful for her foolish stealing at Cyd's. To a large extent, Mrs. Konvitz's shoplifting has been actively driven by her feelings of being out of control and in mental conflict prior to her stealing episodes. This is not to say that she additionally did not reflect intense ego-driven, self-centered feelings fueled by a palpable narcissistic undercurrent.

These psychological components—lacking personal control and self-centeredness—were evidenced on the Locus of Control Scale results, where she affirms that she often has been personally out of control, feeling influenced by external forces that remain confusing to her.

Her externality likewise underscores her psychological victim status as presented on the CPS and from a select analysis of her locus-of-control endorsements. She stated:

Not only didn't I have any real control over my shoplifting, it was like I was somehow compelled to do it by something outside of myself. I had no choice, or really very few good ones as I saw it.

Mrs. Konvitz's externality was indicated on these responses to the Rotter Locus of Control Scale:

1. The trouble with most children nowadays is that their parents are too easy with them.

2. Many of the unhappy things in people's lives are partly due to bad luck.

She did affirm her conviction that sometimes fate, fortuitousness, luck, and chance control people's lives, including, at various times, her own. Her theft behaviors have been motivated by an absence of control, which she intuitively came to realize was both irrational and self-defeating. She additionally connected her repetitive shoplifting to her master irrational belief system: Because of her parents' survival—and hence her own—she needed to be punished just as her German-Jewish family members had been seventy years ago.

Mrs. Konvitz's Case Analysis

Mrs. Konvitz's master psychological trigger for setting in motion her extensive shoplifting career was her unconscious, irrational belief that she deserved to be punished for historic events associated with her family's extermination, a tragedy that was far beyond her personal control. She experienced the world as a place that had taken things from her and her relatives, and now Mrs. Konvitz was intent on taking them back, or perhaps just getting even. This retaliatory justification for her shoplifting qualifies her for inclusion into the equalizer typology (Chapter 3, Typology 8) and fostered her narcissism. She has been negatively impacted by external factors and therefore also falls into the externalizer typology (Chapter 3, Typology 1). Last, she manifests features of the compulsive shoplifter (Chapter 3, Typology 2). Her case presented multiple clinical challenges, and thus was particularly difficult to treat. It was necessary to penetrate the layers of defense armor that she had shrouded herself in for ego protection for so many years.

In this analysis, it was established that Mrs. Konvitz had become fixated or frozen in the Stage 3 shoplifting level, action/theft. During her shoplifting episodes, it was as if she was outside of herself looking back at a stranger who perpetrated illogical and illegal theft. These were actions she would not have dared to do if she had really thought about it. On several occasions, she drove a long distance from her home, picked stores in shopping malls, and stole inexpensive items with no intent to return them. "I found myself driving in L.A and one time I ended up on Wilshire Boulevard and couldn't remember how I got there or how I got home," she recalled. Her psychological confusion and transient disorientation fits with a dissociative fugue state that has been identified with Stage 3, action/theft. In treatment she saw how this dissociative state (not knowing where she was at the time of her thefts) served as an additional ego defense mechanism protecting her from the self-disclosure that perhaps in the end she was no better than a common thief. At one point, seeking to stop her shoplifting, she was convinced that using Paxil prescribed by her psychiatrist might provide a shortcut, enabling her to correct her direction. During therapy it was explained that there are no shortcuts to stop theft episodes. Her use of medication did not in any way reduce her internal drive to shoplift, nor did it reduce her depression or unhook her from the past. Shortly after entering treatment, Mrs. Konvitz lost confidence in the use of medication and discontinued her misplaced reliance on Paxil.

During her recent theft of corned beef at Cyd's, Mrs. Konvitz had to realize that she would surely be apprehended and punished. The act was irrational and out of control. But based on her irrational thinking, she believed, why should others (her relatives) be punished and even be murdered while she and her parents escaped and were not punished? This reaction is characteristic of survivor guilt patterning as illustrated in Frankl's analysis. Mrs. Konvitz's wish fulfillment, entailing the need to be punished, was satisfied via her commission of multiple high-risk, low-reward theft offenses, ultimately leading to her arrest and then to punishment by the criminal justice system.

To date (October, 2013), Mrs. Konvitz has not been rearrested. She has begun to develop increased insight into her self-defeating, self-punishing brand of masochism and self-generated narcissism, having made the decision to "stop sneaking around and come clean with my family about the dumb things I've done, and that I'm sorry for it and will try to not let it happen again."

Case Disposition

Mrs. Konvitz was arrested on July 6, 2009, for California Penal Code 3488/666, petty theft with a prior by the Santa Barbara Police Department. If she had received the maximum sentence, she could have been remanded to the California Department of Corrections and Rehabilitation (CDCR) for a three-year prison term. Her defense attorney presented my psychological evaluation to the district attorney as a mitigating document and was able to negotiate for her a probationary status for two years combined with two years of mandatory outpatient shoplifting therapy. She is working on disclosing her shoplifting background to her family. She remains in treatment and is no longer shopping at Cyd's.

During one therapy session, she was given the homework assignment of engaging in some form of spontaneous laughter. She reports that she was successful, feeling better than she had in years.

Case 3. Mrs. Chow: When the Cradle Will Rock

Case Introduction

Mrs. Chow's major mental issue was her intense feelings of personal inadequacy. This included a large measure of self-blame for being childless when all her friends and family had children. The initial psychological trigger that led her into and through the four stages of shoplifting was her inability to bear children. This fueled her depression and feelings of inadequacy. As a result, she unconsciously desired to punish herself for a situation she could not control, an obvious irrational belief.

Mrs. Chow is a successful 50-year-old accountant who has operated a large corporate tax practice in San Francisco. Her husband is a highly paid electrical engineer at Google. When queried by the police, Mrs. Chow had no idea why she had stolen innumerable baby and children's clothes; she even dropped several items throughout the store immediately prior to her arrest. Mrs. Chow captured it this way: "Dr. Brady, it was like I wanted to get caught or something. Do you think I have a wish to get arrested and go to jail?" I responded: "Yes, maybe for some reason you wanted to get caught because perhaps you are punishing yourself for certain issues beyond your personal control." It was as if she wanted to be caught, and punished. Mrs. Chow has been motivated by external locus-of-control forces unknown to her for many years as well as by what Cupchik has defined as "substituting for perceived loss" (1997, p. 66). Cupchik terms this type of shoplifter the *atypical offender* (see Chapter 3, Typology 3).

Mrs. Chow also engaged in a type of collecting, but not trophy theft behavior. To some extent, she was also driven to steal by selfish, narcissistic forces. She began shoplifting later in life and progressed through the four shoplifting stages quite quickly. She then could not stop her shoplifting until she was apprehended and received intensive shoplifting treatment. During her fourth or fifth counseling session, she told me how devastating her shoplifting ordeal has been for her and her husband: "This shoplifting situation has gotten out of hand. Never in my life did I ever think I would get caught stealing, particularly at my age." She then asked me if beginning to shoplift at a later age was typical based on what I knew about her mental state. I told her that can only be explained when we both discovered what had driven her to steal in the first place. The reason did surface later, and at that point she began to develop insight into her theft history. She had no initial understanding that her shoplifting was driven by intense feelings of overcompensation and guilt related to her not having children.

Dates of Testing: October 27 and November 2, 2010

Client's Name: Mrs. Malinn Chow

Birthplace: Natong, China

Age: 50

Date of Report: November 10, 2010

Place of Examination: Milpitas Impulse Control Center, 615 S. Main Street, Milpitas, CA 95035

Prior Arrests: None

Criminal Charges: Grand theft

Prior Psychiatric Treatment: San Francisco County Jail,

Psych-Unit

DSM–IV–TR Diagnoses	
Axis I:	300.40 Clinical depression, dysthymic reaction, chronic, moderate to severe at times
Axis II:	71.09 No personality disorder diagnosis
Axis III:	None; no confounding general medical issues
Axis IV:	Psychosocial and environmental problems, occupational concerns, legal concerns
Axis V:	Global Assessment Functioning = 67–75; some issues related to repetitive theft patterning, family issues, in general Mrs. Chow has many positive full-functioning personality traits but needs to remain in treatment.

Mrs. Chow's Personal History

Mrs. Chow had a history of pathological stealing followed by collection. Her theft history, however, has been differentiated from identified hoarding behavior. Mrs. Chow came to my office after her arrest for shoplifting. She was referred to me for a psychological assessment by her defense attorney. Born in Natong, China. Mrs. Chow presently lives in South San Francisco with her husband, Tom. Mrs. Chow understood the serious nature of the criminal charges brought against her. She has two sisters and four young adult nieces who live locally.

Mrs. Chow moved to California about 15 years ago to advance her education and for an improved lifestyle for her and her husband. She is a well-educated woman who attended the University of Texas, where she earned combined degrees in economics and accounting. Over the years, she has remained well motivated, commenting that she was always at the top of her academic class.

Mrs. Chow has no history of any remarkable childhood medical or psychological difficulties, nor has she ever been hospitalized for any psychiatric reasons. She and her husband have been married since 1986. They have no children, although early in their marriage they strongly desired to have their own family in keeping with the Chinese tradition of large families. She had seen a psychiatrist after a prior shoplifting event, and he had treated her for depression. At the time, she hoped and prayed that some type of medication might help her stop shoplifting. Her treating doctor completed a thorough mental status examination, and a psychological history confirmed Mrs. Chow's chronic depression.

She was prescribed Paxil for her depression. She continued to use the Paxil for several months, yet reported to me that while taking Paxil she became anxious, could not focus, had problems with concentration, and experienced an interrupted sleep cycle. In addition to Paxil, she was then prescribed the antianxiety drug Xanax (a benzodiazepine) twice per day. She remained in psychotherapy, reporting that while using these medications she felt even less focused, more anxious, and had more manic symptoms. More germane to her case was her assessment that the frequency of her theft impulses dramatically increased rather than decreased when she combined these two drugs. This combination of antidepressants and tranquilizers may paradoxically potentiate a patient's production of manic symptoms, resulting in an increase rather than a decrease in shoplifting episodes. At a later date in treatment, she was slowly withdrawn from both drugs, contributing to her realization that she could stop stealing without using counterproductive drugs. Sometimes prescription drugs do not reduce the problem, but instead might be the problem.[2]

Mrs. Chow's use of these two medications in combination could have adversely affected her in at least two important ways:

1. Her presenting psychological symptoms of depression did not lift or improve.

2. Her feeling of being out of control, along with enhanced mania, also increased, which in turn increased her theft behaviors as well as her thoughts connected to shoplifting.

It is obvious that taking prescription pills didn't help Mrs. Chow with her multiple issues. It has also been established by some shoplifting treatment specialists that prescribing medications in the absence of some type of face-to-face, consistent talk therapy is not efficacious, and for some patients can even make their condition worse. A review of the shoplifting literature reveals that many therapists who treat shoplifters believe this condition is not a medical condition at all, and like many other psychological conditions, it has become over-medicalized. Therefore, prescribing medications without proper therapy for the shoplifter, can do little to alleviate shoplifters' thoughts and fantasies concerning future theft episodes or deter actual stealing. Presently, there are no Food and Drug Administration–approved medications for the treatment of

---

2   Breggin addresses the issue this way describing the negative effects of Xanax. "Sometimes tranquilizers can ameliorate the symptoms of activation (stimulation) caused by antidepressants, including anxiety and insomnia. Unfortunately, the two don't always balance out, and sometimes the combination makes things worse. Tranquilizers have alcohol-like disinhibiting effects and they can be very spellbinding leading to abuse and addiction. Xanax can cause mania. For some people, mixing antidepressants and tranquilizers exaggerates the disinhibiting, spellbinding effects of both drugs, and results in catastrophic episodes of loss of control" (2008, p. 121).

shoplifting, yet doctors consistently prescribe them for these kinds of cases, yielding consistently poor results.

Psychological Test Results

When Mrs. Chow came to for the initial session, she was visibly nervous, angry, and upset. Her immediate affect was appropriate and not restricted. She was well groomed, looked younger than her stated age of 50, and did not appear to be either overweight or underweight. The results of her mental status examination indicated that Mrs. Chow was oriented in person, place, and time and remained alert, although overtly agitated, during the testing and therapy sessions. She demonstrated a normal gait and was not hyperactive, nor was there any psychomotor retardation patterning noticeable. Her speech was clear and comprehensible, yet at times somewhat pressured.

Moreover, she seemed depressed and remained confused. She was responsive to the psychological tests and remained vigilant. Her thoughts were organized, and there were no tangential or loose associations present. There was no indication of any psychotic process at work here. Mrs. Chow felt embarrassed and was upset that she had to see a doctor to help figure out why she stole. She evidenced this by maintaining poor eye contact and initially stated, "I should be able to figure this out on my own. I've gotten this far in life, so why do I need help now?"

Mrs. Chow has clearly demonstrated a depressive profile, which is confirmed by the results of the testing. Her depression is judged to be moderate, and it meets the necessary *DSM–IV–TR* criteria for dysthymic depressive disorder, 300.40. These testing results, confirmed by both the BDI-II and the CPS self-depreciation scale results, meet the dysthymic criteria.

Mrs. Chow's CPS test results confirm a diagnosis of depression (depression elevated to 87%); scoring high in the depression range. Her depressive symptoms are moderate in degree and chronic in nature to the extent that she reports having had these symptoms for at least 10 years. Mrs. Chow has had recurrent acute depressive symptoms during the past few years, but at the time of her assessment she was not suicidal. She stated, "I guess when I'm depressed I steal as a weird outlet or a way to do something exciting, but I don't know why!" Her depressive syndrome was seen on all the psychological tests. For example, on the BDI-II she endorsed these depressive test items:

- I am sad all the time.

- I have thoughts of killing myself, but I would not carry them out.

Mrs. Chow reflects a low energy level as measured on the CPS, and this is consistent with her long history of depression. Her depressive reaction is seen as contributing to and sustaining her theft behavior. As she stated at the time of her shoplifting and arrest, she was at a "low ebb": "I was just lonely and at the end of my rope when I did it this time. I didn't know why, and I couldn't stop."

Mrs. Chow also reports a long history of poor concentration which negatively affects her work performance. She related that she has had many personal losses or setbacks in her life:

Many times it just seemed like the cards were stacked against me. I asked myself, when was I going to get a break? Then I ended up in jail for this stupid stealing. I even thought about ending it all, but that's not the answer.

These personal losses are seen as psychologically connected to her perception of loss and unfairness at not becoming a mother. She went with some detail into her history of desiring children (a desire shared by her husband, especially when they were first married), describing her inability to conceive.

Her sisters, on the other hand, were able to have children (each has two daughters). This fact had a significant and latent impact on her own personal psychology, contributing to her feelings of loss. The view set forth here is that her shoplifting act is interpreted as overcompensatory behavior, a typical characteristic of shoplifting Stage 2, neutralization. Because Mrs. Chow so strongly desired to be a mother, she stole a wide variety of baby and children's clothes to compensate for her perceived loss. Now at midlife, her feelings of loss over not having her own family have become a painful real for her. Her Stage 2 thoughts represented to a large extent factual fabrication (detailed in Chapter 5)—stating, for example,

> I really question how those children's clothes got into that shopping bag. I guess I could have just picked them up by accident at the same time I lifted up the bag. I wouldn't just do that and leave without paying. I'm not a common thief.

It is clear that her repeated theft of children's clothing held symbolic value for her, and she didn't steal merely for excitement.

Mrs. Chow's shoplifting experience is interpreted as an act of symbolic punishment via getting caught in order to persecute herself for the childless void in her life. She told me a rather bizarre story of stealing a number of infant T-shirts that she rolled up, ostensibly secreting them in her hand. As she proceeded to move throughout the Macy's children's department, she dropped several of the T-shirts onto the floor, thinking that it was accidental. In actuality, she was leaving a clear and obvious trail leading to her ultimate apprehension, arrest, and the subsequent punishment she thought she deserved. Mrs. Chow could provide no rational explanation as to why she would steal infant T-shirts. Later she acknowledged she had previously stolen a large number of both infant and children's clothes and afterward "gave them away, donated some items to Goodwill, and simply tossed some other clothes out."

Mrs. Chow's offense is not viewed as an offense of economic gain, since she had $238 in her possession at the time she stole, as well as five credit cards with verified minimal balances. It was my opinion that psychological variables played a major role in her crime and drove her to this shoplifting of children's clothes. Mrs. Chow, of course, understands the difference between right and wrong but, is not yet able to understand why she committed this act. She is not seen as a malevolent person by any measure, including the results of the CPS. In fact, the opposite appears true. Mrs. Chow has been characterized by her husband as a very giving person who has always put the needs of others, especially her family members, ahead of her own needs. She considers herself to be an honest person. So how—or why—did she get herself arrested for shoplifting?

As mentioned, her CPS antisocial scale falls into the low range, negating the presence of attitudes that promote law-violating acts as measured. Her CPS profile is also dissimilar to the Carlson Type 3, typical property offender, to the extent her score was at the 51st percentile and is 25 points lower than the property offender cutoff score (see Figure 1.1). This is especially true of Mrs. Chow's CPS nonpsychopathic profile, which demonstrates that she does not have a wanton disregard for the rights of others, including their property rights. This testing result strongly suggests that she is not predisposed to criminogenic tendencies other than her identified shoplifting deviance. In other words, her offense is seen as being driven by a constellation of psychological factors, including overcompensation, and not by any measurable economic incentives. She stated, "why in the world would I do this? We've got plenty of money. It's very confusing to both me and my husband, and now I might go to jail." Mrs. Chow's lack of personal control over her behavior was evidenced on the Locus of Control Scale, where her responses indicate that she has had difficulty exerting personal control over her own life.

For example, on one of the items on the Locus of Control Scale, she affirmed, "without the right breaks, one cannot be an effective leader." Mrs. Chow believes that outside influences beyond her control have impacted her life negatively. This is fairly typical of an externalizer or out-of-control shoplifter. On another item, she agreed, "Many times I feel I have little influence over the things that happen to me." And on yet another item, Mrs. Chow's externality is again validated: "Many times we might as well decide what to do by flipping a coin." As she stated, "I could just tell that my life was spinning out of control. I thought the medication the psychiatrist gave me would help, but look at me now. I'm doing lots of strange things recently, and stealing is one of them."

Her BDI-II depression scores suggest that she is depressed, but she is not seen as presently suicidal. Her pervasive depression has been recently exacerbated by her arrest and additionally compounded by her recent citations for two traffic violations: one was for not having her headlights on at night, and one was for running a red light. "I must really be losing my mind to run a red light. I just wasn't thinking clearly! In a short period of time, my whole life is coming apart, and I don't know why." Mrs. Chow's testing results also show that her attention span, concentration level, and capacity to focus have been severely compromised, probably by her depression, and this may help explain her recent traffic violations. Combined with her depression, she has a high anxiety level as measured on the CPS test results, and her depression and anxiety levels have had an impact on her theft offense. Moreover, she reported that she has recently experienced some memory deficits, including short-term memory lapses, that are not traceable to either organic-metabolic or drug or alcohol-related causes. There is no clinical finding of brain damage or organic disease in her case. The frequency and duration of her memory lapses will be monitored.

Because of Mrs. Chow's diagnosed moderate depression she is engaged in shoplifter psychotherapy to help her with her depressive and anxiety-related symptoms. She was very willing to participate in therapy. "I know that I need all the help I can get, and I'll do whatever is necessary not to go to jail and stop shoplifting." Mrs. Chow's shoplifting pattern has been recurrent during the last 10 years, and it is hypothesized here that she was depressed and experiencing anxiety, confusion, and considerable tension prior to her theft acts.

Because she unconsciously probably wanted to be caught and subsequently punished for her illegal behavior, her psychological drive to steal is dissimilar from economically driven theft offenders. Her behavior was not engaged in for money or the gain of merchandise she could use. She has expressed sincere guilt and remorse for what she has done and does not want her stealing to recur. It is my impression that her theft behavior has strong symbolic value related to her guilt for not having children, which ties into her personality structure and weakened self-esteem.

A review of Mrs. Chow's shoplifting history indicated that her inappropriate theft behaviors surfaced only when she felt pressured, depressed, lonely, confused, and personally out of control. The Locus of Control Scale results confirm this clinical impression. Her theft behavior serves as a perfect example of a self-defeating action, which suggests that just prior to her offenses, unconsciously, she wanted to be apprehended and then punished.

Mrs. Chow's theft events are viewed as unconscious, developmentally regressive, and symbolic acts. In our conversations, she expressed guilt and remorse for her thefts: "I really feel terrible that I've done such stupid things. I can't believe that it's me that did this." Mrs. Chow wants to not recidivate and to better understand and explore the psychological connection between her unconscious wish fulfillment (not having children) and her act of shoplifting. She recounted that while shoplifting at Macy's, she experienced confusion and disorientation, which resulted in her wandering throughout the store and stealing a diverse collection of clothing items ranging from children's apparel to infant T-shirts. Additionally, she seemed to have lost track of time during her shoplifting episodes. This is reflective of shoplifting Stage 3, action/theft, when disorientation, confusion, and at times memory lapses, have been reported by shoplifters.

In many ways, Mrs. Chow became frozen in shoplifting Stage 3 because the shoplifting event decreased her depression and temporarily lifted her spirits. She also objectified her theft behavior, stating, "It just wasn't like me to do this. I could possibly see it with someone else, but not for me." As stated in Chapter 5, this sort of statement represents a type of mental deflection of personal responsibility away from herself. Mrs. Chow's initial state of confusion and ennui had led her to make the counterproductive decision to steal. For her, the action/theft stage was just that—it provided action for her similar to the way in which the out-of-control gambler seeks excitement at the gaming table to receive the external excitement supplied in the gambling milieu, where the action is central.

Mrs. Chow's objectifying of her theft episode is also consistent with Stage 3 in that shoplifters often describe their stealing "as if it was done by someone else" Elements of a dissociative fugue state may begin to influence the shoplifter's worldview and self-view. According to the *DSM–IV–TR*, the dissociative fugue state is described as "confusion about personal identity or the assumption of a new identity (partial or complete)" (American Psychiatric Association, 2000). Shoplifters' statements such as "It's not something I would do," "It was like someone else stole it, not me," or "That couldn't have been me" are in concert with Stage 3, shoplifter mental disconnection. Mrs. Chow's mental disconnection, separating herself from the shoplifting episode, is likely not a conscious rationalization or justification for her stealing but can be more accurately psychologically interpreted as an unconscious defense to preserve her sense of self as a noncriminal as opposed to acceptance of an implied status of thief.

Special attention in this case was devoted to Mrs. Chow's choice to steal the five infant T-shirts. Because she and her husband have no children and her nieces are young adults, these items selected for theft are all interpreted as having symbolic psychological value for her. Her unconscious wish fulfillment and distorted reasoning may go something like this: "I am unconsciously acquiring (stealing) clothing for the children that I strongly desired and surely deserved yet never had and, at age 50, I probably will never have." The reality of her situation is that she had no conscious control over this, and it underscores the externalizer condition of driving her theft.

The stolen infant T-shirts have great symbolic value to her despite her having no cognition of why she shoplifted these particular items. It is of particular psychological import to her case that she dropped several items, apparently by accident, constituting a visible trail, suggesting she wanted to be caught and subsequently punished. Mrs. Chow's inexplicable dropping of the clothes she shoplifted, her unconscious setting up of events so that in the end she would indeed be unsuccessful, get caught, and then be punished for her perceived deficiency of not having children.

When considering the facts in Mrs. Chow's case, it is apparent that she is in need of intense, continuous cognitive-behavioral shoplifting psychotherapy and follow-up monitoring to insulate her from the possibility of future theft transgressions. She must be encouraged to develop insight into her own unconscious antecedents of her theft of infant's and children's clothing. As might be anticipated from this discussion, her ego strength as measured on the psychological testing is weak and reverifies her underlying depression.

Mrs. Chow's Case Analysis

For Mrs. Chow, the major psychological trigger that drove her and supported her chronic shoplifting episodes was her unconscious and irrational need for punishment because she was childless. Confirmation of her need for punishment is evidenced from her leaving a clear trail of stolen items on the floor at Macy's. Her unconscious wish for punishment became a self-fulfilling prophecy: she was detained, arrested, and jailed, and in her view, she got the punishment she deserved.

Mrs. Chow was referred by her attorney for a comprehensive psychological assessment—now a fairly typical practice for persons charged with petty theft, shoplifting. Specifically, she was referred to me to determine whether she may have a nondiagnosed underlying personal psychopathology that has fueled her superfluous theft behavior of children's clothing, leading to her arrest. Also, the psychological assessment was conducted to assess her probability to recidivate for this or other theft-related offenses. It was evident from the beginning that her theft of baby clothes represented a channel for her to fill a symbolic void in her life as well as to inappropriately deal with her internal feelings of emptiness and estrangement.

It is conjectured that Mrs. Chow's theft of baby clothes may not be recurrent, but only if she continues to participate in a course of cognitive behavioral psychotherapy with follow-up monitoring. The results of the psychological CPS test indicate strongly that she is capable of exercising control over her own impulses (i.e., shoplifting). Her psychological profile is not in keeping with that of an identified property offender or the Type 3 victim offender as specified on the CPS. Mrs. Chow has agreed to remain in follow-up psychotherapy for as long as it takes to better comprehend how she can insulate herself from reengaging in this self-defeating and illegal behavior in the future. She fully understands that what she has done is not only senseless but also wrong and a violation of her personal moral code.

Mrs. Chow is a highly intelligent woman who, while in continuing treatment, has developed insight into her personal motivational patterns leading to her theft and arrest. She is able to control her impulses, including stealing, if she remains in treatment. She has been referred to a Shoplifters Anonymous group in addition to the individual rational emotive interventions I have provided. If she follows through with the recommendations as outlined, Mrs. Chow should be able to conform her behavior and impulses to the requirements of the law. She has certainly demonstrated that she might be viewed more as a sympathetic figure plagued by her own psychological confusion and unconscious drives to steal than as merely a law transgressor. A jail sentence, even local time, for this fragile, depressed, and confused woman at this point in her life would serve no useful end other than retribution. Society's safety, and Mrs. Chow's personal, needs can both be far better served if she is sentenced to a county probation term combined with at least three years of follow-up shoplifter psychological treatment. If she is given this sentence, she needs to stay committed to the recommendations as presented here or be subjected to a more restrictive sentencing regime, quite possibly involving sentencing to jail.

Case Disposition

Although originally charged with grand theft, the court via her attorney, followed my recommendation. Mrs. Chow was given a probation sentence with a commitment to two years of follow-up psychotherapy. The maximum jail term that could have been applied in her case was a five-year sentence to the California Department of Corrections and Rehabilitation prison (CDCR). Mrs. Chow remains in counseling, attends a support group for shoplifters, and she has not recidivated. She stays out of the local shopping malls.

CHAPTER 6

Case 4. Mrs. Nelson: "Blood, Sweat, and Tears"

Case Introduction

Mrs. Nelson's tragic case involves psychologically traumatic antecedent conditions that have forever changed her life and subsequently triggered her shoplifting pattern. Mrs. Nelson's case involved several secret, unique, and grotesque suicide attempts. Above all, she had to hide or, failing this, disguise her self-destructive proclivities and suicidal attempts from her chronically fault-finding and overtly abusive mother, who has been identified as the major negative source of Mrs. Nelson's personal misery and continued sadness throughout her unhappy life.

Mrs. Nelson is a highly motivated hospital executive. Attempted suicide is traumatic enough, but her unfathomable method of attempted suicide, exsanguination (the withdrawal of her own blood with a hypodermic needle), makes this probably the strangest shoplifting case I have ever encountered. Mrs. Nelson's specific suicide plan and attendant methodology represents a kind of masochistic "death on the installment plan." As she came to my office for her initial psychological assessment, her life was not a pretty picture, and it had not been going well for years.

Mrs. Nelson's description of her emotional feelings subsequent to the shoplifting episodes is consistent with shoplifting Stage 4, postexcitation. In this phase the shoplifter's postshoplifting reaction has a positive influence and may momentarily reduce depression, replacing it with feelings that, in Mrs. Nelson's case, she described as a "rush." This psychological flash point of exhilaration is quickly superseded by bouts of recurring depressive thoughts; thus, the shoplifting trap or cycle begins again. This cycle is explained and graphically illustrated in Chapter 5 in the section titled "The Shoplifting Circle." Mrs. Nelson was not exempt from the pull of this psychological noose.

As Mrs. Nelson noted,
> Shoplifting was the only real life thrill I could get to counteract my
> depression. It helped me lift myself up more than the Paxil I was

prescribed by my doctor. To say the least, my entire life had spun out of control, and in a strange way, my stealing helped me from killing myself, and, in an odd way, it made me less depressed, if that makes any sense.

Mrs. Nelson's case establishes that what appears on the surface to be a simple act of shoplifting is often much more than a routine or random act. The multiple motivations underlying her stealing behavior are quite psychologically complex and not easily comprehended initially by either the patient or the therapist. Why would this highly compensated (around $180,000 annually) hospital administrator steal $3,000 worth of designer clothing and jewelry from Bloomingdale's? At the time of her arrest, she had $200 in cash and seven valid, low-balance credit cards in her purse. To aid in her shoplifting she carried a pocket-sized utility tool that she used to cut off the security tags that were attached to the clothing she stole. She had used this tool with considerable success in past theft episodes, and it had become an integral part of her shoplifting routine.

I saw Mrs. Nelson for a comprehensive psychodiagnostic shoplifting assessment, including psychological testing and mental status examination, and for follow-up outpatient therapy that was later ordered by the San Diego Superior Court judge. She was charged with grand theft. She was forthcoming concerning her offense, and did not attempt to lessen, deny, or rationalize her direct personal involvement. She freely participated in the psychological testing and showed a sincere interest in the results of her evaluation. As she said: "Maybe you can help me find out what's wrong with me so I won't do this again." She understood that a comprehensive report would be forwarded to the court and that it would be used to help explain her case to the judge.

The diagnostic assessment of Mrs. Nelson was done to help the court judge determine the following critical areas:

1. Mrs. Nelson's current mental status and suicide potential (non-theft dynamics) because of her history of suicide attempts.

2. Her probability for future theft behavior or other crimes against property.

3. Whether Mrs. Nelson's psychological test scores are consistent with those of an identified offender on a standardized psychological test (the CPS) and to determine what form of treatment is necessary to deter her from subsequent theft episodes. Because of her multiple diagnoses, including a delusional disorder, her shoplifting condition is probably resistant to a medication-based treatment. There are presently no identifiable psychoactive medications that can diminish the production of delusions. Mrs. Nelson will need a combined regimen of rational emotive behavioral therapy and continuous shoplifter therapy.

Mrs. Nelson's Identifying Information

Dates of Testing: July 2010

Client's Name: Mrs. Sharon (Shari) M. Nelson

Date of Birth: April 11, 1960

Birthplace: Tampa, Florida

Age: 50

Date of Examination: July 15, 2010

Place of Examination: The Professional Psychotherapy Center, 1260, Circle Way, San Diego, CA

Date of Report: August 30, 2010

Criminal Charges: Grand theft

DSM–IV–TR Diagnoses	
Axis I:	297.1 Delusional disorder, unspecified, with bizarre suicidal attempts and paranoid ideations
	296.32 Major Depressive Disorder, Recurrent
Axis II:	Deferred, 799.9* Narcissistic personality disorder, NPD
Axis III:	Deferred, 799.9* Cyclothymic disorder
Axis IV:	Psychosocial stressors: moderate to severe
Axis V:	Global Assessment Functioning = 60; chronic depression, suicidal thoughts, issues related to reality testing, intermittent delusions, masochism , somatic fixation, possible "cutting syndrome."

* Axis II and III diagnoses deferred pending the gathering of additional information.

Mrs. Nelson's Personal History

Mrs. Nelson is a 50-year-old woman who was born in Tampa, Florida. She moved to Southern California with her parents in 1965, when she was five years old. Presently, Mrs. Nelson resides in San Diego. She reports that she has no prior arrests or any criminal convictions. She stated that her mother, age 75, who has been a pernicious, controlling, and negative force in her life, lives 30 miles north of San Diego in Carlsbad. She visits her mother infrequently. Mrs. Nelson is extremely religious. She has been a Catholic all of her life and attended both Catholic high school and a Catholic nursing school in the Los Angeles area. She is highly educated, holding a BSN degree and an MBA in hospital management.

Mrs. Nelson stated that most of her childhood problems were centered on her mother's physical abuse, control, and zealous religiosity, which were continuously thrust upon her. She presents an extensive, high-level work history in the nursing field dating back approximately 20 years. For the past five years she has been in hospital management, a position that requires her to rotate from one facility to another several times a year. Mrs. Nelson told me that she has experienced financial stress because she is the sole support for her family. Mrs. Nelson was married in June 1986 and has two children.

Because of the nature of her job, she had to relocate several times a year. Thus, she lives part-time with her husband, Bill, and children in Ohio. Her husband apparently has remained unemployed for a number of years, making Mrs. Nelson the sole provider for the family. Mrs. Nelson presently has been prescribed Paxil, and Premarin, for various medical and psychiatric conditions, including her recurrent depression. She mentioned that while using Paxil, "I still was stealing, so I guess it didn't help me stop. I don't think it made me feel better either." Mrs. Nelson has had previous psychiatric treatment connected to a suicide attempt in 1984. At that time, she was an employee at San Diego Memorial Hospital. That was when she first devised the plan of extracting her blood to cause her own death. She has a history of other minor medical hospitalizations and treatment for asthma and gastrointestinal problems as well as pneumonia, toxic shock syndrome, a miscarriage, food poisoning, and a car accident that resulted in burns to her arms and upper body. Mrs. Nelson consulted a psychiatrist for medication management for approximately eight months subsequent to her first suicide attempt.

Psychological Test Results

To best evaluate Mrs. Nelson's personality and to assess her probability of engaging in future shoplifting, at the request of the superior court judge she was administered the three psychological tests. Each test measured a different aspect of her personality. Her score on the CPS antisocial tendency (AT) scale was compared with that of an identified property offender, CPS Type 3 profile, and her AT scale was checked for any sign of psychopathy as well as criminal behavior.

Mrs. Nelson came for psychological testing deeply depressed, confused, and distressed. She understood that she was facing serious criminal charges, and she had admitted to a long history of shoplifting. Throughout her initial session, she maintained adequate eye contact, while demonstrating some noticeable inappropriate affect. Her physical appearance was well groomed, not disheveled, and she looked younger than her actual age.

Mrs. Nelson's mood was characterized by extreme dysphoric thinking, and suicidal thoughts were evident. Her speech pattern was marginally organized and somewhat pressured. She was not irritable during our sessions. She was lethargic, but for the most part she remained vigilant throughout the entire assessment process. Her thoughts were not well organized as evidenced by some tangential associations. Many of her perceptions were distorted, although there were no hallucinations or active delusional material present. Because of her history of shoplifting, her impulse control system was assessed as limited, and her judgment was also restricted.

Mrs. Nelson does not meet the diagnostic criteria for kleptomania. Specifically, her theft patterning is inconsistent with Criterion D of the *DSM–IV–TR* classification of kleptomania, which states: "the stealing is not committed to express anger or vengeance" (American Psychiatric Association, 2000). She said that at the time of the crime, she was "hostile, angry, mad , and upset." For many months prior to her recent shoplifting incident at Bloomingdale's, Mrs. Nelson felt angry, upset, and depressed for no identifiable reason. She stated, "I just needed to vent." In a paradoxical way, she felt immediate relief of tension after stealing, although it was clear that she was angry during her shoplifting. This is characteristic of shoplifting Stage 4, postexcitation (discussed in Chapter 5).

She has been clinically diagnosed as experiencing a delusional disorder, unspecified and transient, 297.1 *DSM-IV–TR*. It is hypothesized that her intrusive delusional condition is longstanding and has deep psychological, historical roots in her past, extending back to childhood. Her psychiatric condition is differentially diagnosed from schizoid personality and has not been caused by a chemical imbalance or chemical substances, including alcohol, which she denies using. Her mental condition and constellation of psychiatric symptoms are judged to be chronic and fixed, dating back at least 20 years.

Although her delusional disorder remained pervasive, it was intermittent; thus, she was able to perform her responsibilities as a mother and to work at a high professional level in her management position. Her condition is seen as episodic and differentiated from any other psychotic disorders. Her patient history unveils a long-time personal history of intrusive thoughts, and these troubling delusions were based on irrational ideations, including bizarre suicidal thoughts during the past 10 years that would not go away with medication.

Many of her delusional cognitions have centered on situations involving guilt persecution, death, and the administration of masochistic self-punishment contributing to her earlier self-destructive episodes. Her delusional persecutory feelings derive in large measure from her early childhood, overzealous religious experiences, and relentless moral indoctrination by her mother. Mrs. Nelson told me that since early childhood she has had deep feelings of personal guilt and attendant resentment, combined with anger-hostility patterning, directly aimed at her mother.

Mrs. Nelson is the classic adult personality who, as a child, "could do nothing right." She stated that her mother always told her that she "would never be any good or amount to anything in life, and she meant it." Notwithstanding her mother's constant criticism, in reality she has achieved a great deal in her life. Her primary condemnation source, she stated, derives from her mother's rejection tied to her overly religious devotion to the tenets of Catholicism, fostering guilt and shame involving "many brow-beating episodes as well as repeated physical abuse." This persecutory trend of rejection continued into adulthood, with continuous feelings that she could not do anything right with her life—that is, in her mother's opinion.

The results of Mrs. Nelson's psychological testing, especially on the CPS thought disturbance scale indicate that she has, for a long time, been experiencing profound psychiatric symptoms that are consistent with a *DSM–IV–TR* diagnosis, 297.1, of delusional disorder with paranoid ideations. Her delusional disorder can be subtyped as having suspicious, paranoid, or persecutory features. The central theme of Mrs. Nelson's delusions is the punishment meted out by her mother, including both verbal attacks and physical assaults. According to Mrs. Nelson, her mother subjected her to innumerable verbal and physical assaults, on several occasions severe enough to require Mrs. Nelson's hospitalization. Apparently her father was by nature passive, thereby tacitly consenting to what certainly constituted extreme child abuse. This time of her acute unhappiness is when she first had intrusive suicidal ideations, conceived of as a method to ultimately escape from her mother's wrath. Mrs. Nelson's anger at her mother was redirected away from her mother and became refocused inward in the form of self-destructive thoughts that have remained with her into adulthood.

Mrs. Nelson's psychological testing also confirmed a *DSM–IV–TR* diagnosis of major depressive disorder, 296.33 recurrent. Currently, this condition is stabilized.

Mrs. Nelson's continuing depression was verified on both the CPS and the BDI-II test results. On the CPS, her depression score falls into the 90th percentile (indicating extreme depressive symptoms) associated with severely depressive patients. Mrs. Nelson's BDI-II responses also reflect the depth of her depression:

- I feel my future is hopeless and will only get worse.

- I expect to be punished.

During continuous psychotherapy sessions with her, Mrs. Nelson generated a constant verbal menu of negative, critical self-messages. These were likely derived from her mother's innumerable critical castigations, which have fostered her poor self-concept and weak self-esteem patterning, and which ultimately led to an initial suicide attempt in 1984. The psychological circumstances surrounding her suicide attempt confirm her underlying delusional process associated with death. Prior to 1984, she was experiencing increased feelings of worthlessness, depersonalization, rejection, and depression and had irrational thoughts about dying as well as the instrumentality to kill herself. Because of her strict Catholic background and training, as well as a religious prohibition against suicide, Mrs. Nelson devised a bizarre system to secretly attempt taking her own life. She manifested guilt concerning attempting to end her own life and did not want other people, especially her mother and family, to know that she was seriously considering suicide. She devised a macabre methodology involving exsanguination, the extraction of her blood using hypodermic needles.

This plan additionally involved her donating blood to a local San Diego blood bank in her hospital and then progressively extracting additional blood until she would expire of unknown medical etiology, probably attributable to a type of anemia. Mrs. Nelson told me that she would use a large-millimeter syringe inserted into an area of her forearm where there was ample scar tissue resulting from serious burns she experienced in an earlier car crash; this area provided some camouflage for the needle marks.

She stated that she engaged in multiple exsanguination episodes, probably 50 or more, with the goal of dying from a nonspecific and non-detectable medical etiology. This bizarre plan apparently was driven by guilt and depression, as well as a fear that subsequent to her death she would be seen as a failure who ultimately killed herself and, in death, would also be cast as a "bad person, poor mother, and coward." She told me that she had an extensive history of blood donations at the hospital as well as self-bloodletting, which she used as the vehicle toward slowly and progressively ending her life.

Her thought disorder scale on the CPS supports the assumption that she has had a long history of somatic delusions. Her score indicates that she somaticizes many of her complaints and that she has a preoccupation in general with her body and specifically with her death.

Mrs. Nelson's CPS test score on the antisocial scale was not elevated, suggestive of the view that she does not reflect any overt criminal traits other than her illegal drive toward shoplifting. Her score at the 40th percentile is far below an identified property offender (see Figure 1.1). Specifically, her profile is not consistent with that of the Carlson Type 3 criminal property offender's. It is therefore hypothesized that she has no measurable criminal offender traits besides her history theft crimes.

Her major depressive disorder is chronic and dates back at least 20 years, to when she was first hospitalized for her initial suicide attempt. This condition is differentiated from other depressive disorders such as bipolar disorder, although psychotic depression or bipolar disorders cannot be ruled out. Additionally, diagnoses of narcissistic personality disorder and cyclothymic disorder have been deferred at this time.

Mrs. Nelson does not presently manifest any apparent suicidal ideations, but she has a long history of suicidal thought patterning. Her long history of depression antedates her shoplifting and provides a foundation for her motivation to steal. Mrs. Nelson's very complex mental health history as well as the results of her psychological testing confirmed her extreme depression. For example, on the CPS depression scale, her depression is elevated at the 97th percentile, supporting her pessimistic worldview and intense sense of hopelessness.

Furthermore, it was confirmed from the mental status interview that she has a long history of experiencing a deep sense of guilt for what constitute religiously oriented invasive and intrusive or delusional thoughts. It is this examiner's opinion that both her delusional disorder and her dysthymic condition are tied to her history of chronic shoplifting. Her CPS and BDI-II depression scores establish that she maintains a recurrent preoccupation with themes of self-destruction and death.

It is also evident from the psychological testing results that Mrs. Nelson has almost zero self-concept and very poor functional self-esteem. Part of her depression also derives from her external orientation and feeling of being controlled, especially by her mother, who, since she was a child, constantly hurled invectives at her. On the Locus of Control Scale she presents a profile reflecting a belief in being controlled by outside forces. For instance, she affirmed this item on the scale: "Most people don't realize the extent to which their lives are controlled by chance happenings." Part of her depressive reaction has roots in her long-standing feelings of worthlessness and not being in control of many phases of her life, including providing financial security for her children. This is, of course, a false or irrational belief because she has been and will likely continue to be the only provider for her family.

Mrs. Nelson's reliance on an external locus of control substantiates the position that she is an externalizer shoplifter (Chapter 3, Typology 1). This group of shoplifters is motivated, if not controlled, by outside forces that serve as negative psychological drivers, in most cases lowering their moral threshold against not stealing, resulting in theft. Research results from this study have indicated that the preponderance of shoplifters fall into the externalizer category.

Mrs. Nelson presents a well-documented and long history of debilitating depression, and this depression, combined with her external orientation, contributes to her theft offenses. Why would this highly educated, intelligent, professionally successful woman engage in repeated thefts and at the same time have continued, intrusive ideations of her death? Because her crime was not driven by either need or greed, it is essential to provide a psychological interpretation of the factors that drove her to steal. Her psychological profile on the antisocial index on the CPS test is not consistent with a criminal offender's. Her acting-out impulse potential is also at baseline, and no aggressive or psychopathic tendencies were indicated. Other than intrapunitive drives toward self-punishment and eventual suicide, her theft behavior was not influenced by either a conduct disorder or an antisocial-psychopathic syndrome.

She said that two days prior to the theft and arrest at Bloomingdale's, she had just arrived back in Southern California to assume her responsibilities in senior management at a San Diego hospital. At the time, she was feeling very depressed, alienated, and cut off because she was once again away from her home, husband,

and children. Contributing to her mounting financial stress, Mrs. Nelson's husband has been unemployed for the past 10 years. She had the added financial burden placed upon her of being the sole support for her family of four. Several times she mentioned that she feels somewhat cheated that most of her income goes toward the support of her family, thus preventing her from purchasing any nice items such as clothing and jewelry for herself. Not surprisingly, these are the same types of items she stole from Bloomingdale's. She also told me that prior to her most recent theft, she was at one of the mental low points in her life, although she has had innumerable rough spots in the past. She stated that her feelings of depression and the absence of control that she experienced were similar to those when she engaged in her first suicide attempt in 1984:

> I can remember that time and even the day it happened. My life was pretty much spinning out of control. I was at a real low point in my life, and I didn't know if I wanted to live or die. I didn't know what I was doing. I thought I was going insane.

At the time of the Bloomingdale's offense, it is clear that she had engaged in a type of overcompensatory behavior. She felt that she lacked the ability to buy nice things for herself, and to compensate for this troubling situation she engaged in what I have termed *equalization theft*. The equalizer shoplifter's theft pattern (see Chapter 3, Typology 8) is motivated by retaliatory justification for perceived or real things or even an emotional commodity that has been taken from the shoplifter. During the multiple hours of her theft spree at Bloomingdale's, Mrs. Nelson reported experiencing tremendous feelings of personal excitement, a "rush," and a general feeling approximating "I'm on top of the world." These heightened emotions were palpably inconsistent with her state of depression. Increased euphoric feelings or a rush are typical of the Stage 4 postexcitation phase (see Chapter 5). She also felt as if she had limitless boundaries: "I felt as if I could almost do anything I wanted."

This phase of shoplifting exhilaration is quickly displaced with intense feelings of despondence leading to depression, resulting in the shoplifting cycle beginning again. As Mrs. Nelson describes this transitory emotional shift, "One moment I felt great, and the next moment I felt suicidal. I guess the stealing rush had worn off, and I felt terrible again. It was an old pattern repeating itself over again." These intensely stimulating high sensations were then replaced with equally intense feelings of sadness, depression, and guilt characteristic of the Stage 4 depression phase. I conjectured that, on an unconscious level, she was greatly relieved to be apprehended and arrested. These events served as a functional equivalent necessarily requiring punishment because she had been "a bad and worthless girl," the very thought her mother instilled in her so many years ago that she had not forgotten. This is the same type of condemnation patterning that had been meted out to her by her mother throughout her childhood and into adult life. Now she was doing it to herself. Almost all of Mrs. Nelson's delusional and depressive behavior derives from her maladaptive childhood. Her crime is tied to her sense of overcompensation, equalization, being out of control, and self-generated guilt as well as having a self-punishment component, the latter being a residual from her persecution as a child.

Mrs. Nelson's progression through the four shoplifting stages brought her into Stage 4, postexcitation/depression (see Chapter 5). Behavior indigenous to this stage's two phases typically reflects intense mania followed quickly by a dramatic psychological letdown, including attendant remorse for stealing. Also of significance is that many of her shoplifting episodes were immediately preceded by a number of large compulsive shopping/buying sprees.

She described her shopping compulsivity this way:

At times when I was extremely lonely and away from home on a hospital rotation for sometimes a month at a time, then I would go out on spending sprees. I bought lots of clothing, boots, shoes, and even some fine jewelry for myself. I felt terrible later because I know I should have spent the money on my kids, but I didn't. In a funny way, my excessive buying of clothes gave me some of the same feelings or, I guess you'd call it the rush, I had when I stole from Bloomingdale's.

Mrs. Nelson's compulsive shopping/buying episodes functionally served as a gateway step to her shoplifting. Shoplifting researchers, including Shulman (2004), contend compulsive shopping/buying is a precursor or a gateway behavior into the later world of shoplifting. Compulsive shopping involves uncontrollable, repetitive shopping that produces negative consequences, although at the same time feelings of exhilaration are manifested. Legality is the principle differ-ence between compulsive shopping and shoplifting. Problems with termination and withdrawal are shared by both conditions.

A type of reverse gateway process has also been identified. The recovering shoplifter may be driven toward the secondary act of compulsive shopping/buying simply because it is not illegal yet still produces similar mental effects, including an increase in serotonin and other neurotransmitters. The temptation to move into this track was one that Mrs. Nelson apparently could not resist. Her shoplifting and compulsive shopping/buying also share common features with the binge-spree shoplifting typology (Chapter 3, Typology 7). Mrs. Nelson reports that she engaged in serial thefts, sometimes several times in one day, and had long periods of abstinence, going up to a year without stealing.

Although she was quite candid concerning the facts of her arrest and the actions leading up to it during the initial treatment sessions, she had little conscious idea of the deeply buried reasons why she stole. Initially she guessed it might in some way be connected to her compulsive shopping/buying syndrome. In the final therapeutic anal-ysis, this was only a single component of a more complicated psy-chological constellation. Mrs. Nelson has expressed unqualified guilt and remorse for her offense and noted: "This just can't happen again, or it'll ruin my family and myself." She wanted her sincere remorse conveyed to the court. At the time of the offense, all test results con-firmed that she was out of control, clinically depressed, and suicidal.

Many offenders I have diagnosed have attempted to diminish the psychological causality of their offenses, instead attributing the thefts to personal rationalizations, such as "I needed the clothes," or "Why shouldn't I have nice things, after all, I deserve them?" Even though Mrs. Nelson did not attempt to justify her stealing, many of her inferences tied into her self-centeredness: "I guess that I was only thinking about myself, but why not? I've deprived myself of stuff for years." This statement reflects a subtle narcissistic edge that she maintained during treatment. Conversely, she admitted that she was wrong to steal clothing and jewelry from Bloomingdale's. No matter the psychological causes for her theft at this point, she does not project away responsibility for her shoplifting but accepts what she has done, knowing that it was both legally and morally wrong, and deserving of punishment. She knows the difference between right and wrong, and she desperately desires to get back on the right path via treatment and to stop stealing.

Mrs. Nelson's Case Analysis

It is evident from Mrs. Nelson's story, culminating in her grand theft charge and arrest at Bloomingdale's, that she was driven by her very human "need to actually be somebody" and, perhaps even more important, to possess nice things she had intentionally denied herself. Her identified psychological trigger was her need to overcome a lifetime of negative-oriented statements constantly hurled at her by her oppressive and abusive mother. The mother's negative impact became so haunting and traumatic that Mrs. Nelson planned to kill herself by extracting her own blood to escape from her mother's echoing voice and cover up the fact that, in the end, she was a thief.

The perceptive attorney representing her in this case, cognizant of the fact that Mrs. Nelson had multiple mental issues, desired to focus on the central issue—Mrs. Nelson's mental status and how it negatively impacted her, leading to her shoplifting—and then present the results to the court as ordered. This question was before the court: Were there psychological mitigating factors in Mrs. Nelson's history that underscored the theft offense for which she is charged?

The results of the psychological testing and interviews indicated that Mrs. Nelson's thoughts are, at times, permeated by a delusional process. Correspondingly, she has been diagnosed with *DSM–IV–TR*

WHY RICH WOMEN SHOPLIFT - WHEN THEY HAVE IT ALL!

297.1, delusional disorder with both somatic and suicidal persecutory identifiers. Mrs. Nelson's psychiatric conditions, including depression and external locus of control, help explain why she engaged in an irrational and illegal act, shoplifting at Bloomingdale's. Her secondary diagnosis of major depressive disorder is also tied to her delusional disorder, further contributing to her shoplifting. Her depressive condition remains chronic, severe, and recurrent and includes self-destructive ideations.

Mrs. Nelson's delusional and depressive conditions were verified from her history and on the CPS and BDI-II depression test results. These patterns confirm that she has a thought system that is vulnerable to intrusive external and irrational reasoning. Her Locus of Control Scale scores indicate that she feels controlled by external forces, which have fueled her depression and subsequent shoplifting. Many of her delusional ideations are tied to her sense of guilt, persecution and self-destructiveness.

On some level, Mrs. Nelson experiences sadness and guilt because she perceives she has abandoned her family due to her work commitments. Quite paradoxically, however, she is the sole support for the family. There is no doubt that at the time of her offense, she was delusional, depressed, out of control, and generally psychologically confused. Mrs. Nelson has presented no reasonable conscious explanation as to why she engaged in the theft at Bloomingdale's or, any of her other previous thefts. The following three psychological reasons for her stealing are put forth:

1. At the time of the offense, she was experiencing an altered-delusional thought process negatively affecting her judgment and subsequent actions.

2. She was seriously, clinically depressed.

3. She unconsciously desired to be apprehended for her theft in order to be punished for her sense of guilt associated with being a perceived failure (in her mother's mind) and being away from her family for long periods of time.

Psychologically, her shoplifting act at Bloomingdale's on April 30, 2010, is interpreted symbolically as a gesture eliciting punishment for her perceived lifelong "sins"; the long-term Catholicism thrust upon her by her mother historically has supported her feelings of guilt and personal shame. Her overwhelming sense of guilt ties into her outré suicidal attempt in 1984, when she methodically began to extract her own blood, filling infant formula bottles with it for later disposal in a parking lot dumpster. Her convoluted goal related to this self-destructive process was to die quietly and obscure the true medical cause of her death.

To a large extent, her fear of guilt associated with people knowing that she was actively suicidal was so powerful that she did not want her family to know how she died—even after she was dead! Thus, she feared guilt and public exposure more than death itself. Mrs. Nelson was additionally concerned with a religious dilemma in the Catholic faith—it's deemed a mortal sin to commit suicide. Therefore, she was faced with a number of equally bad choices. For at least 20 years, she has fought off her emerging mental demons associated with thoughts of guilt and death. I have seen many patients who have committed similar irrational acts fueled by false ideations and delusional thoughts.

Subsequent to her arrest, she no doubt believed unconsciously that she got what was coming to her. Not only was she being punished for her thefts but also for her perceived sense of the sin connected to her thoughts and acts of self-destruction. The road to moral redemption for Mrs. Nelson appeared to be a long and twisting one. Therefore, in agreement with her self-critical statements, she thought she deserved to be punished for her misdeeds and ultimately to perish by her own hand. In her mind, at the time she was arrested, she paradoxically interpreted what had happened to her as representing a positive outcome and said, "I deserve to either die or be seriously punished for my whole life of sins." After her arrest, she manifested sincere remorse for her illegal act, and, ultimately, she sought redemption.

In my professional judgment, Mrs. Nelson is to be viewed as a very complicated psychiatric patient rather than as an ordinary thief or criminal as depicted in the police report. She was provided with a rational emotive behavior therapy framework. This form of intervention improved her sense of self-worth and also helped decondition the negative impact of many years of living while being denigrated by her unsympathetic, if not cruel, mother. Mrs. Nelson's attorney, who presented my report to the court, succeeded in avoiding a prison sentence for his client. Obviously, any prison time would have served no useful purpose for her or society, other than retribution. Mrs. Nelson's subsequent treatment plan did not include the use of Paxil or any other dangerous antidepressants. [3]

Case Disposition

Although Mrs. Nelson was charged with grand theft for shoplifting almost $3,000 in designer merchandise from a Bloomingdale's store in San Diego, the superior court judge and the district attorney, in their collective wisdom, agreed with the conclusions in my psychological report that she did not represent a major threat to recidivate if she remained in therapy. She entered a guilty plea, demonstrating sincere remorse for her theft. The judge agreed that Mrs. Nelson was in need of continued, extended psychological care and not jail—at least not at this time. In concert with this recommendation, she was sentenced to six months of weekend confinement, three years of probation, and two years of compulsory outpatient shoplifter therapy. However, if Mrs. Nelson fails to comply with these sentencing mandates to remain in therapy, she will be directly remanded back into custody and be committed to the California Department of Corrections and Rehabilitation (CDCR) or a three-year sentence. As of September 2013, she has stayed in rational cognitive-behavioral therapy and

---

3   A more detailed description of Mrs. Nelson's treatment using rational emotive cognitive behavioral therapy is presented in my forthcoming books - *Treatment for Rich Women Who Shoplift* and *Klepto-Bismo: The Case Against Using Drugs with Shoplifters*(2014). Breggin(2008, p.271) points out the dangers of using psychoactive medications:

"Drugs are gross intrussions into an infinitely complex and largely unexplored biological system called the brain, so that any given drug ' treatment' is bound to impair normal functioning."

has neither recidivated for shoplifting nor further engaged in compulsive buying/shopping. Since commencing this treatment, she has progressively withdrawn from the use of medications, seeing perhaps for the first time in a long while a bright light at the end of a very long tunnel.

Chapter 6 References

American Psychiatric Association. (2000) *Diagnostic and statistical manual of mental disorders* (4th ed., text rev. Washington, DC: Author.

Breggin, P. (2008). *Medication madness*. New York: St. Martin's Griffin.

Cupchik, W. (1997). *Why honest people shoplift or commit other acts of theft*. Toronto: Tagami Communications.

Frankl, V. E. (1962). *Man's search for meaning*. Boston: Beacon Press.

Grant, J. E. & Kim, S. W. (2003). *Stop me because I can't stop myself: Taking control of impulsive behavior*. New York: McGraw-Hill.

Katz, J. (1988). *Seductions of crime*. New York: Basic Books.

Lorand, S. (1950). *Clinical studies in psychoanalysis*. New York: International Universities Press, Inc.

Peirce, P. (2010, December 31). Shoplifting suspects grabbed filet mignons, Murrysville Police say. *Pittsburgh Tribune Review*. Retrieved, January 18, 2012, from http://www.pittsburghlive.com/x/pittsburghtrib/news/-716043.html

Shteir, R. (2011). *The steal: A cultural history of shoplifting*. New York: Penguin Press.

Shulman, T. D. (2004). *Something for nothing: Shoplifting addiction and recovery*. West Conshohocken, PA: Infinity Publishing.

CHAPTER 7

CONCLUSION AND RESULTS: WHAT HAVE WE LEARNED?

As one reads of the tragic encounters with psychiatry of such people as James Forrestal, Marilyn Monroe, or Ernest Hemingway, one gains the impression that they felt demeaned and deeply hurt by the psychiatric indignities inflicted on them and that as a result of those experiences they were even more desperately driven to suicide.

—THOMAS SZASZ, *THE THEOLOGY OF MEDICINE*, 1977

Part I: They Spoke, I Listened

I am glad I followed the sound advice of my professional colleagues, friends and, of course, family members who encouraged me to do this research and chronicle these shoplifting cases, ultimately putting them into book form. Without their direct impetus, these valuable cases may have been relegated to a dusty file cabinet somewhere in my office. Breathing new life into these stories, of course, was my task; however, most of the work and the real credit must be attributed to the many shoplifting patients themselves, whose varied stories are at times both humorous and tragic. In the end, they are the building blocks of this book.

Shoplifting, as we have seen continuously throughout these pages, is not a unitary psychological concept, nor can it be. It cannot be disconnected from the innumerable psychosocial explanatory variables that affect it. The cases investigated in this book exhibit elements of negative impulse control, locus-of-control dysfunction (externality), poor moral judgment, depression, overcompensation, fetishism, postictal epileptic-type symptoms, and attempted suicide attempt via exsanguination. There is scant evidence that shoplifters are directly affected or driven to steal because of any type of vague biochemical imbalances. However, shoplifters' behaviors and their overt theft actions cannot be interpreted in isolation without a careful examination and quantification of the many psychosocial variables affecting their lives and the motivational components that drive them, sometimes beyond the point of no return.

The strange, sad story of Mrs. Nelson just told (Chapter 6, Case 4) is a case in point because she was literally driven to the edge of the precipice and sought to commit suicide on the installment plan via long-term withdrawal of her blood, a little at a time. Similarly, Mrs. Konvitz's doleful story (Chapter 6, Case 2) of her Jewish relatives' extermination at the Bergen-Belsen concentration camp during World War II precipitated her ignominious theft of one and a half pounds of corned beef from an upscale deli. She had been previously arrested multiple times for shoplifting, yet she had not been accurately diagnosed or tested, nor was she professionally treated for her condition.

CHAPTER 7

A Final Analysis—A Glance Back

Most shoplifting experts are starting to realize the importance of using psychological assessment tools to accurately and creditably diagnose shoplifters on the basis of evidence. The results reported in this book are in accord with the stated goals of this study. The shoplifter stories told throughout these pages—ones that I have personally diagnosed, assessed, and treated—have recorded some measurable past psychological traumas negatively impacting their lives. The results of this study confirm that the four shoplifters profiled demonstrate:

1. A reliance on an external locus of control—that is, they feel they are being pushed around by outside forces over which they have little or no control over. Being out of control was measured using the Rotter Locus of Control Scale.

2. They are clinically depressed. Their depression was clinically assessed using the BDI-II rather than merely assuming it from a five-minute mental status examination conducted in a psychiatrist's office. The shoplifters' depression was also measured on the CPS depression, self-depreciation scale.

3. They move through at least four demarcated stages of a shoplifting zone: anticipation/readiness; neutralization—moral decision versus moral erosion; action/theft; and postexcitation/depression.

4. That they are not predisposed to reflecting criminal personality traits in addition to their shoplifting behaviors. This goal or assumption was tested and confirmed using the CPS, particularly the results from the CPS antisocial tendency scale.

Of course much additional research is necessary to assess shoplifters. It should be conducted using both psychological testing as well as the in-depth interview study method. Both methods were used in this study. The question of why people risk it all by shoplifting needs to be better researched on all levels and employing multiple methods.

It is true that it is a difficult task to extrapolate conclusions from these four shoplifting cases to the larger universe of all shoplifting cases. The goal of this study was to present in-depth narrative analyses of these four shoplifters to determine a reliable diagnosis rather than merely recounting snippets of conversations with them. It should be pointed out that one of the most enduring psychological theories ever formulated was developed using only a handful of in-depth clinical cases, and, amazingly enough, it was accomplished by one person. The theory is psychoanalysis, and its creator was Sigmund Freud.

The detailed narrative case studies, as presented in this book, provide rich and copious clinical information and are one psychological method psychologists can use in the future to construct a more explanatory shoplifting theory. In this book, it has been established that the four shoplifters discussed in these pages are indeed out of control as measured by the Rotter Locus of Control Scale. Would it have been preferable to include perhaps 50 similar shoplifting cases and tested them? The answer certainly is yes; however, these four cases constitute a favorable beginning for the in-depth case analysis and assessment approach to a better understanding of shoplifting. The Freud reference is used to exemplify the impact just a few detailed cases can have in understanding a certain subject matter. In his case, it was psychoanalysis; in this case, it is shoplifting.

A considerable amount of space in this book has been devoted to the identification of the shoplifter stages comprising what I have labeled the shoplifting *zone*. For more than 25 years, I have been both intrigued and perplexed by the underlying psychodynamics of the shoplifter, not so much in a legal sense, because they all steal, but, more specifically, I posed this question: Are there identifiable progressive stages in the shoplifting process? To help explain this process, the shoplifting zone has been identified and then subdivided into four stages. These four sometimes-overlapping stages include: (1) anticipation/readiness, (2) neutralization–decision making, (3) action/theft, and (4) postexcitation/depression. Stage 4 has been further subdivided into two distinct after-theft phases, as noted: (1) postexcitation and (2) depression. As we have seen, these components of Stage 4 are characterized by very different behavioral identifiers.

These stage definitions comprising the shoplifting zone derive from my observation of and research into the shoplifter's criminal decision-making process as well as from the many descriptions shoplifters have provided to me over the years concerning their individual experiences as they progressively entered into the treacherous world of theft. These four stages represent a unique view into the motivation of the shoplifter—a view not addressed previously by shoplifting researchers.

Furthermore, no well-controlled psychological studies using reliable and valid testing have accurately assessed shoplifter recidivism, despite the fact that such recidivism has one of the highest rates of all property offenses. And no psychological studies have tracked shoplifters through these troubling stages comprising the shoplifting zone. I have offered that the reason for the high rates of repeat shoplifting is tied to the shoplifter becoming addicted and trapped in one or more of the four stages. This zone provides intrinsic psychological rewards and more or less freezes the shoplifter into the self-defeating *shoplifting circle.*

Until additional data becomes available concerning the negative constellation of influences experienced by shoplifters, I contend that we will continue to see shoplifter recidivism rates climb. To unlock the progressive and transitional shoplifting stages representing a unique view into the operational dynamics of shoplifting, two further empirical research areas are deserving of attention:

1. A more in-depth, longitudinal study into the shoplifter's criminal and moral decision-making process.

2. An examination of those factors that facilitate the shoplifter's mental mitigation, paving the way for morally unrestrained stealing.

These stages leading into and through the shoplifting zone represent, for the most part, uncharted waters. No prior investigations have been designed to elucidate the phases involved in the shoplifting sequence of events. These psychosocial stages culminate with a shoplifter first going through a moral and ethical crisis—to steal or not to steal? And then, no doubt, contrary to their own best self-interests, they elect to commit a criminal act. A review of the academic shoplifting literature prior to commencing this study evidenced very limited examination of the shoplifting experience per se; however, hundreds of often vivid anecdotal descriptions of shoplifter behaviors are recounted to counselors and journalists interested in the subject.

In this book, I have striven to show that a person's progression through the four stages of shoplifting is emotionally traumatic, especially because the mental elements in the shoplifting chain involve a perceptual reshaping of the shoplifter's self-identity from a law-abiding, nontheft identity to an identity as a shoplifter. The Rotter Locus of Control Scale scores for individuals who make this transition demonstrate the degree to which they were out of personal control at the time they made the choice to steal. In this process, shoplifters become reluctant converts to a new way of perceiving themselves and their world, controlled by intrusive negative thoughts and actions and increasing the probability that they will continue to commit theft offenses some time in the future.

It was demonstrated through the interpretation of the four cases in this study that at some point shoplifters gradually begin to surrender their conforming, noncriminal identities and progressively begin to accept a reformatted self-image that promotes deviant theft behaviors. They engage in a particular type of self-image conversion fueled by the generation of negative thoughts that, for the most part, they are powerless to comprehend, control, or stop. As this deviant conversion commences, the career shoplifter becomes disillusioned with his or her old self-image, carrying with it the strict observance of society's laws against stealing. Subtly, he or she converts to or accepts law-violating behaviors, including multiple acts of theft, thereby replacing their original prolaw beliefs with newly formulated ones that are consistent with law violation. This disillusionment with laws and perhaps with society at large sets the shoplifter up for more negative theft episodes.

The results of this study support the supposition that the newly acquired deviant beliefs are compatible with thought patterns characterized by an external locus of control. Previous research has demonstrated that persons who show external scores on the locus of control scale are more likely to have impulse control problems, commit crimes, abuse alcohol, take drugs, and engage in multiple acts of shoplifting (Brady, 1990).

For a large percentage of shoplifters, these newly adopted negative, external beliefs serve as pervasive forces that produce psychological confusion and often enhance shoplifter resentment, as in," having always been a nice conformist, now I have crossed the line and see what I have done to myself," as one shoplifter put it. Toch (1965) comments on this deviant personal disillusionment and states that, once disillusioned, the person "becomes actively involved in life situations [theft in this case] for which he has been ill-prepared by socialization" (p. 128).

Toch goes on to describe the deviant's disillusioned belief system, which can easily be applied to shoplifters, by stressing the perceived discrepancy between what a person should do based on his or her moral belief system versus what he or she actually does. This conflict between the acquired deviant belief system and the original nondeviant one is characterized with new beliefs that are:

a. Premised on distortions of social reality.

b. Nonresponsive to personal needs.

c. Insufficiently flexible to accommodate emergent needs.

d. Challenging to existing interpretations of society.

e. Frustrating to existing personal needs.

f. Designed to create new need systems.

g. Representative of problems that differ from conventional ones.

h. Intensely concerned with applying their acquired beliefs.

i. Premised on disillusionments from the past. Disillusionment is involved at all levels of the shoplifter's identity change.

j. Overcompensation for past deviant acts (p.128).

Shoplifter Disillusionment

Direct proof of this shoplifter disillusionment as described by Toch is consistently available once the shoplifter enters treatment and begins to disclose his or her history. Consider the statements in Table 7.1 made by shoplifters who have undergone this deviant identity surrender and attendant transformation.

Table 7.1. Shoplifter Disillusionment Statements

Statements	Case
1. "My whole life was changing, and I didn't like where it was going."	Mrs. Nelson, Case 4
2. "Never in a million years did I expect this to happen to me."	Mrs. Konvitz, Case 2
3. "I had zero idea how much I changed, to the point it [shoplifting] was easy for me."	Mrs. Chow, Case 3
4. "All of a sudden I couldn't tell the good me from the bad me."	Mrs. Daio, Case 1

5. "Everyone in my family has noticed how negative I got after my arrest."	Mrs. Konvitz, Case 2
6. "I really didn't know when I got this bad attitude, but I don't like it because it's just not like me."	Mrs. Konvitz, Case 2
7. "I got so unbelievably out of control" I didn't know if I wanted to live or not."	Mrs. Nelson, Case 4
8. "I became a nonconformist, and then stealing the purses was easy."	Mrs. Daio, Case 1

It is my professional position that the majority of shoplifters undergo this disillusionment via thought realignment. The gradual acceptance of this new self-image (i.e., pro–law violation) makes the shoplifters' acknowledgment of their antisocial theft patterning easy to accept, adapting it into a new lifestyle marked by an increase in legal transgressions. All four cases described in this book represent serial offenders who have experienced this process of being reformulated.

What Can Be Done About Shoplifting?

From an examination of previous research, it became apparent that there is a lot of work remaining both to reduce the incidence of shoplifting for first-time offenders and reduce the high recidivism rates for serial shoplifters. Up to eighty percent of all offenders repeat their thefts either on a continuous or intermittent basis until ultimately they are caught, sometimes resulting in jail sentences. Arrest and periods of incarceration have historically proven to be ineffective deterrents to shoplifters. Most shoplifting researchers, including myself, have called for further exploration into the confusing personality dynamics of the shoplifter as one key to reducing shoplifter recidivism.

One proven area of interest is to encourage more in-depth study of the relationship between the locus-of-control variable and the shoplifting phenomenon. It has been established from the results in this study that shoplifters are influenced or directed by external control factors. This variable appears to be an explanatory, causative psychological construct notwithstanding the fact that innumerable other unresearched psychological reasons in addition to external locus of control may be directly affecting career shoplifters. For example, this study also confirmed, using two psychological tests, that most shoplifters reflect high levels of clinical depression.

Whether shoplifters present other quantifiable criminogenic personality traits or show crossover deviant patterns was also addressed. It was established that the shoplifters in this sample in general do not present evidence of serious criminal traits other than their identified theft pathology. This was established by the direct measurement of antisocial tendencies and psychopathy levels. In a related study, Moore (1983) also found little evidence that any serious psychopathological conditions played a significant role or could be identified as a direct pathway to shoplifting. The results in this study support Moore's earlier findings.

Additionally, and somewhat surprisingly, the four shoplifting patients I have analyzed here were certainly financially secure, if not wealthy by today's standards. They had an average net worth of nearly $2 million. Because of this secure financial status, the act of shoplifting has not proven to be indigenous to any specific social class. Shoplifting, then, for the tested sample appears to be unrelated to the amount of disposable income available to a shoplifter at the time she made the choice to steal, nor is it tied to financial net worth (Kraut, 1976). Each of the four shoplifters highlighted here were definitely not driven by economic gain; therefore, psychological pathways to help explain their stealing were sought out and assessed.

It is essential that society become involved in the increasing problem of shoplifting, which reportedly costs retailers more than $20 billion in net losses per year, an amount that has risen dramatically during the past decade. Notably, these reported financial losses are approximately equal to the amount paid for all methods of theft detection, security, and prevention. This is a good example of how merely throwing money at a complicated social-psychological problem does not provide a solution. Arrest records examined from Santa Clara County, California, indicate that the preponderance of shoplifting crimes are committed by recidivists.

As a number of attorneys have strongly suggested, there is a real need for every shoplifter to have a complete psychological assessment to determine the hidden psychological drivers or triggers that motivate this crime. I suspect that if accused shoplifters, including the well-publicized celebrity cases, were comprehensively evaluated by psychologists, that millions of dollars in defense and court costs could be saved and that judicial outcomes could mirror the court sentences meted out in the four cases elaborated here. It is worth reiterating, from Chapter 1, San Jose–based criminal lawyer William Chestnut's words regarding the Importance of conducting a comprehensive shoplifter assessment with his clients: "It's been my experience with almost all of my shoplifting, petty theft cases that a psychological assessment can make all the difference with the judicial outcome for these defendants" (2013).

This study has taken a special look at the social-psychological categorization of shoplifters, developing sixteen shoplifter typologies. Shoplifting researchers in future investigations will no doubt identify psychological evidence to support the inclusion of new or modified typologies not described here. However, this research has served to expand the identifiable shoplifter typologies to 16 from the previous six or seven. Of particular note is the inclusion of Typology 6, the trophy-collector shoplifter. My colleagues and I are finding more shoplifters referred for evaluations that fit into this new typology. Arrest records also indicate that many of today's shoplifters are stealing high-value items not for their everyday utilitarian purposes but for psychological gain. They admire these objects at a later date, in some cases, derive from them direct sexual pleasure similar to what they would for a fetish, a type of sexual fixation.

These sexual attachments to inanimate objects are more frequently reported and mostly occur during the Stage 4 postexcitation phase of the shoplifting process. Mrs. Daio's (Chapter 6, Case 1) case is a good example of this phenomenon, as she told me that by holding and caressing her stolen purses she began immediately to experience mental stimulation accompanied by an increase in her libidinous impulses and a noticeable lifting of her depression. Her particular type of offense patterning underscores just how complicated and varied shoplifters' motivations, including sexual payoffs, are. Truly one size does not fit all when examining these motivations and shoplifters' idiosyncratic psychological reward systems.

Postarrest Shoplifter Syndrome, PASS

Although there have been many detailed descriptions of shoplifters' behavior, usually provided by the police or paramedics, few attempts have been made to explain or interpret the often bizarre behaviors exhibited by shoplifters at the point of their arrest. Furthermore, a review of the shoplifting literature reveals that no attention has been directed to an interpretation of the shoplifter's behavioral symptoms immediately after his or her arrest.

It has been estimated that approximately 1% of shoplifters apprehended by store security personnel or police exacerbate their already bad situation by making an ill-conceived decision to attempt to elude going to jail. Typically, they run from the scene of the shoplifting to their cars and then drive away. Routinely, these attempted escapes involve a police chase resulting in the shoplifter's ultimate arrest. After their arrests, a large percentage of these shoplifters begin to manifest varied psychological symptoms that appear to be similar to the ones experienced by certain seizure patients.

After personally interviewing shoplifters who elected to make a run for it and in consultation with various paramedics who have witnessed the odd behavior of this subset of shoplifters, I have labeled this phenomenon *postarrest shoplifter syndrome*, or PASS. In some shoplifter cases, the shoplifters reported psychological and physical symptoms mimicking the medically-influenced symptomatology usually associated with a specific set of epileptic symptoms, the post-ictal state. These symptoms tied to PASS are listed as follows: feeling out of control, fugue symptoms, confusion, anger, amnesia, visual attention deficit, hypomanic behavior, delusions/hallucinations, childlike actions, feelings of invincibility, altered states of consciousness, memory lapses, disorientation, mental confusion, incontinence, headaches, suspiciousness, and unexplained aggression.

How We Can Change Things: The DSM Doesn't Work for Shoplifter Diagnosis!

The issue concerning the applicability (or nonapplicability) of the current diagnosis of kleptomania in the American Psychiatric Association (2000) *Diagnostic and Statistical Manual of Mental Disorders* (4th ed., text rev.) *DSM–IV–TR* is an important one to address. In Chapter 2, I made the case for modifying, changing, or perhaps eliminating entirely this diagnostic category from inclusion in future DSM's (DSM-5-TR?). Many peer-reviewed investigations into the nonspecificity of the diagnosis of kleptomania as currently (2012) defined in the *DSM–IV–TR* strongly suggest that it has outlived whatever value it may have once had. Extending back more than 40 years, researchers and practicing clinicians began to question the validity of this ill-defined category that does not accurately capture the exact psychological state of the theft offender's behaviors, especially for the nonkleptomaniacal shoplifter, who represents 95% of cases.

This questioning of the kleptomania diagnosis was exemplified by Cameron's pioneering study of shoplifting (1964 p.117), in which she put forth the notion that *kleptomania* is merely a descriptive term that does not adequately explain why most people engage in theft offenses. Concerning her own research in Chicago, she states: "At this point it seems worthless to discuss a term I have not found necessary or useful to employ often in this study, kleptomania." Kleptomania does represent a guilt-eliciting event that carries with it a damaging social stigma, but it continues as a meaningless category that is not explanatory to clinicians who are forced to use it. At one time, kleptomania was the only category professionals had available to them to diagnose people who steal. It's different today.

Moving forward in time, I have emphasized that the real problem with the present use of the *DSM–IV–TR* diagnosis of kleptomania is that there is clinical evidence that it continues to fail to accurately diagnose up to 95% of people who steal. In large measure, this is true because the shoplifter's specific psychological behaviors do not consistently fit within this *DSM–IV–TR* diagnostic category of kleptomania. Obviously, this is not a positive finding, nor are there many good reasons to continue its use except perhaps for those very few cases where all the specific criteria are met, accounting for perhaps 3–5% of theft offenders.

When diagnosing theft violators, in lieu of the *DSM–IV–TR* kleptomania category 312.32, substitute impulse control disorder, not otherwise specified, 312.30. This diagnosis is able to better capture the recurrent, maladaptive failure to resist stealing that is characterized by, but not limited to, the following features:

a. Preoccupation with shoplifting

b. Unsuccessful efforts to stop

c. Using shoplifting as an escape device

d. Repeat their thefts, even when caught

e. Jeopardizing everything to steal

f. Shoplifting equals excitement

g. Irritability, anger, and hostility

h. Feeling helpless to stop; feeling controlled by external factors

i. Lying about or covering up shoplifting events

j. Sudden gratification and mood elevation after the shoplifting episode

k. The use of "synthetic reasoning"(see Chapter 5, Synthetic Reasoning)

Part II: Case Results

In this study I have put forth the first step toward a unified psychosocial theory to explain shoplifter psychodynamics. The issue of shoplifter treatment presents questions about which treatments work and which treatments don't. There are even questions about whether some interventions actually exacerbate shoplifter symptoms, making them resistant to behavioral change. Prior to conducting this study, the general impression I had of shoplifters was that because of their weak impulses they had to be out of control, although somehow direct measurement of this control factor has eluded most previous researchers. The results presented herein confirm that shoplifters as assessed on the Rotter Locus of Control Scale reflect highly external scores, confirming that, at least in one area, shoplifting, they demonstrate weak impulse control.

Although innumerable attempts have been made to describe and diagnose shoplifters, no serious studies have addressed an important missing aspect: can we identify or somehow classify the psychological steps or stages that a shoplifter passes through on the way to becoming a career shoplifter? One goal was to identify and describe the sequence of the shoplifting stages comprising what I call *the shoplifting zone.*

The results of this study strongly suggest that shoplifters do not necessarily demonstrate psychopathic, antisocial, or criminogenic tendencies in addition to their identified theft actions. This variable was assessed using the Carlson Psychological Survey (Carlson, 1982), especially the Type 3 property offender profile (see Figure 1.1). Carlson describes this type of person as "immature and rebellious but not decidedly antisocial...their offenses are generally unplanned, impulsive reactions to situations with little financial gain" (Carlson, 1982, p.11**).**

None of the four cases had percentile ranks above 50% on the CPS antisocial tendency scale, whereas Type 3 property offenders typically score in a range between 75% and 99%. This finding supports the position that shoplifters, as assessed in this study using this one measure, do not present additional criminogenic conditions such as psychopathy or antisocial tendencies beyond stealing.

The four shoplifters scored as highly external, with an average external score of 17.8 on the IE scale, generally affirming that they perceived their lives were directed by chance, fate, luck, fortuitousness, "powerful others," or additional vaguely defined outside factors. This finding confirms the significance of the externalizer shoplifter classification (Chapter 3, Typology 1). For instance, the four shoplifters assessed in this study responded positively to statements indicating an external locus of control.

In addition to the Rotter Locus of Control Scale, each shoplifter was given the Beck Depression Inventory II to tap depressive symptoms. The results demonstrate that shoplifters have a wide variety of serious depressive symptoms ranging from moderate depression to severe suicidal depression. Each shoplifter scored in the high depression range of the BDI-II.

Shoplifter depression was additionally measured using the CPS depression, self-depreciation scale. All four shoplifters tested had scores consistently within the depressive range, confirming that goal number two—to determine whether shoplifters reflect negative self-identities (depression)—was achieved.

More Work Remaining

It is obvious that much more research is needed to both reduce the incidence of shoplifting for first-time offenders and impact the alarmingly high recidivism rates for serial shoplifters. As stated, a large percentage of all offenders repeat their thefts over and over again until ultimately they are caught. It is only then that they come to my attention.

When apprehended and arrested, the next step for shoplifters involves the adjudication of their cases. If they are fortunate, as in the four cases described in this book, treatment hopefully can be the last stop for them to get back on the path to living without stealing.

The goal of *Why Rich Women Shoplift—When They Have It All!* is to present psychosocial information concerning the psychology of the shoplifter, including the regressive shoplifter zones. Specifically, the aim of this book has been to help explain the multiple pathways leading to the shoplifting event. The current study does not specifically address the dynamics of shoplifter treatment and recovery; however, the explication of how shoplifters become societal outsiders goes hand in hand with the principles of shoplifter treatment, recovery, and change.

The key for successful shoplifting recovery is the development of personal insight and deconditioning, often challenging the illogical thoughts supporting the shoplifter's motivational and denial systems. These denial systems are recurrent patterns using a variety of unconscious defense mechanisms. For example, the neutralization process (Stage 2, described in Chapter 5) is characterized by a twisting and convoluted series of psychological steps whereby shoplifters begin to negate or neutralize their moral reluctance to theft. Therefore, effective treatment must counteract this personal, moral erosion and contaminated decision making.

The journey into and through shoplifter treatment is a very long one, involving too many complex aspects to address here. Because I have been involved with shoplifter assessment and treatment for such a long time, I have collected hundreds of pages of therapy notes. Rather than presenting all of this data here, I have instead elected to gather it, analyze it, and put it into two separate books specifically directed to shoplifter treatment, with the working titles, *Treatment for Rich Women Who Shoplift* and *Klepto-Bismo,* the case against using drugs with shoplifters (in press 2014). The latter book investigates why the use of drugs with shoplifters and why they are not only inappropriate but may cause many undesirable outcomes. The use of certain drugs may actually increase the probability that shoplifters will recidivate. Currently, I am conducting a series of expanded shoplifter studies of a larger sample of 100 shoplifters. These soon to be released books will present the results of these ongoing studies.

Chapter 7 References

American Psychiatric Association. (2000) *Diagnostic and statistical manual of mental disorders* (4th ed., text rev.). Washington, DC: Author.

Brady, J. C. (1990). *Drug addicts: Are they out of control?* San Mateo, CA: Western Book/Journal Press.

Cameron, M. O. (1964). *The Booster and the snitch: Department store shoplifting.* New York-London: The Free Press of Glencoe, A Division of The Macmillan Company.

Carlson, K. A. (1982). *Carlson psychological survey.* Port Huron, MI: Research Psychologists Press.

Chestnut, W. (2013, June 10). Personal communication.

Kraut, R. (1976). Deterrent and definitional influences on shoplifting. *Social Problems, 25*, 350–358.

Moore, R. H. (1983). College shoplifters: Rebuttal of Beck and McIntyre. *Psychological Reports, 53*, 1111–1116.

Toch, H. (1965). *The social psychology of social movements.* New York: Bobbs-Merrill.

INDEX

INDEX

Made in the USA
Columbia, SC
06 May 2018